Contents

W9-DEG-808

Preface

Prelesson: How to Study and How to Learn

How to Use *Grade Aid*

Exam Preparation: How to Pass Your Exams

HOW TO STUDY AND HOW TO LEARN

What does it take to learn and remember?

Educational psychologists focus their attention on instruction and academic learning and know a lot about what it takes for a person to learn. The information in this section comes primarily from their research findings about teaching, thinking, and learning.

The three most important characteristics of effective study are:

➤ Being actively involved in the learning process.

➤ Making new information meaningful by linking your existing life experiences and knowledge (what you already know) to new information (what you are learning for the first time).

➤ Taking responsibility for your own learning.

These characteristics are important to learning for several reasons. The first characteristic, *active learning* or *active participation*, means that you interact with new information so that it becomes alive and challenging. Instead of passively yawning over lifeless facts that refuse to stay in mind long enough to even pass a test, an active learner makes the facts alive and important by wrestling and dancing with them and really getting to know them. By simply using your own thoughts, asking and answering your own questions, and organizing information in ways that make sense to you, you become an active learner. When you are an active learner, the facts become more than facts, they become meaningful and stay with you. This suggests the second characteristic of effective learning.

To *make new material personally meaningful* (so that it becomes relevant to your life and needs), you must find ways to connect yourself, your knowledge, and your life experiences to the material you are studying. People have a natural tendency to do this, but by knowing that learning and memory are enhanced when you create personal meaning, you will be more likely to do it intentionally in the future. When you can relate new information to your own life by connecting it to your past or present, to problems you need to solve, or to events in the world, you make it important, and you are much more likely to understand it, remember it, and use it.

The third characteristic of effective study, *taking responsibility for your own learning*, is essential because no one can do your learning for you. We do not learn much just by being present in class and skimming over printed words on a page. To learn means to change, and to change we must experience things for ourselves. Teachers (and textbooks) can present ideas and try to make them interesting; but only you can learn those ideas for yourself, and only you can make them meaningful to your life. For this reason, it is important to take responsibility not only for how you go about learning, but also for how you will shape and mold the ideas that are presented to you.

DEVELOPING GOOD STUDY SKILLS

Remember trying to use a computer for the first time? You knew it could perform wonders, but you did not understand the new language required to operate it, or you tried the mouse and felt like you were suddenly totally uncoordinated. The first time you made a mistake or got a strange error message on the screen, you probably did not feel so bad, but by the second or third time, you began to feel like maybe you were not cut out

Preface

Grade Aid Study Guide has been written with one goal in mind: to help you learn more from *Psychology, Ninth Edition*. Proven learning strategies are incorporated throughout the study guide in an easy-to-use format that will encourage you to become an active participant in the learning process. The focus will be on learning, not on memorizing. Each chapter will begin with an overview of the chapter and a presentation of the key terms and learning objectives of that chapter. The most efficient learning process involves distributed practice, and the learning objective provide logical breaks during the learning process. Mastering the learning objectives will increase your confidence, and being confident and relaxed are keys to successful learning and examination preparation.

This *Grade Aid* study guide prepares you by providing various exercises designed to maximize learning. The study guide contains dozens of learning exercises tied to the learning objectives in the text. In addition to teaching students to learn, *Grade Aid* challenges you to become *critical thinker* by encouraging you to evaluate the research and generate personal meaning for the concepts presented in *Psychology*.

Grade Aid uses several techniques to optimize your learning, including:

1. Establishing clear learning objectives that are logically linked to the textbook.

2. Providing various methods of learning such as self-paced exercises, *Practice Tests* that prepare you to evaluate your learning, internet links to expand and apply your knowledge beyond the information presented in the textbook, and a crossword puzzle that challenges you to use the key words from the textbook in a fun and interactive way.

3. Encouraging you to establish schedules and goals for studying, to take breaks from studying, and to evaluate and reward yourself for your progress.

4. Encouraging critical thinking about facts, issues, and methodologies.

for computers. If you had friends who were catching on more easily, you probably began to feel still more frustrated).

The point is this: lacking the appropriate skills makes any task harder than it should be. In *Chapter 12* of your textbook, you will learn about the key factors in motivation. You will learn that when people do not have the necessary skills or do not know what is expected of them, they experience failure, become frustrated, and lose their motivation to try. A lack of motivation is neither innate nor necessarily a fault in the individual; it may just mean that someone never learned the skills or values necessary to make the job worthwhile. When you have the necessary skills, your task, even though it may be difficult, will become easier and more rewarding. It may even be fun. This lesson is designed to teach efficient and effective study skills which, assuming that you use them, will help you with this and other courses as well.

Review Your Educational and Professional Goals

Each time you begin a new class, you will find it useful to think about why you are taking the class and decide how it fits in with your long-term educational and professional goals. For example, you are currently enrolled in introductory psychology. Will this class help you with your professional goals? With your personal life? Is it a class required for your major? If so, why? Decide what value this class has for you and try to keep it in mind throughout the term.

Knowing how the class is meaningful to you will help motivate you to study and master the material presented. If you cannot think of a personally or educationally meaningful reason for taking the class, perhaps you should talk to your teacher or a school counselor. Almost every class has value, but pinpointing the value may be difficult. In any case, a lack of interest in the class from the outset will probably lead you to struggle through, feel frustrated, and continually wish the semester would end. This attitude is not conducive to good study skills.

Scheduling Study Time

Once you have attended the first session of each of your classes, plan a study schedule based on the workload you expect to have for each class, your personal needs, your family's needs, and any other obligations you may have. Frequently people are not realistic about their time and think they can do more in a given period than they actually can. When planning your class and study schedule try hard to be reasonable: allow time for the unexpected and remember that you have obligations other than school. If you do not plan for these things and for "play/relax" time, you will end up having to take time for them anyway, and be forced to break or readjust your educational commitments. Remember, your study schedule is just as important as your class schedule. If you commit yourself to a realistic study schedule, you should be able to fulfill all your obligations, including school, much more smoothly.

If you work full or part-time, it is important to plan your class schedule so that you are enrolled in a few classes each semester that have little or no homework along with one or two classes that do. A student who works full-time should seriously consider being a part-time student since it is almost impossible to study four or five subjects well without a full-time commitment.

Some of the most successful students are also the busiest students in class: students with jobs or family obligations and students carrying an extremely heavy courseload. What separated these students from the rest was their ability to organize. To be a well-organized student you begin each term by making a calendar of the due dates for every course. You should include all tests, papers, projects, personal dates to remember and most importantly, personal time. Personal time is time you set aside for yourself to relax and reward yourself for your hard work. This time does not have to be alone, just personal.

When planning your class and study schedule, try to mix your subjects. Also, when constructing your study sessions, plan to study several subjects at a time, each for about one hour, rather than one subject for several hours. Research indicates this is a much more efficient study tactic.

You will find it easier to fulfill your study schedule if you have a specific place to study. Select a quiet, well-illuminated place and always sit at a desk or table. If you study at home, be sure to move away from the television and family activities.

How to Deal with a Short Attention Span

The average college student can read for only twelve minutes before drifting away from a book and falling into a daydream. Since daydreaming interferes with learning, knowing how to control it helps. You will find that using the *As you read...* section of the study guide will, to some extent, automatically decrease the number of daydreams you have while reading *Psychology*. In addition, if you set small goals, take breaks from your study sessions, and reward yourself, you should learn more efficiently. Use these techniques over the next three or four years, gradually increasing your attention span so that you can study for a full hour without daydreaming.

READ ACTIVELY. When a study guide is not available, formulate and answer your own questions as you read. When using a study guide, follow the prepared exercises as outlined. With this study guide, you are encouraged to find many of the answers yourself and write them into the area provided. This outline approach will help you develop this skill for courses without study guides.

SET SMALL GOALS. In the beginning, do not expect yourself to read a complete chapter or finish an entire in chapter in your study guide in one study session. If you can do an entire chapter in one session, GREAT! But do not feel you have to. Set a goal of answering seven to ten questions and plan on taking a break when you have accomplished it. Over the next few years, gradually increase your goals.

TAKE BREAKS FROM YOUR STUDY SESSIONS. When you have answered or read the number of questions you set as a goal, take a break for 5-10 minutes. If you notice you are daydreaming a lot before you reach your goal, perhaps it was too large a step, and you should start out with a smaller one the next time. If you should discover you are daydreaming more than you are studying, *answer one more question* and take a 10 minute break. When you go back to studying, review the questions you have answered and then continue. You should strive to study at least 30 minutes for every 10 minute break.

REWARD YOURSELF. You will discover in *Chapter 8* of *Psychology* that behavior followed by reward tends to be repeated. Of course earning a good grade, feeling proud of yourself, and having your teachers, family, and friends recognize your achievements are rewards, but why not go one step further? Make your hobbies, special activities, and favorite foods contingent (dependent) upon completion of your homework. The problem with self-reward is that it is easy to cheat. It is easy to watch a football game and plan to study afterward; but this can have a negative effect on your study habits. Instead, *always* plan your time so that reward comes *after* you study. This way you really will increase your studying and learning rates. The other way around (sports or computer games--and then studying) only increases your procrastination rate! Reset you priorities and reinforcement schedule.

Memorization versus Understanding

Meaningful learning is much more permanent than rote learning (memorization). So, whenever you can, try to apply the concepts you are studying to your own experiences, look up words you are not familiar with, pay attention to examples given by your instructor if necessary. It is your responsibility to make everything you are trying to learn meaningful. Others can help you, but you will have to take the initiative to ask about any concepts giving you trouble.

In some cases memorization is an efficient way to help you recall information. This is so when you have made the information meaningful and are trying to remember names or lists of words. An effective way to memorize lists of material is to use mnemonic (nuh-MON-ik) devices. Mnemonic devices allow you to organize meaningless material into meaningful stories or words. In the textbook, *Chapter 9*, you will learn many interesting rudiments about human memory and forgetting. For example, if you wanted to remember the words cat, dish, punishment, nowhere, man, song, and gruesome you could create a story incorporating the word list. Try this: A *cat* was drinking milk from a *dish* when *punishment* fell upon him from *nowhere*. Turning his head the cat saw it was the *man* singing the *song* that had delivered the *gruesome* blow. Or if you wanted to remember the names Sabrina, Ulysses, Romeo, Pandora, Raina, Isis, Sebastian, and Ezekiel, you could simply remember the word SURPRISE. Mnemonic devices provide you with cues for recalling necessary information. You will find more about mnemonics and other memory strategies in *Chapter 9* of your *Psychology* text.

DEVELOPING EFFECTIVE CLASSROOM BEHAVIORS

Active Listening

Although entertainment, socializing with your peers, and conforming to the norms of going to college may be among your reasons for attending classroom lectures, one would hope that your primary reasons are to listen and learn. As with reading, to be a successful learner through listening you must be an active participant. Here are some tips that might help:

1. Exercise control over your thoughts by consciously directing your attention toward what is being said.
2. Allow the speaker's lead-in statements to act as cues that important information is about to be given. Lead-in statements will begin with phrases like "The main idea ...," "There are four approaches ...," "Another viewpoint ...," "In conclusion ...," and so on.
3. Silently ask yourself questions about what is being said and, as the lecture proceeds, try to answer them.
4. Ask questions in class, when the lecturer is ready for them, to clarify anything you missed or did not understand.
5. Try to make connections between what is being said now and what you recall from previous lectures or text material.

Taking Notes

Listening and writing at the same time can be somewhat distracting. If you are listening actively and intently you may find it difficult to write down as much as you would like; if you are writing a lot down you may find yourself falling behind and missing parts of the lecture. For these reasons it is important to give some thought to your listening/note taking approach, and during the first few lectures of a course adapt your listening and note taking skills to the style and pace of the lecture.

As with reading and listening, note taking can become merely a passive activity. If your approach to note taking involves trying to write down, word for word, just about everything that the lecturer says, you will be more involved in getting words on paper than in focusing your attention and asking questions about what points are important. An effective approach for successful classroom learning is to be an active listener, take well-organized and brief yet explicit notes, making them complete enough to provide you with an overview of the entire lecture. Here are some ideas that may help you take good class lecture notes.

1. Use an 8 1/2" x 11" three-ring binder that allows you to add and remove pages. This will allow you to keep all of your notes in one place and in order.
2. Develop an outlining system that works well for you. Your outline of what is said in the lecture should reflect major ideas, minor points that follow those ideas, and the relationship between ideas. Complete sentences take time to write and, for the most part, are unnecessary. Try to catch the lecture ideas in short phrases that include key words.
3. Make some notation of all ideas brought out in the lecture, even those you have read about in the text or already know, so that you can be reminded of all the ideas the lecturer felt were important to the main lecture topic.
4. Use multiple color highlighters to reflect your outline. Try different colors for major and minor points.
5. If you are a "doodler," then turn your doodles into meaningful *icons* for emphasizing important material. Being a good student does not come naturally or easily for most. It takes self-discipline, realistic scheduling, and a true desire to succeed. The important thing to remember is that almost anyone who wants to be a good student can be.

HOW TO USE GRADE AID

HOW TO USE THIS STUDY GUIDE

You may want to think of your study guide as a "How to Do It" manual or a carefully tested "recipe" that will help you succeed in your psychology class. As you work with it over the next few months and come to understand its purpose through practice, you will probably also find yourself using the formula it provides in most of your other classes. *Grade Aid* is designed to compliment Lefton and Brannon's *Psychology, Ninth Edition*. It will assist you in learning the essential terms, concepts, theories, and important research in the field of psychology. It is not meant as a substitute for *Psychology,* but rather as an adjunct to your learning process.

BEFORE YOU READ...

At the beginning of each study guide chapter, you will find a brief introduction to the chapter. Research studies on learning and memory have shown it is much easier to learn if you have some idea of the topic and the specific areas you will be learning. Having an overview prepares you for what is about to be read and gives you a glimpse into the exciting topics you are about to learn.

KEY TERMS

As with any other topic, understanding psychology requires that you learn certain terms that are specific to the discipline. The list of key terms guides you to specific terms that you will need to know.

LEARNING OBJECTIVES

The chapter learning objectives serve four purposes. First, they tell you specifically what you should expect to know when you have completed studying the chapter. Second, they give you an overview of what is in the chapter. Third, help you identify important material when you begin test preparation. Fourth, they can be used as practice essay questions.

AS YOU READ

People, terms, concepts, and ideas will be presented throughout this section in a variety of formats. These exercises will be a good indicator of how quickly you are getting the information. The exercises in *Grade Aid Study Guide* will allow you to test your understanding by applying the text's concepts to new situations. If you can transfer your textbook knowledge successfully to these exercises, what you are learning is taking on meaning. Meaningful learning is much more permanent than simple memorization. Other ways that you can make the things you are learning meaningful include applying the concepts you are studying to your own experiences, looking up unfamiliar words, and paying attention to examples given in your text and during lecture.

PRACTICE TESTS

At the conclusion of each chapter you will be provided with three practice tests and a comprehensive self-test. The practice tests will give you immediate feedback on how well you have learned. If you miss more than one or two questions on the self-test you need to study the chapter lessons more thoroughly. When preparing for your exam, the comprehensive test will give you a more thorough test of your knowledge, as these tests challenge you to demonstrate your knowledge in answering multiple-choice, true-false, and essay questions. If you are preparing for a comprehensive exam in your course, you can combine chapter tests to simulate a real course exam. It has been my experience that providing students with a sample of what a test will be like in their course relieves much of the pre-test anxiety and allows them to concentrate on the material in a much more efficient manner.

Grade Aid was written with the student in mind. I welcome your comments, opinions, and suggestions for future editions. My address is Jim A. Haugh, Ph.D., Department of Psychology, Rowan University, 201 Mullica Hill Road, Glassboro, NJ 08028, or you can contact me via my email address at haugh@rowan.edu.

EXAM PREPARATION

HOW TO PASS YOUR EXAMS

FACING EXAMS. Students often dread preparing for exams. However, students also recognize that the most prevalent method of assessing acquired knowledge is to administer exams. Therefore, one of the most important things you can do it to improve your test taking ability and how you approach exams. There are a number of simple steps you might use to accomplish these goals. First, realize that successful *learning and memory* of information requires preparation, practice, and application. This means you need to start early, accurately assess what you do and do not know, and review the information that you are struggling with. Second, try to reduce your own test anxiety, as this anxiety can interfere with your ability to learn and accurately recall information during the exam. There are a number of methods to reduce your test-anxiety. One of the best is to be confident in your ability to recall the information you have studied. This comes with extensive preparation. The other key to relieving test anxiety is monitoring your own thoughts and realizing that one test grade does not define whether you are a success or a failure. A final way of reducing the tension about exams is to give yourself a chance to simulate the exam without the pressure of failing or the shock of a tough question causing you to block on the correct answer. This practice tests in this study guide, and the online practice tests, are excellent ways to accomplish this goal.

PREPARING FOR EXAMS. Preparing for exams should be an *ongoing process*. As you read your text, listen to class lectures, and take notes, keep in mind that an exam is coming and begin preparing as early as possible. Do not wait until the day (or even the weekend) before the exam, because time pressures, low energy, and unexpected events are likely to interfere with your ability to prepare and get the grade you want on your exam. To avoid this problem, you should begin studying approximately one week before the exam date. During this week, you should take the following steps:

1. Ask your instructor what the exam will cover, what material will be omitted, and what kinds of questions will be used. This information is also likely on your course syllabus; check it first before asking these questions.
2. Make a list of things you must know and rank them according to their importance. You will want to give the most important and difficult concepts more preparation time.
3. Spend some time predicting test questions: How might they be worded? How general or detailed might they be? How might two or more concepts be combined into one question? You might even want to generate your own questions to help this process along.
4. Begin reviewing. Your text, lecture notes, *study guide questions and answers*, *chapter learning objectives*, *key terms, and practice tests* will become extremely useful tools at this time. If you are studying as you should, you will have most of this material already completed when it comes time for your final studying. In other words, your studying

should not consist of note taking, it should be spent trying to understand and remember the material you are studying.

5. Schedule group study sessions with other students. Sharing ideas about what might be covered on the test and talking out loud about the things you have learned will help clarify and solidify your understanding.

ANSWERING ESSAY TEST QUESTIONS. Essay test questions require that you know the material well enough to be able to recall both major and minor points from memory in an organized fashion to provide an answer. The *Practice Tests* in this study guide will let you know if you have grasped the concepts beyond rote memorization. When presented with an essay test, keep these steps in mind.

1. Before you begin to answer any test questions, read all of the questions and make some quick notes about the major and minor points you will want to cover when answering them.
2. Estimate how much time you should give to each question and try to stick to your schedule. You will want to allow more time for difficult questions and questions that carry more points toward scoring of the test. If possible, plan to have some time in the last minutes of the class session to review and polish your answers.
3. Answer the easier questions first.
4. Answer each question as directly as possible and avoid wandering and writing too much or too little.
5. Leave a few blank lines between answers so that you can go back if time allows and add ideas.

ANSWERING OBJECTIVE TEST QUESTIONS. Objective test questions include multiple-choice, true-false, and matching questions. These questions require you to recognize and discriminate between correct and incorrect answers. The *Practice Tests* at the end of each chapter and the *"As You Read…"* exercises should give you good practice at this. When taking an objective test keep the following in mind:

1. Read each question carefully and completely; do not jump to conclusions and assume that you have the correct answer until you have read and considered the entire question.
2. Give careful thought to questions that include words such as *always*, *never*, *all*, *tendency*, or *sometimes*. The first three terms may indicate that the statement is too extreme and perhaps false; the last two terms show more qualified conditions, suggesting that the statement may be true; however, these rules are not absolute.
3. Treat each alternative in a multiple-choice question as a true-false statement. Eliminate those alternatives that are definitely false and if more than one answer seems to be true, choose the one that most thoroughly and directly answers the question.
4. Do not spend too much time on any one question. If you are unsure of an answer, put a check mark in the margin next to the question and go back to it later.
5. The rule of thumb about changing answers is to stick with your original answer unless you have *strong* second thoughts about it. If you feel reasonably sure that your second thoughts are correct, then go ahead and change the answer.

SIMULATING YOUR EXAMS. You can prepare better for your course examinations if you follow a couple of proven review steps. First, in *Psychology* you are presented with a new glossary of terminology. In the *Key Term* section, you are provided with a list of new or difficult terms and asked to define each to enhance your memory for these terms. This technique is a proven way to increase your ability to recall the correct test answer in many test formats such as matching or short answer type questions. The next, more difficult task is to recognize the correct answer when you are given less than the complete definition, as in multiple-choice items or scenarios, where the item stem is lengthy, and you need to determine what the salient points are before attempting to answer. What if you could be given bits of information about specific topics and asked to correctly identify and spell the topic? What if you could learn difficult concepts, increase your confidence and also have some fun doing it? I have provided a sample of multiple-choice test items similar in content to the items your instructor may choose for your exam. These *Practice Test* items are real and an excellent method of practicing for an exam.

Although Lefton and Brannon's *Psychology,* Ninth Edition is written in a very logical format, many instructors choose to alter the chapter sequence to better fit individual instructor goals. Preparing for a multiple chapter exam is difficult, but there is a way to put together your own practice exams and build your confidence prior to the real exam. For example, if your instructor assigns Chapters 1, 2 and 5 for the next exam, you would remove the *Practice Tests* for Chapters 1, 2, and 5 and combine them to make a simulated exam covering the same material as your instructor's exam. Be sure to grade yourself on the simulated tests to review the material that is causing you difficulty. If you feel like you need to practice more than once, simply make copies of the pages before you begin or write your answers on a separate sheet of paper versus on the tests themselves.

After creating your own simulated exams, you can also test your knowledge by taking the sample exams provided via the internet. The Companion Website, an internet resource for *Psychology*, Ninth Edition, is located at www.ablongman.com/lefton9e. **Remember, you cannot get better without practice, so check it out and use all the resources available to you!**

Chapter 1

What Is Psychology?

Before you read...

Maybe you are a psychology major, maybe you are taking this class because you are required to at your university or college, or maybe you just have an interest in psychology. Whatever your motivation, the goal of this chapter is to provide you with a broad overview of what psychology is.

The chapter begins with a brief definition of how psychology is defined and an overview of the early history and traditions in psychology. You will then learn about the various current perspectives in psychology, such as behavioral and cognitive psychology. This overview will be important as these various schools of thought will appear over and over again as you explore topics in later chapters. In addition, you will find out about the contributions of women and ethnic minorities to the current and past history of psychology. Along the way, you will explore some fascinating new research that looks at how psychologists are beginning to understand and study the relationship between the brain and behavior!

In the second part of the chapter, you will be introduced to the various types of professionals that are working in the field of psychology. You will find answers to such questions as: What is the difference between a psychologist and a psychiatrist? If I wanted to be a psychologist, how many years of schooling do I need? What do psychologists do? In addition, the areas of applied research, human services, and experimental psychology are explained, and the subfields that encompass these exciting careers are examined. You might find the debate between psychologists and psychiatrists regarding who should be able to prescribe medications to be particularly interesting in this section!

To finish out the chapter, you will be introduced to four recurring themes in the field of psychology. These themes will come up throughout the textbook, and you will be encouraged to think about these themes as you review the rest of the chapter.

In summary, the science of psychology is as diverse as the behaviors and mental processes it seeks to understand. Chapter 1, like the discipline itself, is meant to give a broad understanding of this diversity and open your mind to the theories and issues relevant to psychologists. The authors of your text (i.e., Lefton and Brannon) provide a broad base from which the rest of the text will develop, as you begin this fascinating journey through the field of Psychology.

Key Terms

Psychology
Structuralism
Introspection
Functionalism
Gestalt Psychology
Behaviorism
Humanistic Psychology
Cognitive Psychology
Psychoanalytic Approach
Biopsychology Perspective
Positive Psychology
Industrial/Organizational Psychology
Evolutionary Psychology
Psychologist
Clinical Psychologist
Counseling Psychologist
Psychiatrist
Psychoanalyst

Learning Objectives

After reading this chapter, you should be able to:

1. Discuss the common misperceptions about psychology, understand the limitations of these perceptions, and come to an understanding of how psychology is currently defined.
2. Define the early schools of thought and traditions in psychology, including structuralism, functionalism, Gestalt psychology, psychoanalysis, behaviorism, humanistic psychology, and cognitive psychology. Who are the psychologists associated with these traditions and what do these traditions believe and study?
3. Name the women and ethnic minorities who have been contributors in psychology and discuss their contributions to the field.
4. Define behaviorism, humanistic psychology, cognitive psychology, and the biological perspective. Include the similarities and differences between them.
5. Name and describe the major perspectives within psychology, including the psychoanalytic, behaviorist, humanistic, cognitive, biopsychology, and social and cultural. For each of these perspectives, you should be able to discuss the main idea associated with each and the emphasis or technique used within that perspective.
6. Name and describe the current trends in psychology, including positive, industrial/organizational, and evolutionary psychology.
7. Define and differentiate between the major types of mental health practitioners and describe what psychologists do.
8. Describe and differentiate between the subfields of applied research, human services, and experimental psychology and discuss the focus and activities in each subfield.
9. Identify and summarize the four recurring themes in psychology that can be used to help you understand how the many content areas of psychology relate to one another.

As you read...

How Accurate Is the Image of Psychology?

1. Psychology is defined as the science of _____ and _____.

2. What are some of the common images of psychologists and how are these images inconsistent with what psychologists really do?

How Did Psychology Begin?

1. Compare and contrast structuralism, functionalism, and Gestalt psychology.

2. Analyzing and describing thoughts as they occur is called _____.

3. Define psychoanalysis, behaviorism, humanistic psychology, and cognitive psychology and describe how they are different from one another.

What Trends Currently Shape Psychology?

1. _____ was the first women president of the American Psychological Association.

2. In psychology today, women earn _____ percent of bachelor's depress and _____ percent of doctorates in psychology.

3. Francis C. Sumner is an African-American psychologist who is best known for what?

4. _____ was the first Latina to earn a Ph.D. in psychology in the United States.

1.1 Be An Active Learner: Major Perspectives in Psychology

Fill in the missing information that describes the perspectives on psychological issues.

Perspective	Main idea
Psychoanalytic	
	Uniqueness of each human being's experience is central, as is the idea that human beings have free will to determine their destiny
Cognitive	
	Combines an emphasis on human values such as optimism and well being
Biopsychological	
	Explains behavior by analyzing how specific behaviors have led to adaptation and survival of the species
Behaviorism	
	Social and cultural context influences a person's behavior, thoughts, and feelings
Industrial/Organizational Psychology	

Who Are These People Called Psychologists?

1. What are the differences between a Clinical Psychologist, Counseling Psychologist, and Psychiatrist?

2. A _____ is typically a psychiatrist who is trained in the technique of psychoanalysis.

3.   Describe applied research, human services, and experimental psychology, and name the areas of psychology that belong under each subfield.

4.   _____ psychologists try to identify and understand the basic elements of behavior and mental processes, whereas _____psychologists use research findings to solve practical problems.

5.   Of all the jobs in psychology, which are the two most popular?

How Should You Use This Textbook?

1.   Identify the four recurring themes in psychology.

1.2 Be An Active Learner: Using Psychological Knowledge to Become a Better Student

You might have been tempted to skip over the text box on page 24 of your text. However, before you are done, take some time and read through the tips provided by the authors of your text regarding how to improve your academic performance.

a) Make a list of the things you do regularly, which you need to do more of, and which you do not do.
b) When you have completed this list, set a schedule for yourself for the coming week and at the end of the week evaluate how well you were able to stick to your plan.
c) Finally, make a plan for yourself that addresses how you can continue to improve your study skills.

After You Read, Practice Test #1

1. Psychology is defined as the science of behavior and _____ . (5)
    A. Society
    B. Mental processes
    C. Emotions
    D. Biology

2. _____ was an early proponent of functionalism, whereas _____ was an early proponent of structuralism. (6)
    A. Sigmund Freud; William James
    B. William James; Wilhelm Wundt
    C. Edward Titchner; Wilhelm Wundt
    D. B.F. Skinner; Sigmund Freud

3. Which perspective in psychology argues that thoughts and mental process are the essence of psychology? (9)
    A. Behaviorism
    B. Structuralism
    C. Gestalt psychology
    D. Cognitive psychology

4. In the 112-year history of the American Psychological Association, only _____ women have been elected to serve as the president. (10)
    A. 25
    B. 45
    C. 10
    D. 2

5. A researcher is interested in exploring whether or not depression is genetically transmitted. This researcher is likely affiliated with what psychological perspective? (13-14)
    A. Humanistic
    B. Social and cultural
    C. Evolutionary
    D. Biopsychological

6. _____ psychology is concerned with the study of human strength and virtue. (15)
    A. Health
    B. Positive
    C. Strength-based
    D. Industrial/Organizational

Psychology

7. Traditionally, psychoanalysts have training in both _____ and _____. (18)
    A. Cognitive psychology and medical school
    B. Social work and humanism
    C. Psychoanalysis and medical school
    D. Cognitive psychology and social work

8. Individuals trained in the areas of behavioral medicine, clinical psychology, and school psychology belong to what subfield in psychology? (20)
    A. Human services
    B. Experimental research
    C. Applied research
    D. Biopsychology

9. Which of the following statements about the psychology major is not true? (20-21)
    A. It is one of the most popular undergraduate majors in the united states
    B. Unemployment among psychology graduates tends to be low
    C. You need a masters degree in psychology to do anything with the degree
    D. Many psychology major go on to work in business settings

10. For years, psychologists have argued about whether intelligence is something you are born with our something that can be influenced by the experiences you are provided in your life. This argument best represents which of the four recurring themes in psychology? (23-25)
    A. Relationship between nature and nurture
    B. The role of human diversity
    C. The action-oriented quality of research and practice in psychology
    D. The interaction between brain and behavior

After You Read, Practice Test #2

1. _____ is the science of mental processes and behavior. (5)
   A. Philosophy
   B. Psychology
   C. Cognitive psychology
   D. Behavioral psychology

2. You are speaking to a psychologist, and he states that "studying thoughts is a waste of time because thoughts cannot be observed and measured like behaviors can." This psychologist is associated with what perspective in psychology? (8)
   A. Psychoanalysis
   B. Functionalism
   C. Humanistic psychology
   D. Behaviorism

3. Which of the following is most consistent with Psychoanalytic perspectives? (7)
   A. Stresses the importance of human growth motives
   B. Focus' on studying positive human values
   C. Stresses the importance of unconscious thought
   D. Explores the basic structure of the mind

4. _____ was the first Latina to earn a Ph.D. in psychology in the United States. (11)
   A. Martha Bernal
   B. Jorge Sanchez
   C. Manuel Barrera
   D. Gail Wyatt

5. A clinical psychologist is working with her client to help the client think more realistically and change their negative thoughts about themselves. This psychologist is likely a _____ psychologist. (13)
   A. Behavioral
   B. Social and cultural
   C. Cognitive
   D. Psychoanalytic

6. Which of the following research questions is likely to be of interest to a behavioral psychologist? (13)
   A. How do children learn to use violence?
   B. Are unconscious thoughts related to dreams?
   C. Is aggression behavior adaptive to humans?
   D. Does the pay employees receive influence their motivation?

7. This perspective in psychology emphasizes the importance of free choice and the perspective that people are born with a desire to fulfill their potential. (13)
    A. Positive psychology
    B. Humanistic psychology
    C. Cognitive psychology
    D. Psychoanalytic psychology

8. _____ are physicians who have chosen to specialize in the treatment of mental or motional disorders. (17-18)
    A. Psychiatrists
    B. Psychoanalysts
    C. Counseling psychologists
    D. Psychologists

9. _____ psychologists try to identify and understand the basic elements of behavior and mental processes. (19)
    A. Applied
    B. Clinical
    C. Experimental
    D. Counseling

10. Which of the following is *not* one of the four recurring themes in psychology? (23-25)
    A. The interaction between nature and nurture
    B. The importance of scientific understanding in psychology
    C. The emphasis on conducting research and putting that research into practice
    D. The relationship between the brain and behavior

After You Read, Practice Test #3

1. You are talking to your friend and they argue, "psychology is nothing more than common sense." You know this is not true because psychologists use _____. (5)
    A. Science
    B. Observation
    C. Experience
    D. Mental telepathy

2. The focus of John Watson's research was on _____. (8)
    A. The basic elements of consciousness
    B. Stream of consciousness
    C. Observable behaviors
    D. The useful functions of the mind

3. _____ was a school of psychological thought that was based on the premise that it was insufficient to examine the individual parts of the human mind and/or behavior, but that it was necessary to examine the total experience of the individual. (7)
    A. Structuralism
    B. Functionalism
    C. Gestalt psychology
    D. Humanistic psychology

4. Today, women earn ____ percent of doctorates in psychology. (10)
    A. 20%
    B. 70%
    C. 90%
    D. 50%

5. A psychologist in the field of _____ psychology would likely be interested in the role of hope in recovering from a severe mental illness? (15)
    A. Industrial/Organizational
    B. Positive psychology
    C. Psychoanalytic psychology
    D. Social and cultural psychology

6. You friend is interested in being a therapist and states that he believes the key to understanding mental illness is exploring unconscious thoughts. Your friend would likely enjoy which perspective in psychology? (13)
    A. Cognitive
    B. Evolutionary
    C. Biopsychology
    D. Psychoanalytic

7.   Which of the following statements is incorrect? (17-18)
     A. Clinical and counseling psychologists tend to do very similar things
     B. Psychologists can be trained as psychoanalysts
     C. Most psychoanalysts are psychiatrists
     D. Psychologists are medical doctors

8.   The majority of psychologists are employed _____. (22)
     A. As counseling service providers
     B. In colleges and universities
     C. As a clinical service provider
     D. In industry

9.   _____ psychologists use research findings to solve practical problems. (19)
     A. Applied
     B. Experimental
     C. Human Service
     D. School

10. The authors of your textbook present you with a number of tips on becoming a better student. Many of these tips are based on psychological research that examines what helps students learn. This material reflects which of the recurrent themes in psychology? (24)
     A. The interaction between brain and behavior
     B. The importance of learning on success in psychology
     C. The role of human diversity in learning
     D. The action-oriented quality of research and practice in psychology

After You Read, Comprehensive Practice Test

1. Psychology can be defined as the study of _____. (5)
    A.   Humans and other animals
    B.   Stimulus and responses
    C.   Behavior and mental processes
    D.   None of the above

2. Who founded the school of structuralism and the first psychological laboratory? (6)
    A.   Sigmund Freud
    B.   Ivan Pavlov
    C.   John Watson
    D.   Wilhelm Wundt

3. Humanistic psychology is not associated with _____. (8)
    A.   Uniqueness
    B.   The unconscious mind
    C.   Free will
    D.   Abraham Maslow

4. Introspection is _____. (6)
    A.   Used by behaviorists
    B.   Involves describing and analyzing thoughts as they occur
    C.   Is part of the cognitive revolution
    D.   Was developed by Koffka

5. Ethnic minorities comprise _____ percent of the membership in the American
    Psychological Association. (11)
    A.   23
    B.   10
    C.   50
    D.   35

6. The biopsychology perspective does not look at _____. (13)
    A.   Introspection
    B.   Central nervous system problems
    C.   How behavior changes brain structure and function
    D.   Genetic abnormalities

7. Cognitive psychology is a school of psychological thought that emphasizes the
    importance of _____. (13)
    A.   Biological and chemical processes in the brain
    B.   Measuring overt, observable behaviors
    C.   Mental processes such as thought and memory
    D.   Unresolved conflicts and forces in the unconscious

8. Compared to a clinical psychologist, a psychiatrist's training makes him or her better prepared to _____. (17)
   A. Engage in research about psychological problems
   B. Prescribe the appropriate medications for a patient
   C. Understand the biological causes of disorders
   D. Explain psychological disorders to their patients

9. A medical doctor who has chosen to devote their efforts to the treatment of emotional or mental disorders is known as a _____. (17)
   A. Clinical psychologist
   B. Psychiatrist
   C. Counseling psychologist
   D. Psychoanalyst

10. The fields of counseling and clinical psychology _____. (17-18)
    A. Have responsibilities that are converging
    B. Cover completely different types of problems
    C. Are both decreasing in popularity
    D. Would not deal with the problem of spousal abuse

11. Individuals in the fields of engineering, educational, forensic, and industrial/organizational psychology demonstrate skills in _____ psychology. (20)
    A. Applied
    B. Human service
    C. Experimental
    D. Health

12. A psychologist who is interested in testing children to determine whether or not they have a learning disability would be a member of which subfield in psychology? (20)
    A. Experimental
    B. Applied
    C. Human services
    D. Counseling

13. People who choose psychology as a career can expect _____. (21-22)
    A. Salaries ranging from $500,000 to $1,000,000 annually
    B. To find a wide variety of job opportunities
    C. Some difficulty finding a job since employment opportunities have recently stabilized
    D. All of the above

14. The two most popular work settings for psychologists are _____ . (22)
    A.   Schools and research positions
    B.   Clinical service providers and industry/organizations
    C.   Faculty members at universities and clinical service providers
    D.   Research positions and industry/organizations

15. Some psychologists are interested in studying the impact that cultural norms have on emotional expression. These psychologists reflect which of the following themes in psychology? (23-25)
    A.   The importance of research in psychology
    B.   The interaction between the brain and behavior
    C.   The importance of emotion as a basic element of being human
    D.   The role of diversity in understanding psychological experiences

True or False

1.   Psychology is a science. (5)

2.   In psychology today, more psychologists tend to label themselves as cognitive versus behavioral psychologists. (9)

3.   Latinos receive a greater percentage of doctoral degrees in the United States compared to Asian Americans. (11)

4.   The humanistic perspective in psychology emphasizes self-actualization, which is the process of realizing one's unconscious thoughts. (12)

5.   Evolutionary psychology is based on the work of Charles Darwin. (16)

6.   According to many practitioners and researchers, counseling and clinical psychology are converging and are very similar. (17)

7.   Most psychoanalysts are psychologists. (18)

8.   One of the recurrent themes in psychology concerns the interaction between human behavior and unconscious processes. (24-25)

Essay Questions

1.   Discuss the role of women and ethnic minorities in the history of psychology, making sure to include important events and individuals in this history. (10-12)

2.   Identify the four recurring themes in psychology and provide an example of a psychological topic/question that might be addressed using each theme. (23-25)

When You Have Finished!

Surf's Up!!

After you've read and reviewed, try these web sites for additional information about some of the topics covered in this chapter.

1. **Considering A Career in Psychology? The American Psychological Association** (http://www.apa.org/students/student1.html)
   This is part of the website of the American Psychological Association, the largest organization of psychologists in the United States. The particular site has a variety of information for students who are thinking about pursuing a career in psychology. You might also want to search the APA website when you are done! There is a lot of information on this site for those interested in psychology.

2. **The American Psychological Society** (http://www.psychologicalscience.org/)
   APS is another large group of psychologists with a more scientifically focused membership base. There is also a section devoted to students in psychology.

3. **Today in the History of Psychology** (http://www.cwu.edu/~warren/today.html)
   The American Psychological Association Historical Database is a collection of dates and brief descriptions of over 3100 events in the history of psychology. Type in the date and see what happened in psychology today!

4. **The History of Psychology Website** (http://elvers.stjoe.udayton.edu/history/welcome.htm)
   This website contains information related to the history of psychology. You can search psychologists alphabetically, by birth date, or by searching various categories of interest. You can even play history of psychology trivia!

5. **Psychology Online Resource Center** (http://www.psych-central.com)
   This site contains valuable information for psychology students and covers a wide variety of topics. Some topics of interest to beginning students include a section on careers in psychology, study tips, and student organizations in psychology.

6. **Positive Psychology Center** (http://www.positivepsychology.org/).
   The Positive Psychology Center is an organization located at the University of Pennsylvania. There is information about the emerging field of positive psychology, measures that are used in research on positive psychology, and even a link where you can find out about the positive traits that you possess!

7. **The Society for Industrial and Organizational Psychology** (http://www.siop.org/)
   This is an organization that is affiliated with both APA an APS and promotes the field of industrial/organizational psychology. One of the many links available contains information related to graduate education in I/O psychology.

Cross Check: What is Psychology?

Psychology

Across
1. Looking inward
2. Study of mental processes and behavior
3. How behavior serves a survival function
4. Interest in how people think
5. Mental health practitioner with focus on less sever problems
6. Focus on the unconscious
9. Use of psychological information in an applied setting
10. Study of the mind's structure
14. Medical doctor focusing on mental health issues
15. Professional with advanced psychoanalytic training
16. Founder was William James
17. Integrates biology and psychology

Down
1. Study of work environments
7. Rebukes psychology's normal focus on the dysfunction and disorder
8. Focus on human potential
11. Focus is on the whole
12. Interested in measuring only what is observable
13. Mental health practitioner with focus on more severe problems

Created by Puzzlemaker at DiscoverySchool.com

Chapter 2

The Science of Psychology

Before you read...

Many people think of psychology as being akin to common sense. However, psychology, like other sciences such as biology, physics, and sociology, uses science to inform what we know about human thought and behavior. In this chapter, you will be introduced to the science of psychology and you will learn about the methods that psychologists use to collect scientific knowledge.

In the first part of the chapter, you are introduced to the basic principles that underlie all scientific endeavors. In addition, you will be introduced to the steps involved in designing and implementing a research project. As you will see, this knowledge allows you to think critically about research reports that you hear about on a daily basis. In doing so, you can be an active receiver of information versus a passive recipient of information people want you to know.

After a basic introduction to the process of scientific inquiry, you are then introduced to the specific types of methods that psychologists use in conducting research. These methods are broadly classified into experimental and descriptive methods. As you will see, the type of method used by a psychologist is directly related to the types of conclusions that can be made from the results of these studies.

A third topic that you will be introduced to in this chapter is how psychologists evaluate their data once it is collected. In exploring this issue, you will explore two issues: (a) the role of statistics and (b) the importance of considering human diversity when interpreting research findings. With regard to statistics, you will be introduced to basic statistical terms and information that will allow you to more clearly understand research conducted in psychology. With regard to human diversity, you will learn how considering such factors as race, culture, gender, and disability status serves to reduce bias in our research.

The chapter concludes with a discussion of ethics in psychological research. Ethics help guide psychologists decision-making when designing and implementing research projects and serve to protect human and animal participants. In this section, you will learn what your rights are as a participant in a research study and you will explore important questions such as, "Can we deceive participants about what will be required of them when they do research?" Happy science to you!

Key Terms

Empiricism
Theory
Scientific Method
Hypothesis
Experiment
Variable
Independent Variable
Dependent Variable
Sample
Operational Definition
Participant
Experimental Group
Control Group
Descriptive Research
Case Study
Naturalistic Observation
Correlational Study
Ex Post Facto Study
Statistics
Descriptive Statistics
Measure of Central Tendency
Mean
Median
Mode
Range
Standard Deviation
Correlation Coefficient
Inferential Statistics
Significant Difference
Ethnocentrism
Ethics
Informed Consent
Debriefing

Learning Objectives

After reading this chapter, you should be able to:

1. Explain how psychologists discover the underpinnings of human behavior and mental processes through the conduct of empirical research and theory development.
2. Summarize the three principles that underlie the scientific endeavor.
3. Identify and describe the five basic steps of the scientific method.
4. Define the key elements of the experimental method and be able to identify these components in a research study.
5. Identify and describe the various types of descriptive research methods and state the strengths and limitations of each.
6. Compare and contrast the strengths and limitations of experimental and descriptive methods of research.
7. Define and differentiate between descriptive and inferential statistics.
8. Provide examples of some of the commonly used descriptive statistics.
9. Compare and contrast the idea of statistical significance and meaningfulness.
10. Identify factors that contribute to human diversity and that potentially may be related to bias in psychological research. Summarize each and explain why universal statements about human behavior are not always true.
11. Describe how human participants in research experiments are safeguarded by ethics.
12. Discuss the use of deception in psychological research and the conditions that must be met when deception is used.

As you read...

What Makes Psychology a Science?

1. The science of psychology, like other sciences, is based on the premises of _____ and _____.

2. Define Empiricism and state how it is different from logic or intuition.

3. A theory is a collection of interrelated ideas that together _____, _____, and _____ behavior or mental processes.

4. List the 3 principles that underlie the scientific endeavor.

5. Give the 5 basic steps involved in the scientific method and generate an example at each stage.

What Research Methods Do Psychologists Use?

1. An _____ is a procedure in which a researcher systematically manipulates and observes elements of a situation in order to test a hypothesis.

2. How are participants and samples similar to one another?

3. A researcher is interested in the effects of stress on academic performance. He defines stress by the number of stressful events the person has experienced in the past three months. This would be an example of an _____ _____.

4. A _____ group is exposed to the independent variable, whereas the _____ group is not.

2.1 Be An Active Learner: Identifying the Parts of a Research Study

Identify the independent and dependent variables in each of the following experiments.

A psychologist investigates the effects that level of background noise has on the time it takes subjects to complete a series of analytical problems.

➢ Independent_____

➢ Dependent _____

A researcher conducts a study in which she measures academic performance among students who do and do not eat breakfast regularly.

➢ Independent_____

➢ Dependent _____

Hospitalized individuals with schizophrenia are rewarded for cooperative behaviors, and a clinical psychologist observes to see if their rate of being cooperative increases as a result.

➢ Independent_____

➢ Dependent _____

5. What are extraneous variables and why are they important to identify and control?

2.2 Be An Active Learner: Descriptive Research Methods

Match the following terms with the correct definition

A. Correlational Study   _____ Involves observation of behavior in its normal setting versus in a laboratory

B. Descriptive Research   _____ Attempts to determine the strength of a relationship between two variables

C. Survey Method   _____ type of research that involves summarizing events rather than performing a manipulation of variables

D. Case Study   _____ Allows researchers to describe differences among groups of participants based on a naturally occurring difference

E. Ex Post Facto Study   _____ Involves intensive observation and analysis of an individual

F. Naturalistic   _____ A method in which a set of questions is posted to a large
Observation   group of people

6. State the strengths and weaknesses of the 5 types of descriptive methods.

How Do Psychologists Evaluate Their Research Findings?

1. Statistics is _____.

2. _____ statistics are used to summarize, condense, and describe sets of data, whereas _____ statistics are used to make statements regarding the meaningfulness of the data.

3. List and define the three measures of central tendency and two measures of variability.

4. When would you use the mode or median instead of the mean?

5. A correlation coefficient assesses the _____ of _____ between two variables.

6. A research finding could be statistically significant but not meaningful. Explain how this could be true.

2.3 Avoiding Bias in the Research Process

1. Identify the six areas discussed in the text that should be considered when evaluating potential bias in research.

2. Define Ethnocentrism and give an example.

3. Compare and contrast race and ethnicity and state why psychologists should study ethnicity over race.

4. _____ reflects a person's ethnic background, religious and social values, artistic and musical tastes and scholarly interests.

5. The United States is a _____ culture, while many Asian countries have a _____ culture.

6. What are the 4 ways that social class is defined?

7. What is the difference between sexual orientation and sexual behavior?

8. Disability can be defined from the _____, _____, and _____ perspectives.

9. When it comes to understanding diversity, we need to realize that there are usually more differences _____ a group than between groups.

What Ethical Principles Guide Psychology Research?

1. _____ consists of rules concerning proper and acceptable conduct that investigators use to guide their studies.

2. List the information that should be included in informed consent.

3. Debriefing a research participant should happen _____, and it should include _____.

4. Discuss whether deception in psychological research is ever appropriate.

Psychology

After You Read, Practice Test #1

1. Dr. Feelgood is a strong proponent of drug therapy to treat mental illness. As a result of this bias, he tends to overlook the value and effectiveness of traditional talk-therapies. Which of the basic principles of scientific endeavor has he violated? (30)
    A.   Replicability
    B.   Thoroughness
    C.   Systematic Observation
    D.   Objectivity

2. Which of the following is not one of the steps in the scientific method? (32-34)
    A.   Collecting the data
    B.   Developing a hypothesis
    C.   Interviewing other scientists
    D.   Designing a study

3. A set of procedures that specifies exactly how a particular variable is to be measured is called a(n) _____. (36)
    A.   Operational definition
    B.   Experimental document
    C.   Subjectivity report
    D.   Hypothetical statement

4. A condition or characteristic of a situation or person that can change over time or that can be different between different situations or people is called a(n) (35)
    A.   Variable
    B.   Hypothesis
    C.   Correlation
    D.   Experiment

5. A researcher is interested in the effects of cell phone use on driving ability. He gives the participants in the experimental group 3 different types of cell phones and monitors their cell phone use and driving every afternoon from 2-4 pm. The dependent variable in this study would be _____. (35)
    A.   Whether or not someone had a cell phone
    B.   Driving performance
    C.   Time of day
    D.   Type of cell phone

6. The primary advantage of which of the following studies is that it allows us to study unique events or phenomena in great depth. (39)
    A.   Correlational study
    B.   Naturalistic observation
    C.   Surveys
    D.   Case study

7.   _____ statistics allow a researcher to conclude that the results of their research form meaningful patterns and confirm the hypotheses of the study. (46)
   A.   Inferential
   B.   Descriptive
   C.   Insight
   D.   Pattern

8.   For many years in psychology, behavioral phenomena were interpreted from the world-view of Caucasian, European American males. This would be an example of _____. (47)
   A.   Ethnorelativism
   B.   Caucasian bias
   C.   Cultural blindness
   D.   Ethnocentrism

9.   When considering bias in the research process, all of the following factors should be evaluated except _____. (47-52)
   A.   Age
   B.   Gender
   C.   Intelligence
   D.   Race

10.   At the end of a person's participation in a research study, they should always be _____. (53)
   A.   Thanked
   B.   Told the results of the study
   C.   Debriefed
   D.   Given informed consent

Psychology

After You Read, Practice Test #2

1. A good theory should allow a scientist to do each of the following things with regard to behavior, except _____. (30)
    A. Predict
    B. Explain
    C. Describe
    D. Interpret

2. A tentative statement expressing a causal relationship between two events that will be evaluated in a research study is called a(n) _____. (33)
    A. Operational definition
    B. Theory
    C. Hypothesis
    D. Variable

3. A researcher is interested in how manipulating the name on an employment application might influence the decision of the person doing the hiring. In this study, the independent variable is the _____. (35)
    A. Decision that is made
    B. Name on the application
    C. Date the application was received
    D. Gender of the applicant

4. In an experiment, the _____ variable is manipulated by the experimenter and the _____ variable is expected to change due to the manipulation. (35)
    A. Dependent, extraneous
    B. Extraneous, independent
    C. Independent, dependent
    D. Dependent, independent

5. Before conducting an experiment, a researcher must provide a(n) _____ definition for each of the variables they are interested in studying. (36).
    A. Independent
    B. Operational
    C. Experimental
    D. Control

6. A correlation _____. (41)
    A. Exists when two events are regularly associated with one another.
    B. Means a change in one variable causes a change in another variable.
    C. Is found only through controlled laboratory experiments
    D. Is an experimental variable

7. Which measure of central tendency is less sensitive to extreme scores within a distribution? (44)
    A. Standard deviation
    B. Mean
    C. Range
    D. Mode

8. Statistics is the branch of mathematics that deals with _____. (43)
    A. Analyzing data from case studies
    B. Classifying and analyzing data
    C. Determining only measures of central tendency
    D. Conducting only inferential statistics

9. Race is more tied to biological and genetic factors, whereas ethnicity is more related to _____. (47-48)
    A. Culture
    B. Age
    C. Disability status
    D. Geographical region

10. When a researcher uses deception as part of a research project, it is especially important that there should be _____. (54)
    A. A meaningful rational for doing so
    B. Both informed consent and payment of the participants
    C. A second piece of research that does not use deception
    D. A careful record of all responses

After You Read, Practice Test #3

1. _____ is the idea that knowledge should be acquired through careful observation. (30)
   A. Theory
   B. Empiricism
   C. Science
   D. Replicability

2. A researcher predicts that males would be more likely to agree with stereotypes based on attractiveness compared to women. This would be an example of a _____. (33)
   A. Research question
   B. Hypothesis
   C. Objective observation
   D. Distorted thinking

3. In an experiment, only the experimental group _____. (36)
   A. Is given an informed consent
   B. Receives some level of the independent variable
   C. Must represent the population being studied
   D. Is debriefed

4. A _____ is a group of individuals who represent a larger group. (36)
   A. Population
   B. Sample
   C. Control group
   D. Representative group

5. One of the biggest strengths of the experimental method over other methods of psychological research is _____. (37)
   A. It allows us to make cause-effect statements
   B. It is the easiest and most time efficient method
   C. We can make statements about the relationship between variables
   D. The conclusions are based on observations from the natural environment

6. In an experimental study, variables are _____, whereas in an ex post facto study variables are _____. (42)
   A. Manipulated; selected
   B. Observed; correlated
   C. Correlated; manipulated
   D. Selected; observed

7. A significant difference is a difference _____. (46)
   A. That is statistically unlikely to be due to chance
   B. Can be inferred to be the result of the manipulation of the dependent variable
   C. Researchers ignore
   D. That is not used to confirm the hypothesis

8. One caution in interpreting significant differences is _____. (46)
   A. Sometimes significant differences are not meaningful differences
   B. A significant difference can be incorrect if the statistics are inferential
   C. One must make sure the research is ethical
   D. Making sure the differences are not too large

9. Sexual orientation is different from sexual behavior because sexual orientation _____. (50)
   A. Refers to self-perception and self-concept
   B. Is specifically related to gay and lesbian individuals
   C. Cannot be studied scientifically
   D. Is more misunderstood by scientists

10. A(n) _____ is conducted at the conclusion of the experiment and serves to inform the participant as to the true nature of the study. (53)
    A. Informed consent
    B. Demand characteristic
    C. Self-fulfilling prophecy
    D. Debriefing

After You Read, Comprehensive Practice Test

1. Empiricism is the view that knowledge should be acquired through _____. (30)
    A.   Observation
    B.   Logic
    C.   Intuition
    D.   Personal experiences

2. Theories are _____. (30)
    A.   Rarely used in psychology
    B.   Used to describe, explain and predict behavior
    C.   Not formed from empirical observations
    D.   Used to test hypothesis

3. A factor in an experiment that might affect the results but is not of interest to the experimenter is called a(n) _____. (36)
    A.   Dependent variable
    B.   Extraneous variable
    C.   Replication variable
    D.   Theoretical variable

4. A procedure in which a researcher systematically manipulates and observes elements of a situation in order to test a hypothesis and tries to establish a cause-effect relationship is called a(n) _____. (35)
    A.   Experiment
    B.   Independent variable
    C.   Correlation
    D.   Survey

5. A researcher has people in the experimental group watch a sad movie before having them engage in a series of academic tasks. Their hypothesis is that being sad will cause people to perform poorly in comparison to those who are not made to feel sad. Sadness in this study would be considered the _____ variable. (35)
    A.   Dependent
    B.   Control
    C.   Contextual
    D.   Independent

6. A researcher is interested in the impact of alcohol use on driving for older adults. They randomly select 200 adults age 55-75 for their study. The group of people they select represent the _____ of the study. (36)
    A.   Control group
    B.   Population
    C.   Experimental group
    D.   Sample

7. A new drug for the treatment of Alzheimer's disease is being studied. Two groups are randomly selected. The first group gets the drug, and the second group does not. The group that does not get the drug is referred to as the _____ group. (36)
   A. Control
   B. Experimental
   C. Confound
   D. Placebo

8. Which of the following is not a descriptive research method used in psychology. (38-42)
   A. Surveys
   B. Experiment
   C. Ex Post Facto study
   D. Case study

9. One of the biggest limitations of survey research is that _____. (40)
   A. The results are difficult to generalize
   B. They rely on self reports from participants
   C. They are performed in the natural environment
   D. Allow us to collect a great deal of information in a very short time

10. The statistic that assesses the degree of relationship between two variables is a _____ (41)
    A. Mean
    B. Standard deviation
    C. Correlation
    D. Relationship mode

11. Which of the following is a measure of variability in a data set? (45)
    A. Mean
    B. Standard deviation
    C. Distribution
    D. Correlation

12. Which of the following is not involved in determining social class? (49)
    A. Income
    B. Race
    C. Occupational status
    D. Education

13. Disability can be defined from all of the following perspectives, except _____. (51)
    A. Medical
    B. Moral
    C. Social
    D. Cultural

14. _____ consists of rules concerning proper and acceptable conduct that investigators use to guide their studies. (52)
    A. Informed consent
    B. Ethics
    C. Debriefing
    D. Risk statements

15. Which of the following statements regarding research is correct? (53)
    A. Participants can never be deceived in research
    B. Informed consent should be obtained after a person participates in a project
    C. Participants should be able to withdraw their participation from a study without any penalty
    D. Coercion of participants is appropriate if the goal of a study is important

True or False

1. The importance of replicability in the scientific endeavor is that it gives scientists greater confidence in the accuracy of their results. (31)

2. Hypotheses are often used to generate theory in science. (33)

3. If we wanted to make definitive cause and effect statements about the variables we are studying, the best method to use would be the correlational method. (37)

4. The ex post facto design is most similar to a correlational design. (42)

5. The mean and the mode are both measures of central tendency. (44)

6. A correlation coefficient of -.75 is better than one of +.75. (46)

7. When examining diversity within and between groups, it is important to realize that there are usually more differences between groups than within groups. (51)

8. Only research studies that are done using human participants are required to abide by ethical principles of research conduct. (52-54)

Essay Questions

1. Compare and contrast the strengths and weaknesses of the specific types of research methods associated with experimental and descriptive research studies. (35-42)

2. Discuss the importance of avoiding bias in the research process and identify the various aspects of diversity that should be considered when conducting research. (47-51)

When You Have Finished

Surf's Up!!

After you've read and reviewed, try these web sites for additional information about some of the topics covered in this chapter.

1. **A New View of Statistics**. (http://www.sportsci.org/resource/stats/index.html)
   This site contains information about all sorts of statistics and how they are used in psychology. The descriptions are written so that the reader can make sense of what results of specific statistical technique mean versus being bogged down in statistical and mathematical formulas.

2. **Psychological Research on the Net**. (http://psych.hanover.edu/research/exponnet.html)
   At this site, you will find links to known experiments on the internet that are psychologically related. Take some of these studies and find out what being an actual participant in a research study is really like!

3. **The Center for Critical Thinking.** (http://www.criticalthinking.org/)
   This center is devoted to the development of critical thinking in society with the goal of promoting essential change in education and society. There is information here on improving your own critical thinking skills, a place to discuss critical thinking with others, and resources for applying critical thinking to society's problems.

4. **Ethics in Research with Animals.** (http://www.apa.org/science/anguide.html)
   Some students are concerned about animals being used in psychological research. This site, part of the American Psychological Association, discusses ethical treatment of research with animals. In addition, there are links here to other issues related to ethics and the ethical treatment of human participants.

5. **Tutorial: Research Methods in Psychology**
   (http://psychology.about.com/library/bl/blmethods.htm)
   This site is sponsored by about.com. It contains information about a number of topics in psychological research that are included in your text, but also contains a lot of additional information and links. Some of the topics include the difference between correlation and causation, the difference between theory and hypothesis, and different types of research methods.

Cross Check: Science of Psychology

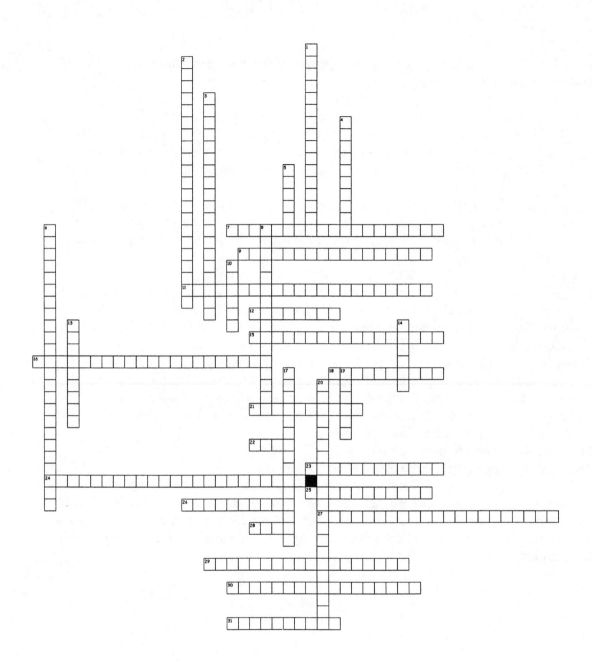

Across

7. Variable that is manipulated
9. They get the IV
11. Ranges for 1.0 to −1.0
12. Something that varies in experiments
15. How much scores vary on average
16. Statistics that allow us to determine meaning
18. Knowledge should be acquired through observation
21. Educated statement about relationships
22. The most frequently occurring score
23. They are a comparison group to the experimental group
24. Watching it as it normally occurs
25. They used to be called subjects
26. Branch of mathematics used in research
27. Describes our data
28. The average score
29. Tells us about relationships
30. Manipulation of IV should influence this
31. Telling you what you did once you are done

Down

1. Process of doing research
2. Not to be confused with meaningful differences
3. Describes versus manipulates variables
4. Systematic manipulation of variables
5. Group of people in a study
6. The mean would be an example of these
8. Subject variables versus manipulated variables
10. Collection of organized ideas
13. Intense study of one
14. Rules that guide behavior
17. Letting you know before you agree to do it
19. Another average indicator; less sensitive to extremes
20. How we define and measure our variables

Created by Puzzlemaker at DiscoverySchool.com

Chapter 3

Neuroscience: The Brain and Behavior

Before you read...

We often go through our day without much thought or awareness of the things that our biological systems are doing that allows us to accomplish our goals. In fact, it is only when some of these systems become dysfunctional or break down that we become aware of their extreme importance and influence on our daily lives. In this chapter, you will learn about the basic systems that operate and communicate in your body. In addition, you will be introduced to two other important factors that influence your behavior, your genetic make-up and your evolutionary history. Combined, these factors set the stage for much of what you do, or are capable of doing, as a human being.

The chapter begins with a specific and detailed discussion of the structural and functional aspects of the nervous systems. The journey begins at the "simple" level by looking at the functioning and communication of neurons, and it moves to the more complex level of the brain. As you will see, the brain is a complex and fascinating structure that influences everything from breathing to solving complex problems. In the next section, you are introduced to neural imaging and an exploration of how we know what we do about the functioning of brain. You will also learn about brain specialization and how the brain recovers after injury. You will learn a lot of terms in the beginning of this chapter. Try not to get lost in the terminology as you read, and keep an eye on the importance of these structures and their influence on human behavior.

The other major biological system that is explored in this chapter is the endocrine system. Although it is a bit slower in communicating compared to the nervous system, it is no less important in controlling human behavior. In this section, you will learn about communication within this system, some of the important influences it has on behavior, and some of the things that might go wrong if the system is not functioning properly.

The chapter concludes by looking at two factors that influence our biological and psychological make-up, but at a more indirect level. These factors include the role of genetics and our evolutionary history. You will come to understand how psychologists and other scientists attempt to understand how much of our behavior is related to genes we inherit from our parents. You will also be presented with a thought provoking discussion of the influence of our evolutionary history on human sexuality. In this "point-counterpoint" discussion, the question of whether men are promiscuous by nature is explored!

Because of the importance of biological, genetic, and evolutionary factors on human behavior, Chapter 3 will serve as a foundation for information presented in many of the future chapters. So, take some time and read carefully. You might even want to start thinking ahead and see if you can think of some ways that the information presented here might be related to the chapters to come!

Learning Objectives

After reading this chapter, you should be able to:

1. Review the functioning of the nervous system by specifying the four types of neurons, the parts of a neuron and their functions, and the electrochemical process associated with neuronal communication.
2. Describe the action of a neurotransmitters on the receiving neuron and be able to list the different types of neurotransmitters and what function(s) they are believed to be associated with
3. Explain the field of psychopharmacology and discuss the goals of professionals within this field.
4. Describe the peripheral nervous system, its subsystems, and the role of these systems in human behavior.
5. Identify and describe the structures and functions of the central nervous system.
6. Define the structures and functions of the brain including the substructures of the hindbrain, midbrain, and forebrain.
7. Describe how studying brain damage might allow us to better understand how the brain normally functions.
8. Specify how modern techniques such as CT, PET, and MRI and fMRI scans are making the examination of brain processes more precise.
9. Understand brain specialization and discuss some of the research that has been conducted within this area.
10. Examine the concept of plasticity, discuss factors that may influence the plasticity of the brain, and explain how plasticity may provide hope in altering the effects of neuronal disease.
11. Describe the functioning of the endocrine system, list the endocrine glands within this system, and state how the hormones produced by these glands influence behavior.
12. Understand the difference between nature and nurture and how each affects the expression of human traits.
13. Understand the basic components of genetics including gene(s), chromosomes, genotype and phenotype and heritability.
14. Discuss the role that genetics has on human behavior and traits.
15. What is the evolutionary approach to psychology and how our evolutionary history is believed to influence current human behavior(s).
16. Outline some of the controversies associated with evolutionary approaches and explain how evolutionary psychologists answer these criticisms.

Key Terms

Nervous system
Neuron
Afferent neuron
Efferent neuron
Interneurons
Glial Cells
Myelin Sheath
Dendrites
Axon
Synapse
Threshold
Action Potential
All-or-None
Refractory Period
Neurotransmitter
Synaptic Vesicles
Excitatory Postsynaptic Potential
Inhibitory Postsynaptic Potential
Acetylcholine
Gamma-amniobutyric Acid
Serotonin
Dopamine
Norepinephrine
Endorphins
Psychopharmacology
Agonist
Antagonist
Peripheral Nervous System
Somatic Nervous System
Autonomic Nervous System
Sympathetic Nervous System
Parasympathetic Nervous System
Central Nervous System
Spinal Cord
Brain
Hindbrain
Medulla
Reticular Formation
Pons
Cerebellum
Midbrain
Forebrain
Thalamus

Hypothalamus
Limbic System
Hippocampus
Amygdala
Cortex
Convolutions
Corpus Callosum
Broca's Area
Wernicke's Area
Electroencephalogram (EEG)
Magnetic Resonance Imaging (MRI)
Functional Magnetic Resonance Imaging (fMRI)
Positron Emission Tomography (PET)
Split-Brain Individuals
Plasticity
Hormones
Endocrine Glands
Pituitary Gland
Insulin
Genetics
Nature
Nurture
Chromosome
Genes
Genotype
Phenotype
Mutations
Heritability
Identical Twins
Fraternal Twins
Genome
Genomics
Evolutionary Psychology
Natural Selection
Adaptation

As you read...

How Is The Nervous System Organized?

2-1	The Cellular Level

1.   The _____ system is composed of billions of individual nerve cells called _____.

2.   Define and compare afferent neurons and efferent neurons.

3.   List and briefly describe the 3 types of neurons.

4.   _____ _____ provide nourishment and structure to neurons.

5.   What is a myelin sheath and how does it help neuronal communication?

6.   Draw a neuron, label the primary parts of the neuron, and trace the path of a nerve impulse.

7.   Explain the electrochemical process of a neural impulse.

8.   Mach the following parts of the nervous systems to their correct definition.

Term	Definition
_____ Action Potential	a) transmits signals from cell body through axon terminal to adjacent neurons
_____ Axon	b) the time a neuron needs to recover after firing
_____ Central Nervous System	c) fibers extending from the neuron cell body and receive signals from neighboring cells
_____ Dendrite	d) small space between neurons
_____ Neuron	e) an electrical current that travels down the axon of a neuron
_____ Refractory Period	f) brain and spinal cord
_____ Synapse	g) the basic unit of the nervous system

9.   Neurons communicate with one another through the release of _____, which are defined as _____.

10.   The small structures that are found in every axon terminal and store neurotransmitters are called _____.

11.   Compare and contrast EPSP and IPSP.

12.   Complete the following table.

Neurotransmitter	Behavioral Effect	Inhibitory or Excitatory?
Acetylcholine		Excitatory
	Plays a role in sleep, mood, and appetite.	
GABA		
Dopamine		

13. _____ is a neuropeptide that inhibits certain synaptic transmissions involving pain.

14. Psychopharmacology is the study of _____.

15. When an agonist is present, receptors respond by _____, whereas when an antagonist is present, receptor sites _____.

2-2	**Divisions of the Nervous System**

1. What are the function and structures of the peripheral nervous system?

2. List and describe the two subsystems of the peripheral nervous system.

3. Compare and contrast the sympathetic and parasympathetic nervous systems.

4. Fill in the organizational structure of the nervous system with the correct terms.

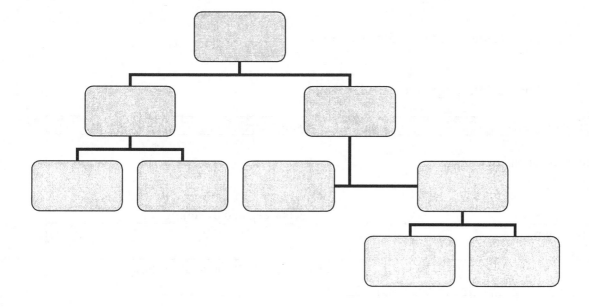

5. Identify the nervous system (central, somatic, parasympathetic, or sympathetic) that is most specifically illustrated by each of the following situations.

   a) _____ In an effort to shape up, John engages in a series of sit-ups and push-ups.

   b) _____ Mary, while walking to her psychology class, comes across a large dog who growls at her. Mary notices her heart beating faster and her breathing increased.

   c) _____ Jane just moved off-campus and must draw up a new budget. She carefully analyzes her assets, her bills, and how she would like to spend the excess after bills.

   d) _____ An increase in the secretion of digestive juices and blood flowing to the gastrointestinal system causes the meal Simon just ate to break down into protein and carbohydrate molecules and nutrients that are eventually absorbed by his blood system.

5. What is the function of the central nervous system?

6. The central nervous system is composed of the _____ and the _____.

2-3	The Brain

1. The brain is divided into three main divisions, called the _____, _____, and _____.

2. What functions does the hindbrain perform?

3. Define the following parts of the hindbrain.

Part of hindbrain	Function
Reticular formation	
	Provides a link to the rest of the brain and affects sleep and dreaming.
Cerebellum	
	Controls heartbeat and breathing

4.   What are the functions controlled by the midbrain?

5.   The authors of the text claim that the forebrain is the "largest and most complex" of the three brain regions. Explain why this is so.

6.   The thalamus has sometimes been refereed to as the "Grand Central Station" of the brain. Why?

7.   Which part of the forebrain might be not working correctly if you found yourself to be suddenly thirsty all the time? What if you were having memory problems?

8.   What is the limbic system involved in? What structures does it include?

9.   The _____ is involved in navigating about the world, learning, and memory.

10.   The amygdala is involved in _____.

11.   Describe the cortex of the brain.

12.   The cortex contains _____ that increase its surface area.

13.   List the 4 lobes of the cortex, their location, and their function(s).

Lobe	Location	Function(s)

How Does the Brain Function?

1. You can read this sentence and understand it, but when someone asks you to repeat it out loud, you cannot. The part of the brain involved in the reading and understanding is referred to as _____ _____, whereas the part of the brain involved in producing language is referred to as _____.

2. Describe the functions and applications of the 4 neural imaging techniques.

3. Split-brain individuals have had what done to them?

4. Discuss the results of research on lateralization in the brain.

5. Are their gender differences in the brain? Answer this question using the results of research findings presented in your text.

6. The capability of the brain to grown and develop through the lifespan is _____.

7. List the factors that influence plasticity.

What Effects Do Hormones Have on Behavior?

1. The nervous system communicates through the release of _____, whereas the endocrine system communicates through the release of _____.

2. Endocrine glands are _____.

3. Why is the pituitary gland often called the body's master gland?

4.   Complete the following table on the endocrine system.

Endocrine Gland	Hormone Released	Effect
	steroid hormones	
pancreas		
	epinephrine (adrenaline)	

How Do Genetic Factors Affect Behavior?

1.   Genetics is _____.

2.   Describe the difference between nature and nurture.

3.   Label each of the following statements as being primarily the product of nature, nurture, or both nature and nurture. Remember, all behavior is ultimately the product of both. However, the statements below *emphasize* (in some cases) nature or nurture. They are designed only to give you practice in discriminating between the two components of behavior. If you cannot determine a *primary* influence, "both" is probably the correct answer.

   a)   _____ Unlike most babies, at the age of seven months, Mario said his first word in the language he had been exposed to by his parents.

   b)   _____ Mary has blond hair and is very tall.

   c)   _____ Having lived in China, France, and Italy, Kim can prepare Chinese, French, and Italian meals.

   d)   _____ Donna's level of dopamine is so low that her body trembles most of the time.

   e)   _____ By the age of twelve, Francis was mastering college-level academic material.

4.   What are genes?

5.   The microscopic strands of DNA that are found on the nucleus of every cell and that contain genetic information are called _____.

6. State the differences between dominant and recessive traits.

7. A _____ is a person's genetic make-up, whereas a _____ is a person's observable characteristics.

8. Unexpected changes in gene replication are called _____.

9. Using the research presented in your text, answer the question "Do genes influence behavior?"

10. How does the study of fraternal and identical twins help us to understand what behaviors might be genetically transmitted?

11. What is the human genome?

12. Behavioral genomics is _____.

Does Our Evolutionary History Influence Our Current Behavior?

1. What is Evolutionary Psychology?

2. Define Natural Selection.

3. _____ has occurred when a trait or inherited characteristic has increased in a population.

4. Outline the controversies associated with evolutionary psychology.

After You Read, Practice Test #1

1. The _____ of the neuron has thin branching fibers and receives information from neighboring neurons. (59)
   A.   Cell body
   B.   Axon
   C.   Dendrites
   D.   Axon terminals

2. What are the basic building blocks of the nervous system called? (58)
   A.   Synapses
   B.   Nerves
   C.   Grey cells
   D.   Neurons

3. After a neuron fires, it generally needs time to recover before it can fire again. This time period is referred to as the _____ period. (61)
   A.   Resting
   B.   Inhibitory
   C.   Sympathetic
   D.   Refractory

4. Endorphins _____. (63)
   A.   Are narcotic drugs
   B.   Excite synaptic transmission of pain
   C.   Inhibit synaptic transmission of pain
   D.   Are incomplete amino acids and ineffective as neurotransmitters

5. Suppose a researcher has determined that a particular illness is caused by excessive action of a particular neurotransmitter. The researcher will probably try to create a drug that will act as a(n) _____ for that neurotransmitter. (64)
   A.   Agonist
   B.   Antagonist
   C.   Neuropeptide
   D.   Synapse

6. Which of the following is NOT one of the three main divisions of the brain? (68-69)
   A.   Hindbrain
   B.   Forebrain
   C.   Midbrain
   D.   Frontbrain

7. Which of the following brain structures serves as a relay station for sensory information? (69)
   A. Amygdala
   B. Hippocampus
   C. Thalamus
   D. Hypothalamus

8. One way in which men and women use their brains differently when performing the same task is that _____. (78-79)
   A. Men process language primarily on the right side, women primarily on the left
   B. Men's brains process more tasks at lower levels, women more at higher levels
   C. Men's brains are less affected by hormones than women's brains are
   D. Women use both sides of their brains more equally on some cognitive tasks

9. The ability of the brain to grow and develop throughout the lifespan refers to the brains _____. (79)
   A. Neurogenesis
   B. Plasticity
   C. Emergence
   D. Lateralization

10. _____ refer(s) to the proportion of a trait's variation among individuals in a population that is genetically determined. (85)
    A. Heritability
    B. Percent mutation
    C. Genomics
    D. Phenotype

After You Read, Practice Test #2

1. The long, slim fiber that extends from a neuron and that carries its message out to other neurons is called the _____. (59)
    A.   Dendrite
    B.   Glia
    C.   Myelin
    D.   Axon

2. A neuron will fire when a rapid reversal of negative and positive ions stimulate the cell and reach a level of intensity that is above the cell's _____. (61)
    A.   Potential
    B.   Threshold
    C.   Spikes
    D.   Resting level

3. Select the neurotransmitter that is especially involved with anxiety. (63)
    A.   GABA
    B.   Acetylcholine
    C.   Serotonin
    D.   Norepinephrine

4. The sympathetic nervous system is primarily responsible for _____. (65)
    A.   Helping relax and conserve energy
    B.   Processing sensory inputs to the brain
    C.   Muscular coordination and movements
    D.   Coping with emergency situations

5. The parasympathetic nervous system is primarily responsible for _____. (66)
    A.   Helping relax and conserve energy
    B.   Coping with emergency situations
    C.   Muscular coordination and movements
    D.   Processing sensory inputs to the brain

6. Which of the following parts of the brain is most heavily involved in regulating emotions? (69)
    A.   The cerebellum
    B.   The reticular formation
    C.   The limbic system
    D.   The corpus callosum

7. Mark has suddenly begun to experience problem with his ability to learning and remember new information. Which of the following brain areas is likely involved? (69)
   A. Thalamus
   B. Hypothalamus
   C. Hippocampus
   D. Pons

8. Which of the following is not knowledge garnered through split-brain patient studies? (75-78)
   A. Not every behavior or function is associated with a single part of the brain
   B. Severing of the corpus callosum produces ambidextrous abilities
   C. Specific localization of certain functions
   D. Performance on certain tasks is reduced due to the inability of the left and right hemispheres to communicate

9. The endocrine system operates through the release of _____ into the bloodstream. (81)
   A. Neurotransmitters
   B. Hormones
   C. Action potentials
   D. Serotonin

10. In response to the nature versus nurture debate, most psychologists agree that _____. (83-84)
   A. Heredity is more important than environment
   B. Environment is more important than heredity
   C. Ultimately, all behavior is the result of the environment
   D. Both heredity and environment are important, but the question of which is more important has not been resolved

After You Read, Practice Test #3

1. _____ neurons carry information from the central nervous system to the glands and muscles. (58)
   A. Inter
   B. Sensory
   C. Efferent
   D. Afferent

2. When a postsynaptic potential (PSP) is received by a cell, if it is excitatory it will _____, while if it is inhibitory it will _____. (62)
   A. Trigger the release of neurotransmitters; trigger the absorption of neurotransmitters
   B. Trigger the absorption of neurotransmitters; trigger the release of neurotransmitters
   C. Make the cell fire more easily; make the cell fire less easily
   D. Make the cell fire less easily; make the cell fire more easily

3. Which of the following neurotransmitters is believed to play a key role in arousal reactions and possibly hunger, eating, and sexual activity? (63)
   A. Norephinephrine
   B. Dopamine
   C. Serotonin
   D. Endorphins

4. The _____ includes brain areas such as the cortex, a thought oriented structure, and the thalamus, which routes information to different parts of the brain. (69)
   A. Corpus callosum
   B. Hindbrain
   C. Midbrain
   D. Forebrain

5. The peripheral nervous system consists of two parts, which are _____. (65)
   A. The brain and spinal cord
   B. The parasympathetic and sympathetic nervous systems
   C. The somatic and autonomic nervous systems
   D. The afferent and efferent nervous systems

6. The _____ is directly related to the development of disorders involving the over or underproduction of insulin. (82)
   A. Pituitary gland
   B. Pancreas
   C. Adrenal gland
   D. Salivary gland

7.   The relationships between the endocrine glands, the brain, and behavior can best be summarized by saying _____. (81-82)
   A.   The endocrine glands control the brain through the hormones they secrete into the bloodstream
   B.   The brain controls the endocrine glands and the hormones they produce through nerve signals
   C.   Hormones produced by the endocrine glands affect behavior through their effect on the brain
   D.   The endocrine glands, the brain, and behavior all interact and affect each other

8.   Genes are _____. (84)
   A.   The units of heredity transmission consisting of DNA and protein
   B.   Strands of genetic material
   C.   Used to describe the development of twins
   D.   Found only in ova and sperm sex cells

9.   The term *nature* refers to _____. (83)
   A.   Life experiences
   B.   Heredity
   C.   Personality
   D.   The environment

10.   _____ refers to the study of the entire pattern of genes in an individual. (87)
   A.   Genomics
   B.   Genome
   C.   Genetics
   D.   Genocide

After You Read, Comprehensive Self Test

1. Name the part of the neuron that carries information toward the cell body. (59)
    - A.   Dendrites
    - B.   Synapse
    - C.   Axon
    - D.   Myelin

2. The _____ is the small space that separates the signal transmission center from one neuron and the receptor centers of another neuron. (59)
    - A.   Axon
    - B.   Dendrite
    - C.   Synapse
    - D.   Action potential

3. How can the electrochemical process that produces an action potential be best described? (61)
    - A.   A chemical change that occurs as a result of electrical stimulation
    - B.   An exchange of ions through the cell membrane
    - C.   A molecular chain reaction
    - D.   The creation of chemical transmitters by electrical energy

4. Your body assumes a "fight-or-flight" condition, preparing you for emergency situations, when the _____ nervous system is activated. (65)
    - A.   Central
    - B.   Somatic
    - C.   Sympathetic
    - D.   Parasympathetic

5. An individual with an impaired somatic nervous system may have difficulty with which of the following activities? (65)
    - A.   Mentally adding two numbers together
    - B.   Digesting food
    - C.   Spading a garden
    - D.   Daydreaming

6. Which of the following is not a spinal reflex? (67)
    - A.   Knee jerk
    - B.   Removing your hand from a hot object
    - C.   Reaching for a candy bar
    - D.   Pulling your foot from the cold water in a swimming pool

7. The reticular formation that extends through the hindbrain, the midbrain, and forebrain is thought to be involved in _____. (68)
    A. Coordination of smooth muscle
    B. Experiencing pain
    C. Controlling heart beat
    D. Arousal and sleeping

8. Which of the following is likely to be disrupted in an individual with a damaged cerebellum? (68)
    A. Sleeping
    B. Playing basketball
    C. Thinking
    D. Homeostasis

9. A CT scan (computerized tomography) is created using _____. (73)
    A. Electrodes attached to the outside of someone's head
    B. Computer controlled and processed X-ray pictures
    C. Radiochemicals injected into the patient's blood
    D. The magnetic fields of varying strength and direction

10. _____ is a brain monitoring technique that tracks the regional blood flow during various mental tasks using radioactive markers. (74)
    A. Magnetic Resonance Imaging
    B. Computerized Tomography
    C. Positron Emission Tomography
    D. Functional Magnetic Resonance Imaging

11. The central nervous system affects the release of _____ which then impact _____ to ultimately impact human behavior. (81)
    A. Glands, organs
    B. Organs, hormones
    C. Hormones, glands
    D. Hormones, organs

12. The hormone produced by the pancreas that controls the body's sugar production is called _____. (82)
    A. Glucose
    B. Insulin
    C. Diabetes
    D. Sucrose

13. A person's eye color is best understood by which of the following? (85)
    A. Phenotype
    B. Genotype
    C. Mutations
    D. Both phenotypes and genotypes

14. _____ _____ refers to the principle which states that characteristics and behaviors which serve adaptive functions will be those that are passed on to successive generations. (89)
   A.   Genetic parsimony
   B.   Evolutionary adaptation
   C.   Genomic fitness
   D.   Natural selection

15. Each of the following represents a controversy associated with evolutionary psychology, except _____ (91).
   A.   Evolutionary psychologists assert that there are human universals
   B.   The assumption that many of our behaviors are biologically determined
   C.   Evolution is more important to psychology than other theories of human behavior
   D.   The methods that are used to study evolutionary psychology are difficult to disprove

True or False

1.   Myelinated neurons carry information through the nervous system at a higher speed than do unmyelinated neurons. (58)

2.   After firing a number of times, some neurons are only able to fire at a lesser strength. (61)

3.   The nervous system operates at a slower speed than the endocrine system. (81)

4.   The parietal lobe is located in the back of the brain and is associated with the sense of touch and body position. (71)

5.   Damage to Wernicke's area in the brain is associated with difficulties in language comprehension. (72)

6.   Research findings generally do not support the fact that there are masculine and feminine sides of the brain. (78)

7.   The brain is able to produce new neurons to replace damaged or destroyed neurons. (79)

8.   The effects of genes on behavior are generally considered by scientists to be direct versus indirect. (85)

Essay Questions

1.   Describe the action potential of the neuron. (59-61)

2.   Describe the interaction between the sympathetic and somatic nervous system during the fight-or-flight syndrome. (65-66)

When You Have Finished!

Surf's Up!!

After you've read and reviewed, try these web sites for additional information about some of the topics covered in this chapter.

1. **Brain Explorer** (http://www.brainexplorer.org/)
   A site packed with visual images of the brain, neurons and neuronal control. Also contains a glossary with definitions related to the brain and information on common brain disorders.

2. **Exploring the Brain, Neuronal Communication, and Drugs**
   (http://science.education.nih.gov/suppliments/nih2/addiction/activities/activities_toc.htm)
   Interactive video and audio presentations related to the brain, communication between neurons, and the effects of drugs on the brain. The site is sponsored by the National Institutes of Health and National Institute on Drug Abuse.

3. **Basic Neural Processes** (http://psych.hanover.edu/Krantz/neurotut.html)
   On this site, you will find a collection of tutorials that describe the basic neural functions. In addition, there are some quizzes and ways to test your knowledge of the nervous system and neuronal communication.

4. **Society for Neuroscience** (http://web.sfn.org/)
   An organization for scientists who student the brain and nervous system.

5. **A Neuropsychologist Homepage** (http://www.tbidoc.com/)
   This site is devoted to understanding and explaining brain injury from the standpoint of a neuropsychologist.

6. **Center for Evolutionary Psychology** (http://www.psych.ucsb.edu/research/cep/)
   This site is developed to provide support and information about evolutionary psychology. You will find information about research topics in the area, research methods that are used, and information about places where you might study more about this emerging area in psychology.

7. **The Endocrine System** (http://www.ama-assn.org/ama/pub/category/7157.html)
   This is part of the American Medical Association website. You will find a nice diagram of the endocrine system here that you could use to practice labeling the glands of the endocrine system. In addition, there is a nice, brief description of the endocrine glands, the hormones they produce and their function(s).

Cross Check: Neuroscience: The Brain and Behavior

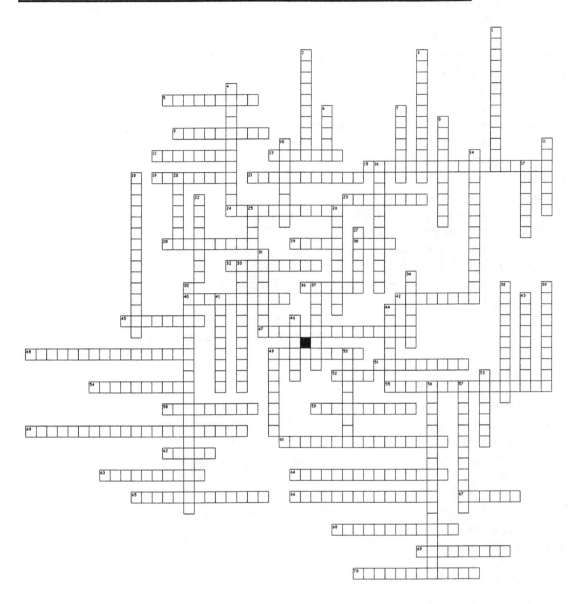

Psychology

Across

5. Person's observable characteristics
9. Unexpected changes in genes
12. Chemicals produced by endocrine glands
13. Part of nervous system consisting of the brain and spinal cord
15. Involved in regulation of arousal
19. Person's genetic makeup
21. Microscopic strands of DNA
23. Routing station for sending sensory information
24. Important to learning and memory
28. Receive messages from other neurons
29. Part of CNS located in skull
30. Sends out messages to other neurons
32. Level of stimulation required for activation of a neuron
36. Total sequence of the genes on an organism's DNA
40. Capability of the brain to grow and develop throughout the life span
42. Neurotransmitter related to emotion, feelings of reward and pleasure
45. Receives and interprets signals from other parts of the brain
47. Secrete hormones
48. Chemical substances that are stored in synaptic vesicles
49. Part of nervous system that controls physiological actions and reactions and proceeds automatically
51. Gland that is known as the master gland
52. Functional unit of hereditary transmission
54. A trait that has increased in a population because it aids survival
55. Small structures found in every axon terminal that store neurotransmitters
58. Lowest of three main divisions of the brain
59. Part of nervous system that carries information to and from the central nervous system
60. Inhibitory neurotransmitter related to anxiety
61. Principle that states characteristics that have helped the species survive are likely to be passed on
62. Types of cells that serve support functions
63. Influences balance and coordination
64. Electrical current that travels along the axon of a neuron
65. An excitatory neurotransmitter that is involved in many functions
66. Thick band of nerve fibers connecting the left and right hemispheres
67. Basic building block of nervous system
68. Type of neuron that connects other neurons
69. The largest of the three main areas of the brain
70. Important to emotional experiences

Down

1. Structures and organs that facilitate electrical and chemical communication
2. Chemical that opposes the actions of a neurotransmitter
3. Affects eating, drinking, and sexual activity
4. Protective coating of axon
6. Area of brain critical to language production
7. Part of nervous system that responds to the senses of sight, hearing, touch, and smell
8. The period of time needed for a neuron to recover after it fires
10. Study of the entire pattern of genes in an individual
11. Space between axons
14. Neurotransmitter related to arousal, hunger, eating, and sex
16. Area of psychology that seeks to explain behavior by examining how the brain developed over long periods of time
17. Hormone produced by pancreas
18. Part of nervous system that controls normal operation of the body
20. Person's experience
22. Part of limbic system and related to emotional experiences
25. Affects sleep and dreaming
26. Part of CNS that relays signals from the sensory organs
27. Person's biological makeup
31. Area of brain critical to language comprehension
33. Proportion of a trait's variation among individuals in a population
34. Chemical that mimics or facilitates the actions of a neurotransmitter
35. People whose corpus callosum has been severed
37. Type of neuron that sends messages from brain and spine to other parts of body
38. Part of nervous system that responds to emergency situations
39. Neuropeptide that exerts effects similar to opiate drugs
41. Neurotransmitter related to mood, sleep, and appetite
43. Type of twin also known as dizygotic twin
44. Study of heredity
46. Convoluted exterior covering of the brain's hemispheres
49. Type of neurons that sends message to spine and brain
50. Type of twin that shares all genetic material
53. Part of hindbrain the controls heartbeat
56. Study of how drugs affect behavior
57. Folds in the cortical tissue in the cerebral hemispheres

Created by Puzzlemaker at
DiscoverySchool.com

Chapter 4

Child Development

Before you read...

From the moment that we are conceived, we go through constant development and change. In this chapter, you will be introduced the field of developmental psychology, and you will review the types of changes associated with continued development. Child development has received the most widespread research attention within psychology. The chapter begins by exploring some of the common issues that come up when exploring human development. It is likely that you have considered many of these same issues in your own thinking about human behavior. For example, one such issue is the question of how much our development is influenced by genetics versus the environment. In this introductory section, you will also be introduced to research methods that are used to answer specific developmental questions.

In the following sections of the chapter, you will explore specific aspects of child development. The first area you will study is physical development. The prenatal period is the first developmental stage, and it extends from conception to birth. During this critical period, development may be affected by environmental variables such as diet, infection, radiation, and drugs. These substances are known as teratogens, and they can have significant negative effects ranging from birth defects to early infant death. In contrast, normally developing newborns can hear, see, smell, and respond to the environment immediately after leaving the birth canal. In addition, newborns exhibit several reflexive behaviors at birth which allow them to function and adapt to their new environment. After reading this section, you will have a good idea of the important and exciting changes that are a part of the child's early development!

In the next part of the chapter, you will learn about the exciting aspect of cognitive development. In doing so, you will be introduced to two of the most influential theorists of cognitive development, Piaget and Vygotsky. Piaget's theory focuses on the individual child and how that child comes to understand and integrate new learning about his or her environment. Vygotsky's model is also concerned with such factors, but focuses more on the influence of social and cultural factors on the development of thought.

We are all born as social beings and we rely heavily on other people in our lives. The fourth part of the chapter focuses on how children learn about and adapt to the social and emotional demands of the environment. Attachment and temperament are two key concepts that are related to social and emotional development, and you will learn about the importance of these concepts to childhood development and adaptation. In addition, you will learn about the moral development of children, and you will come to understand how children learn to make decisions in their environment.

Finally, you will explore some of the more important environmental factors that impact social development. These factors include the child's early interactive learning, parents, peers, and gender-roles. In addition to these factors, you will also be introduced to Erik Erikson's model of psychosocial development, which explores how children develop a sense of self.

Learning Objectives

After reading this chapter, you should be able to:

1. Explain the five key issues in developmental psychology and understand how they operate to frame the questions developmental psychologists ask.
2. Compare and contrast cross-sectional and longitudinal research designs and outline the strengths and weaknesses of each.
3. Describe prenatal development as it proceeds through the zygote, embryonic, and fetal stages.
4. Identify some of the environmental factors that might negatively impact prenatal development and the role of critical periods in determining the type of potential impact.
5. Discuss the infant's ability to perceive and interact with the world, paying particular attention to the research that informs our knowledge about this interaction.
6. Describe the central concepts of Piaget's theory of cognitive development, list each of the key stages in this theory, and summarize the changes that are evident at each stage.
7. Summarize some of the criticisms of Piaget's cognitive development theory.
8. Describe Vygotsky's sociocultural theory and differentiate it from Piaget's theory.
9. Explain the theory of mind.
10. Define attachment, discuss some of the classic work on attachment theory, and explain modern theories of attachment style and its impact on childcare.
11. Define temperament, list the different categories of temperament, and discuss the impact of temperament on the child's developmental environment.
12. Explain Kohlberg's levels and stages of moral development.
13. Summarize Gilligan's criticisms of Kohlberg's theory of moral development.
14. Describe some of the influences on early social development.
15. Understand gender roles and the influence of these roles on development and socialization.
16. List and describe Erikson's first 4 stages of psychosocial development.

Key Terms

Developmental Psychology
Cross Sectional Research Design
Longitudinal Research Design
Zygote
Embryo
Fetus
Placenta
Critical Period
Teratogen
Fetal Alcohol Syndrome
Babinski Reflex
Moro Reflex
Rooting Reflex
Sucking Reflex
Grasping Reflex
Schema
Assimilation
Accommodation
Sensorimotor Stage
Object Permanence
Preoperational Stage
Egocentrism
Decentration
Concrete Operational Stage
Conservation
Formal Operational Stage
Zone of Proximal Development
Theory of Mind
Attachment
Socialization
Separation Anxiety
Strange Situation
Temperament
Morality
Sex
Gender
Gender Role
Gender Stereotype

As you read...

What Are the Central Issues of Development?

1. Developmental psychology is _____.

2. List and describe the five main issues in developmental psychology

3. How does the transactional model explain and incorporate the impact of both nature and nurture on development?

4. The authors of your text claim that _____ might have the strongest impact on development. Why do they state that, and what do you think about their argument?

5. Define and differentiate between a cross-sectional and longitudinal research design.

6. You are interested in studying the effect of playing video games on aggressive behavior. Your hypothesis is that the more time you spend playing video games, the more violent you will be. How would you test your hypothesis using a cross-sectional design? A longitudinal design?

How Does Physical Development Proceed?

1. Briefly describe the time period and event(s) associated with the following prenatal periods:
    a. Zygote

    b. Embryo

    c. Fetus

2. The mass of tissue that provides oxygen, food, and antibodies to the fetus and eliminates waste is called the _____.

3. The _____ connects the zygote to the placenta.

4. List the known factors that can affect the baby and mother, and state the importance of a critical period as it relates to exposure to these factors.

5. A _____ is a substance that can produce developmental malformations.

4-1	Newborns Are Ready to Experience the World

1. Infancy is considered to be the time period between _____ and _____.

2. There are two typical growth patterns. Describe each.

3. List and describe the 5 primary reflexes of a newborn.

4. The _____ reflex is an outstretching of the arms and legs and crying in response to a loud noise.

5. The _____ reflex occurs when one touches the sole of the foot of an infant and the toes turn upward and out.

6. Describe the Fantz's viewing box and how it is used to study infant perception

7. According to research using the visual cliff, infants develop depth perception at what age?

How Does Thought Develop?

1. Piaget's theory focused on _____ people think versus _____ they think; thus, making it more applicable _____.

2. What is a schema and how it is related to Piaget's theory of cognitive development?

3. What are the three processes by which a schema can change?

4. List Piaget's four stages of intellectual development, the age range that each state encompasses, and the major intellectual accomplishment associated with each stage

Stage	Age	Major Accomplishment
_____	_____	_____
_____	_____	_____
_____	_____	_____
_____	_____	_____

5. The realization that objects continue to exist even when they are out of sight is called _____ _____.

6. The inability to perceive a situation except in relation to oneself is called _____.

7. Name the three primary criticisms of Piaget's theory of cognitive development.

8. What are the differences between Vygotsky's and Piaget's approaches?

9. According to Vygotsky, the zone of proximal development is _____.

10. Provide an example of decontextualized thought.

11. Define Theory of Mind.

12. What type of research is used to study the theory of mind?

13. Why are program such as Head Start important to early development?

How Do Social and Emotional Development Proceed?

1. Attachment is _____.

2. _____ is the process by which a person's behaviors, values, skills, plans, and attitudes conform to and are adapted to those desired by society.

3. Describe the results of Harry Harlow's research on the importance of attachment.

4. _____ _____ is a fear response that occurs when an attachment figure leaves an infant.

5. Describe the four attachment types demonstrated in the Strange Situation technique.

6. What does the research show about the effects of leaving children in the care of someone other than their parents?

7. What is the evolutionary perspective on attachment?

4-2   Temperament

1. Define *temperament*.

2. List the 4 broad categories of temperament.

3. Describe the relationship between biology and temperament.

4. Does parenting have an impact on temperament?

4-3   Moral Reasoning

1. Define morality.

2. Moral relativity _____.

3. Compare and contrast Piaget's and Kohlberg's theories of moral development.

4. List the 3 levels with their 2 stages of Kohlberg's theory of moral development.

5. What is the distinction between sex and gender?

6. _____ _____ are differences between men and women on behaviors or mental processes.

What Environmental Factors Are Important for Social Development?

1. Outline the research that examines the relationship between fathering and development.

2. Describe the social interactions of the child during their first two years of life.

3. A _____ _____ is a set of expectations in a given society about behaviors and responsibilities that are appropriate for males or females.

4. What is a gender stereotype?

5. Describe the first 4 stages of Erikson's psychosocial development.

6. At what age does each stage of Erikson's stages occur?

After You Read, Practice Test #1

1. What branch of psychology focuses on change in an individual's lifetime? (98)
   A. Social
   B. Developmental
   C. Motivational
   D. Personality

2. Dr. Grau believes that development is a process of change that occurs at various critical periods and changes appear abruptly. Dr. Grau then, believes that development is a _____ process. (100)
   A. Stable
   B. Volatile
   C. Continuous
   D. Discontinuous

3. A researcher tests a group of the same children at ages 2, 4, and 6. What experimental design is being used? (100)
   A. Cross-sectional
   B. Longitudinal
   C. Tri-sectional
   D. Continuous

4. Before a fertilized egg implants into the uterine wall, it is called a _____. (102)
   A. Zygote
   B. Embryo
   C. Fetus
   D. Neonate

5. What did Frantz use his "viewing box" to study? (107)
   A. The visual preferences of infants
   B. Recognition memory in infants
   C. Stimulus generalization in infants
   D. The depth perception of infants

6. The process by which new ideas and experiences are absorbed and incorporated into existing mental structures and behaviors is _____. (113)
   A. Accommodation
   B. Interpretation
   C. Assimilation
   D. Understanding

Psychology

7. Piaget's theory focuses on _____. (111-113)
   A. Thought processes
   B. Content
   C. Intellectual development
   D. Social development

8. A child who begins to engage in make-believe play is in which of Piaget's cognitive stages? (114)
   A. Sensorimotor
   B. Concrete operational
   C. Formal operational
   D. Preoperational

9. The only reason Leo does not take a hot cookie off the plate is because his mother would yell at him. Leo is operating at which level of morality? (128)
   A. Pre conventional
   B. Post conventional
   C. Mid conventional
   D. Conventional

10. Six-month-old Sydney is a baby who does well on a set routine. However, when Sydney and her parents went out of town on vacation Sydney did not react well and appeared "out of sorts" the entire time. Which category best describes Sydney's temperamental style? (125)
    A. Slow-to-warm-up
    B. Difficult
    C. Easy
    D. Unique

After You Read, Practice Test #2

1. A developmental theorist who believes that early childhood experiences are shaped primarily by one's biologically based urges, subscribes to a theory based more on _____. (98)
    A. Nurture
    B. Impulses
    C. Nature
    D. Behavior

2. The basic function of the placenta is to _____. (102)
    A. Cushion the baby against damage
    B. Serve as the baby's life support system
    C. Provide stimulation to the prenatal environment
    D. Protect the mother from the baby's system

3. Infancy is defined as ending and toddlerhood as beginning when the child _____. (102)
    A. Is 18-24 months old
    B. Can stand without support
    C. Begins to use language to describe experiences
    D. Drops the rooting reflex and uses learned behaviors in its place

4. Which of the following situations will cause the Moro reflex to occur in newborn infants? (106)
    A. A touch on the cheek
    B. Pressure on the kneecap
    C. A touch on the bottom of the foot
    D. A sudden change in environmental stimulation

5. Research on the visual cliff indicates that infants develop the ability to perceive depth at what age? (108)
    A. One month
    B. Six months
    C. Twelve months
    D. Nine months

6. When a child learns that a toy continues to exist when it is out of sight, that child has mastered _____. (114)
    A. Conservation
    B. Egocentrism
    C. Decentration
    D. Object permanence

7. The major difference between children in the concrete operational and preoperational stage of development is that in the concrete operational stage child _____. (114-115)
   A. Understand the concept of conservation
   B. Develop a sense of object permanence
   C. Are generally more egocentric
   D. Can think logically about hypothetical things

8. In which of Piaget's cognitive stages would an individual develop the ability to engage in abstract reasoning and hypothetical events that are not directly experienced? (116)
   A. Concrete operations
   B. Preoperational
   C. Formal operations
   D. Sensorimotor

9. Some researchers claim that Piaget may have underestimated the extent of _____ in young children. (117)
   A. Egocentrism
   B. Maturity
   C. Cognitive development
   D. Age

10. Which of the following is the central concept in Kohlberg's theory of morality? (128)
    A. Justice
    B. Property rights
    C. Truth
    D. Reciprocity

After You Read, Practice Test #3

1. A time in the development of an organism when it is especially sensitive to certain environmental influences is called a(n) _____. (104)
    A. Sensitive stage
    B. Critical period
    C. Impact stage
    D. Sensory period

2. The _____ reflex consists of an infant turning the head toward a light touch on their lip or cheek. (106)
    A. Moro
    B. Rooting
    C. Babinski
    D. Sucking

3. Megan knows her daddy's real name is John and she is introduced to a family friend who is also named John. When introduced she says, "Your name isn't John that's my daddy's name." According to Piaget, Megan's error is an example of _____. (115)
    A. Role confusion
    B. Egocentrism
    C. Assimilation
    D. Accommodation

4. The preoperational stage occurs from _____. (114)
    A. Birth to age two
    B. Age seven to age eleven
    C. Age two to age six
    D. Age eleven

5. What is the focus of Lawrence Kohlberg's moral development theory? (128)
    A. The morality of young children
    B. The morality of adults
    C. Moral behavior
    D. Moral reasoning

6. Carol Gilligan found that women are more likely to use _____ when reasoning moral conflicts. (129-130)
    A. Justice
    B. Information relevant to potential harm to people
    C. Logic and reasoning
    D. Caring, relationships, and connections with other people

7. Most babies have a _____ attachment; they become distressed when their mother leaves, but they are easily comforted. (123)
   A. Avoidant
   B. Resistant
   C. Secure
   D. Disoriented

8. Long –lasting differences in the intensity and quality of a person's emotional reactions is referred to as _____. (125)
   A. Conditioning
   B. Attachment
   C. Egocentrism
   D. Temperament

9. _____ is the biologically based category of male or female. (129)
   A. Gender
   B. Hormone
   C. Sex
   D. Sex role

10. The stage of Erikson's psychosocial development in which the child must deal with learning many new skills or risk a sense of inferiority is called _____. (136)
    A. Initiative vs. guilt
    B. Industry vs. inferiority
    C. Trust vs. mistrust
    D. Autonomy vs. shame and doubt

After You Read, Comprehensive Self Test

1. The disadvantages of longitudinal studies are _____. (101)
    - A.   Subjects' backgrounds differ
    - B.   Subjects may move, withdraw, or even die
    - C.   Behavior or performance of a task or ability may reflect their subjects' predisposition, i.e., liking of the task
    - D.   Individual differences are impossible to assess

2. _____ are substances that can cause developmental malformations. (104)
    - A.   Schemas
    - B.   Malformers
    - C.   Teratogens
    - D.   Placenta

3. Which reflex is important to a child's nutrition and eating? (106)
    - A.   Sucking
    - B.   Rooting
    - C.   Babinski
    - D.   Moro

4. Newborn babies prefer to stare at _____. (107)
    - A.   Random patterns
    - B.   Simple patterns
    - C.   Human faces
    - D.   Breasts

5. The visual cliff is applied to a baby to measure _____. (108)
    - A.   Primary reflexes
    - B.   Visual preferences
    - C.   Depth perception
    - D.   Cognitive development

6. According to Piaget, during which developmental stage do children begin to learn to manipulate the environment? (113)
    - A.   The preoperational stage
    - B.   The sensorimotor stage
    - C.   The formal operational stage
    - D.   The concrete operational stage

7. Decentration is _____. (115)
   A. The ability to recognize that objects may be transformed visually or physically, yet represent the same amount of weight or volume
   B. The ability to understand the difference between their interests and those of others
   C. The belief that the world exists solely to satisfy the needs and interests of the child
   D. The ability to recognize that objects continue to exist even when they are out of sight

8. The ability to recognize that objects can be transformed in some way, yet still be the same in number, weight, or volume is referred to as _____. (115)
   A. Assimilation
   B. Conservation
   C. Decentration
   D. Egocentrism

9. Vance and his mother bought a puzzle at the store. The puzzle was harder than any Vance had previously worked. Vance's mother sat on the floor with him and gave instructions when Vance could not make any more progress on his own. According to Vygotsky, Vance's mother was _____. (119)
   A. Interfering with Vance's learning
   B. Not giving Vance enough observational help
   C. Being overly intrusive to the learning process
   D. Scaffolding Vance's skills

10. Charles believes it is acceptable for a starving man to steal food because even though stealing is against the law, a man must do whatever it takes to survive. At what level of moral reasoning is Charles? (128)
    A. Preconventional
    B. Postconventional
    C. Conventional
    D. Relative

11. Gilligan's work dealing with gender differences in moral reasoning suggests that _____. (129)
    A. Boys gravitate more toward morality of domination
    B. Boys gravitate more toward morality of caring
    C. Girls gravitate more toward morality of justice
    D. Girls gravitate more toward morality of caring

12. According to Bowlby, a baby's interactions with parents during the first few months of life _____. (122)
    A. Are primarily focused on food and safety
    B. Are more meaningful for the parents than the baby
    C. Are crucial to survival and normal development
    D. Will be replaced by stronger feelings at the end of the year

13. The social development of infants is the first year of life is largely focused on _____.
    (132)
    A.   Developing a sense of self
    B.   Forming relationships with other children
    C.   The infant's own needs
    D.   Learning to share and take turns

14. A fixed, overly simple attitude and behavior about being male or female is referred to as
    gender _____. (135)
    A.   Discrimination
    B.   Inconsistency
    C.   Stereotype
    D.   Schema

15. At which of Erikson's stages is toilet training and mastery of skills important? (136)
    A.   Initiative vs. guilt
    B.   Autonomy vs. shame and doubt
    C.   Trust vs. mistrust
    D.   Industry vs. inferiority

True or False

1. Most psychologists believe that development can be best understood by using a
    transactional model in which parents, children and situations mutually influence one
    another. (99)

2. The proper order of prenatal development is zygote, fetus, and embryo. (102)

3. At birth, infants tend to have relatively poorly developed sensory systems. (104)

4. Accommodation refers to the process of changing existing ideas to adapt to new
    information from the environment. (113)

5. One of the criticisms of Piaget's theory is that he focused too much on the social
    environment in cognitive development. (117)

6. Research indicates that a child develops a theory of mind around the age of three years old.
    (119)

7. The majority of infants tend to show distress when separated from their parent, and they
    are not easily comforted when their parents return. (123)

8. Research indicates that having a child cared for outside of the home tends to result in
    negative effects to the child. (124)

Essay Questions

1. Compare and contrast the strengths and weaknesses of cross-sectional and longitudinal research designs. (100-102)

2. Discuss the role of fathers on child development. (131-132)

When You Have Finished!

Surf's Up!!

After you've read and reviewed, try these web sites for additional information about some of the topics covered in this chapter.

1. **National Academy for Child Development** (http://www.nacd.org)
   An international organization devoted to spreading information and conducting research related to childhood development.

2. **March of Dimes** (http://www.marchofdimes.com)
   This organization is aimed at improving the health of infants and providing resources to keep infants health and to prevent birth defects. Lots of information about children, prenatal care, and even careers.

3. **Freud's Stages of Psychosexual Development at AllPsych Online**
   (http://allpsych.com/personalitysynopsis/psychosexual.html)
   A brief overview of Freud's stags and a variety of other links to information about Freud and his theories.

4. **Positive Parenting.com** (http://www.positiveparenting.com)
   Devoted to providing information and tips to parents that will help them provide a positive and nurturing environment for their child's development.

5. **Harry Harlow and The Nature of Love** (http://psychclassics.yorku.ca/Harlow/love.htm)
   This is a re-print of the classic article written by Harlow that describes his classic work with monkeys and attachment.

6. **Temperament: Different Drums, Different Drummers** (http://keirsey.com/)
   Wondering what your own temperament is? You can take a test here. In addition, you can explore a wealth of information about temperament and even find out the temperament patterns of past presidents!

7. **Vygotsky Resources** (http://www.kolar.org/vygotsky/)
   A wealth of different resources devoted to Vygotsky's theory of sociocultural development.

Cross Check: Child Development

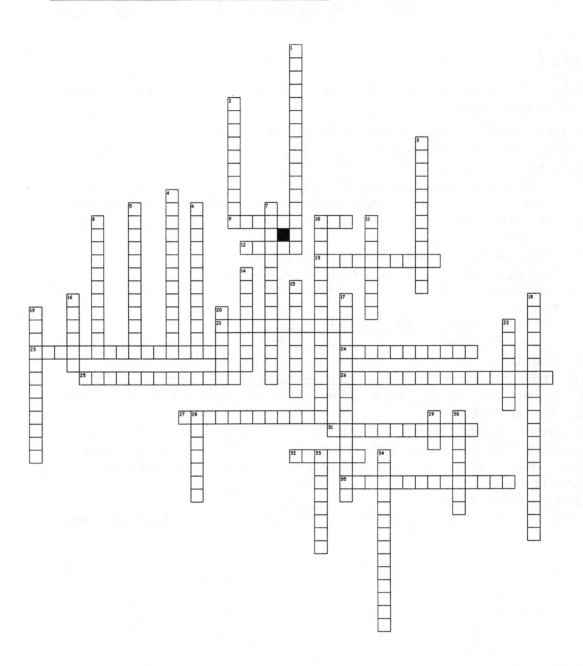

Across

9. The prenatal organism from 5th to 49th day
10. Biologically based category of male or female
12. Prenatal organism from 8th week to birth
13. The strong emotional bond or connection that a person feels toward special people in his or her life
21. Ability to recognize that objects can be transformed in some way, yet still be the same
23. Realization that objects continue to exist even when they are out of sight
24. Inability to perceive a situation except in relation to oneself
25. Area of psychology devoted to the study of lifelong changes
26. Distress at being separated from caretakers; more extreme than normal
27. Process where new ideas are absorbed into existing mental structures
31. Syndrome with a characteristic set of physical, mental, and neurobehavioral defects that is associated with alcohol use
32. A fertilized egg
35. Stage where child begins to represent the world symbolically

Down

1. Individual can think hypothetically at this stage of development
2. Set of expectations in a given society about behavior and responsibilities that are appropriate for males or females
3. Research design that compares groups over time
4. Process by which a person's behaviors, values, and attitudes conform to those that are socially desired
5. Stage Involves motor coordination and memory for past events
6. Change from self-oriented to recognizing other's feelings
7. Sensitive time where fetus is at risk to environmental hazards
8. Early emerging and long lasting pattern in an individual's disposition and in the intensity and especially the quality of his or her emotional reactions
10. Technique used for assessing attachment
11. Connected to fetus by umbilical cord and supplies fetus with oxygen and nutrients
14. Reflex where toes fan out
15. Substances that can produce developmental malformations
16. Socially and culturally constructed set of distinctions between masculine and feminine behaviors expected by society
17. A fixed, simple and often incorrect idea about traits, and behaviors of males or females
18. Third stage of Piaget's developmental theory
19. Process where existing mental structures are modified to new experiences
20. Mental structure that helps us organize information
22. Reflex that cases newborn to turn head toward touch
28. Reflex associated with feeding and eating
29. Reflex that causes baby to stretch out arms and legs and cry in response to sound
30. System of learned attitudes and practices about what is right and wrong

33. Reflex to grasp an object
34. Research design that compares individuals of different ages at one time

Created by <u>Puzzlemaker</u> at
DiscoverySchool.com

Chapter 5

Adolescence and Adulthood

Before you read...

All of you who are reading this will be intimately familiar with the content of this chapter, as you are likely in the midst of experiencing some of the interesting, challenging, and sometimes stressful transitions that will be discussed. In addition, you will also learn what to expect as you continue to transverse life on the road to the inevitable "final transition." As you read, try to compare your own experiences to those outlined in the chapter and think about how you might handle some of the challenges that await you as you continue in your own development.

The chapter begins with a discussion of the developmental changes that occur during adolescence, the period of time between childhood and adulthood. As you are likely intimately familiar with, adolescence is a significant time of growth and development. You will learn about the various aspects of development, including physical, cognitive, emotional, and social development. In doing so, you will come to understand some of the common challenges faced in adolescence and learn how these events can and do impact adolescents. You will also explore how a person's gender identity and sex roles develop during adolescence and take a look at how sexual behavior among American adolescents is changing.

In the second part of the chapter, you will focus on an understudied area in psychology, adult development and change. As with adolescence, you will explore the physical, cognitive, social, and personality changes that occur as someone transitions through his or her adult year. In addition, you will be introduced to two stage theories of development, those of Erik Erikson and Daniel Levinson. As you will see, adulthood is far from a static time of development like psychologists once thought. Instead, you will find that adulthood involves facing many demands and challenges related to relationships, work, and family commitments.

The chapter finishes with the final transition into late adulthood. In this section, you will first learn about some of the numerous myths and stereotypes about older people, and you will come to understand some of the harmful and negative effects they have. In addition, you will learn about some of the common health challenges that are faced in late adulthood. Finally, you will end your journey, as we all do, with the final transition: death. In doing so, you will briefly examine an understudied area, namely how people prepare for and transition into the end of life.

Learning Objectives

After reading this chapter, you should be able to:

1. Understand adolescence and discuss why it must be considered in multiple contexts.
2. Describe the physical development that occurs during adolescence, and discuss how it can affect the self-image of an adolescent.
3. Understand cognitive development in adolescence, and explain its impact on social and academic functioning.
4. Discuss key aspects of emotional and social development during adolescence and compare how each might be related to positive and negative outcomes.
5. Understand the factors that contribute to the development of gender identity and gender roles, and outline the impact of gender stereotypes on the development of self.
6. Explain the significance of friendships in adolescence, and trace the importance of friends throughout the developmental spectrum.
7. Discuss adolescent sexual behavior and state some key statistics related to sexual behavior.
8. Understand how attitudes about sexuality influence social development and personal behavior.
9. Outline the physiological, sexual, and sensory changes that occur during adulthood.
10. Describe the various theories of aging.
11. Describe the cognitive changes that take place during adulthood.
12. Compare and contrast Erikson's and Levinson's stage theories of adult development.
13. Discuss how myths and stereotypes have led to biases against the elderly.
14. Describe the symptoms of specific brain disorders such as dementia, and define the different types of dementia.
15. List the symptoms of Alzheimer's disease, and discuss some of the risk factors for developing this disorder.
16. List the common causes of death and discuss some of the factors related to this final life transition.

Key Terms

Adolescence
Puberty
Secondary Sex Characteristics
Anorexia Nervosa
Bulimia Nervosa
Imaginary Audience
Personal Fable
Ethnic Identity
Gender Identity
Gender Intensification
Gender Schema Theory
Androgynous
Osteoporosis
Life Expectancy
Ageism
Dementia
Alzheimer's Disease
Thanatology

Psychology

As you read...

Does Adolescence Bridge the Gap to Adulthood?

1.   The period of adolescence extends from _____ to _____.

2.   What are the characteristic signs of puberty?

3.   Many psychologists have thought of adolescence as a period of storm and stress. Based on the information presented in your text, would you say that this an accurate portrayal of adolescence? Support your argument.

4.   Why must adolescence be viewed in cultural context?

5-1   **Physical Development in Adolescence**

1.   The average age at which a person reaches sexual maturity is _____.

2.   _____ sex characteristics are the genetically determined physical features that differentiate the sexes but are not directly involved with reproduction.

3.   List the male and female secondary sex characteristics.

4.   Does development during puberty affect males and females differently? Explain.

5.   _____ nervosa is characterized by repeated episodes of binge eating followed by purging, whereas _____ nervosa is characterized by an obstinate and willful refusal to eat, a distorted body image, and in intense fear of being fat.

5-2	**Cognitive Development in Adolescence**

1. An imaginary audience refers to what phenomenon in adolescence?

2. A cognitive distortion experience by adolescence, in which they believe that they are so special and unique that other people cannot understand them is called the _____ _____.

3. Are there ethnic differences in cognitive development?

4. Explain the relationship between parenting styles and cognition in adolescence.

5-3	**Emotional and Social Development in Adolescence**

1. Children whose early emotional or social adjustment is ____ are less likely to make good adjustments as adolescents.

2. The results of the Carolina Longitudinal Study indicated that _____.

3. _____ _____ refers to a feeling of membership in an ethnic or cultural group.

4. Describe how ethnicity influences emotional and social development.

5. What impact does involvement of sports have on social and emotional development?

6. Explain how peers and parents influence self-esteem.

7. Over the last three decades, suicide rates for American teens have _____; likely the result of what factors?

Psychology

5-4   Who Am I? The Search for Gender Identity
---

1.   Who tends to reach developmental milestones faster, males or females? Does it stay this way throughout development?

2.   Gender identity refers to _____.

3.   A sense of one's gender as permanent is usually reached at what age?

4.   _____ _____ is the exaggeration of traditional male or female behaviors.

5.   Describe gender schema theory and label the following aspects of gender schema theory.

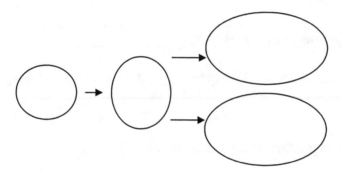

6.   _____ refers to behaviors that represent a blend of stereotypically male and female characteristics.

7.   Outline the effects of gender roles and stereotypes on males and females, noting the positive and negative aspects.

5-5   Friendship and Sexual Behavior
---

1.   Friendship is _____.

2.   Adolescencents report spending approximately _____% of their time with friends, compared to adults who spend _____% of their time with friends.

3. The development and maintenance of friendships is related to the development of what two types of skills?

4. Outline some of the consequences of having or not having friends during one's development.

5. When are American teenagers most likely to have intercourse? Cite the relevant statistics in your answer.

6. Each year over _____ unmarried teenage girls become pregnant in the United States.

7. List the risk factors for a teenager becoming pregnant.

8. What are the consequences of childbearing for teenage mothers?

Is Adulthood a Time of Stability or Change?

1. Between the ages of 25-44, the most common cause of death is _____.

2. Describe the physical changes that occur as a person moves through adulthood.

3. _____ is a condition in which bone mass and strength decrease.

4. What sensory changes occur in adulthood?

5. Many people can no longer hear _____ _____ sounds by age 65.

6. The cessation of ovulation and menstruation in women is called _____.

7. List the sexual changes that occur in adulthood?

8.   Compare and contrast the genetic, wear-and-tear, and homeostatic theories of aging.

9.   How might external, or _____, factors affect how long a person lives?

10.   _____ aging refers to the normal, inevitable change that occurs in every human, whereas _____ aging refers to _____.

11.   Compare primary aging and secondary aging and provide one example of each.

5-6   Cognitive Changes in Adulthood

1.   What cognitive changes occur after age 65?

2.   What factors are more important than age in predicting cognitive functioning in older adults?

3.   Based on the research on cognitive declines in aging, what would you recommend to someone in order to decrease the impact aging might have on their abilities?

5-7   Social and Personality Development in Adulthood

1.   Characterize the social changes that occur in the following three stages of adulthood.

      a) Young adults

      b) Middle-age adults

      c) Older adults

2.   Describe the "supermom" phenomenon and state its possible impact on women.

3. Complete the stages of Erikson's Psychosocial Stage Theory listed below.

Stage	Age	Events	Description of Conflict
Identity vs. Role Confusion	Adolescence		
Intimacy vs. Isolation	Young Adulthood		
Generativity vs. Stagnation	Middle Adulthood		
Ego Integrity vs. Despair	Late Adulthood		

4. Describe the 4 eras outlined by Levinson, including the ages for each.

5. What is involved in the midlife transition and when does it generally occur?

6. How is Levinson's theory different than Erikson's?

7. According to Levinson, how are males and females different with regard to their development?

8. Name and describe some criticisms of stage theories.

Do We Grow Older and Wiser in Late Adulthood?

1. Prejudice, stereotyping, and discrimination of individuals based on their age is referred to as _____.

2.   An older person who appears healthy, bright and alert is _____ likely to be treated with the same respect shown to younger people.

3.   Complete the following table representing development in later adulthood.

Age	Physical Change	Cognitive Change	Work Roles	Personal Development	Major Tasks
Middle Adulthood 40-65					
Late Adulthood 65-75+					

5-8   Health in Late Adulthood

1.   Dementia is defined as _____.

2.   _____% of the people between the ages of 75-79 suffer from dementia.

3.   Compare and contrast reversible and multiple infarct dementias.

4.   Define Alzheimer's disease and describe its symptoms.

5-9	The Final Transition: Dying

1.	The 4 leading causes of death in the United States are _____ .

2.	What is terminal drop?

3.	_____ is the study of the psychological and medical aspects of death and dying.

After You Read, Practice Test #1

1. Puberty is defined by _____. (142)
    A. Psychological changes
    B. Physiological changes
    C. Cultural standards
    D. Behavioral symptoms

2. Facial hair, chest hair, and breasts are all examples of _____. (144)
    A. Gonadotrophs.
    B. Primary sex characteristics
    C. Secondary sex characteristics
    D. Pubertal markers

3. Which parenting style seems to be associated with high achievement among school students? (149)
    A. An accepting, tolerant, permissive style
    B. A stern, uncompromising autocratic style
    C. A warm, loving, but firm authoritative
    D. A distant, managerial leadership style

4. Behaviors that are shared by both sexes are _____. (154)
    A. Gender based
    B. Androgynous
    C. Role based
    D. Stereotypical

5. Which of the following statements is true regarding the sensory changes that occur during adulthood? (159)
    A. Older adults generally have some degree of hearing loss, especially for low frequency sounds
    B. Older females usually have a higher degree of hearing loss than do their male counterparts
    C. Dark adaptation is one of the few sensory capabilities that remains constant through out early, middle, and late adulthood
    D. Older adults need a higher level of stimulation to be able to taste and smell like they did when they were younger

6. It is predicted that John will have a long life because his parents are presently over 85. This prediction is based on the _____ theory of aging. (161)
    A. Congenital
    B. Heredity
    C. Familial
    D. Homologous

7. According to Erikson, _____ is a psychological crisis that middle adults face. (164)
    A. Ego-integrity versus despair
    B. Identity versus role confusion
    C. Generativity versus stagnation
    D. Intimacy versus isolation

8. Identity versus role confusion is the _____ stage of Erikson's theory. (165)
    A. Fifth
    B. Fourth
    C. Seventh
    D. Sixth

9. Which of the following is not a traditionally stereotypical description the elderly? (170)
    A. Inflexible
    B. Financially secure
    C. Incompetent
    D. Unhealthy

10. _____ is a chronic and progressive disorder of the brain and the most common cause of degenerative dementia in the United States. (172)
    A. Alzheimer's disease
    B. Parkinson's disease
    C. Osteoporosis
    D. Neurofibromatosis

Psychology

After You Read, Practice Test #2

1. Most research on adolescence has been conducted on _____. (143)
   A. White teenagers
   B. Black teenagers
   C. Middle class teenagers
   D. Both A and C

2. Just before the onset of puberty, boys and girls experience significant growth spurts, gaining as much as _____ inches in a year. (144)
   A. Four
   B. Five
   C. Six
   D. Three

3. _____ _____ is characterized by repeated cycles of binge eating and purging. (146)
   A. Anorexia disorder
   B. Food refusal
   C. Bulimia nervosa
   D. Eating disorder

4. Peer groups consist of people of the same _____. (152)
   A. Age
   B. Sex
   C. Race
   D. All of the above

5. In the last few decades, what change has occurred in adolescent sexual behavior? (156)
   A. Teens are acting the same but talking about it more
   B. Teens are having sex at earlier ages than before
   C. Only teens from minority groups are having sex earlier
   D. There has been no change in sexual behavior at all

6. The three basic types of theories of aging emphasize _____. (161)
   A. Diet, exercise and stress
   B. Heredity, external factors, and physiology
   C. Lifestyle, the physical environment, and attitudes toward life
   D. Medical care, social integration, and personality

7. The theory of aging that claims that human organisms wear out from overuse is called the _____ theory. (162)
   A. Mechanistic
   B. Wear-and-tear
   C. Homeostatic
   D. External factors

8. New dilemmas, challenges, and responsibilities that require reassessment, reappraisal, and development of new skills are _____. (165)
    A.   Transitions
    B.   Mid-life crisis
    C.   Transition-crisis
    D.   None of the above

9. What is one of the major problems of being older? (170)
    A.   Society's negative attitudes toward the elderly
    B.   Lack of friends
    C.   Experiential aging
    D.   Finding useful and interesting things to do

10. All but which of the following causes reversible dementias? (172)
    A.   Toxins
    B.   Alcoholism
    C.   Strokes
    D.   Malnutrition

After You Read, Practice Test #3

1. When discussing the psychology of adolescence, it is very important to keep in mind that _____. (142-143)
    A. Adolescence is invariably a time of severe discord between parents and their adolescent child
    B. Individuals experience more psychological problems during adolescence than during any other developmental period
    C. Adolescence, by definition, is invariably a time of storm and stress
    D. The majority of youths do not experience major psychological disturbances during the adolescent period

2. Fourteen-year-old Sara had a zit on her cheek one day. Sarah tried hard to hide her face all day at school. She thought that everyone she came into contact with would be disgusted if they saw her blemish. Sarah's thinking illustrates the adolescent cognitive distortion of _____. (148)
    A. Hypothetical-deductive reasoning
    B. The imaginary audience
    C. Latent egocentrism
    D. The personal fable

3. A person's sense of being either male or female is their _____. (153)
    A. Gender identity
    B. Gender schema
    C. Gender role
    D. Gender stereotype

4. Which of the following activities would make one suspect that Susan is an androgynous individual? (154)
    A. Dancing with another girl
    B. Changing the spark plugs in her car
    C. Helping her father clean the kitchen
    D. Helping her mother do the grocery shopping

5. Physically, human beings are at their peak of agility, speed, and strength between ages _____. (158)
    A. 11-17
    B. 20-30
    C. 18-30
    D. 18-25

6. About what percent of adults aged 60 and older report engaging in sexual activity at least once a month? (160)
    A. 20%
    B. 30%
    C. 40%
    D. 50%

7. In Erikson's theory of psychosocial development, young adulthood is a time when people struggle with the issue of _____. (164)
    A.   Intimacy versus isolation
    B.   Generativity versus stagnation
    C.   Identity versus confusion
    D.   Ego integrity versus despair

8. According to Levinson's theory we can think of a person's life as _____. (164)
    A.   The development of stable life structures to get them through life
    B.   Made up of several stages
    C.   A period during which individuals work out various developmental tasks
    D.   Alternating between stable periods and transitional periods

9. Ageism is exceptionally prevalent in _____. (170)
    A.   The media
    B.   Everyday language
    C.   Housing
    D.   Both A & B

10. Terminal drop is _____. (173)
    A.   The year before death
    B.   Rapid physical decline
    C.   Rapid intellectual decline
    D.   Both A & C

After You Read, Comprehensive Self Test

1. _____ is the period of human development that bridges childhood and adulthood. (142)
    A. Puberty
    B. Menarche
    C. Idiosyncrasy
    D. Adolescence

2. Tommy, a seventeen-year-old male, knew that he probably shouldn't get in the car after having had four beers to drink. However, as he turned on the ignition to the car, he thought to himself, "I won't have a wreck." Tommy's thought process illustrates the adolescent cognitive distortion of _____. (148)
    A. Hypothetical-deductive reasoning
    B. The imaginary audience
    C. Latent egocentrism
    D. The personal fable

3. Research has shown that negative feelings that arise during puberty can be reduced by involvement in _____. (150)
    A. Athletics
    B. Hobbies
    C. Clubs and organizations
    D. Religious groups

4. The exaggeration of traditional male or female behaviors is called _____. (153)
    A. Gender identification
    B. Gender intensification
    C. Gender differentiation
    D. Gender pluralization

5. Gender schema _____. (153)
    A. Is a person's sense of being male or female
    B. Is a social category
    C. Asserts children use gender as an organizing theme to help them understand their world perceptions
    D. States that the way a person is raised and taught has a profound impact on behavior and seems to have a gender related component

6. According to your text, more than _____ unmarried adolescent girls in the United States get pregnant each year. (156)
    A. 250,000
    B. 500,000
    C. 750,000
    D. 1,000,000

7. Decreases in bone mass and strength, especially in women after menopause is called _____. (158)
   A.   Osteogenesis
   B.   Osteobiflex
   C.   Osteodisintegration
   D.   Osteoporosis

8. By age _____, most people can no longer hear high-frequency sounds. (159)
   A.   50
   B.   60
   C.   65
   D.   70

9. Menopause occurs when women are approximately _____ years old and results in _____. (160)
   A.   50; loss of sexual desire
   B.   50; cessation of ovulation and menstruation
   C.   40; loss of sexual desire.
   D.   40; cessation of ovulation and menstruation.

10. The external factors theory of aging emphasizes such things as _____. (161-162)
    A.   Where people live
    B.   Whether people smoke
    C.   Whether people are overweight
    D.   All of the above

11. The theory of aging that emphasizes loss of the ability of the body to adjust to changing conditions is called the _____ theory. (162)
    A.   Homeostatic
    B.   Adaptation
    C.   Efficiency
    D.   Biobehavioral

12. Which of the following concepts was originated by Erik Erikson? (164)
    A.   Midlife crisis
    B.   Hospice
    C.   Identity crisis
    D.   Androgyny

13. Seventy-year-old Thomas views his life as a series of "missed opportunities." He feels that he should have done more with his life. According to Erikson, Thomas has developed a sense of _____ regarding his past. (164)
    A.   Confusion
    B.   Despair
    C.   Isolation
    D.   Stagnation

14. The first era in Levinson's theory is _____. (165)
    A.   Infancy and early childhood
    B.   Adolescence
    C.   Youth
    D.   Early adulthood

15. Mark is seventy-five- years old. He is having severe lapses of memory, judgment, and personality changes, and they are progressively getting worse. It is likely that Mark is suffering from _____. (171)
    A.   Ageism
    B.   Parkinson's disease
    C.   Psychosis
    D.   Dementia

True or False

1.   Most adolescents go through some sort of significant psychological difficulty as they adjust to the demands of adolescence. (143)

2.   Girls are more likely to feel good about their bodies during puberty than males. (145)

3.   Anorexia is characterized by starvation, whereas bulimia tends to be characterized by binging and purging cycles. (146)

4.   Involvement in sports is associated with higher satisfaction for boys, but not girls. (150)

5.   A sense of one's gender as relatively permanent is usually realized by the age of 6 or 7. (153)

6.   The number of friends one has growing up is generally a good predictor of how many friends they will have later in life. (155)

7.   As people move from adolescence to adulthood, and ultimately old age, they tend to became psychologically healthier. (158)

8.   Research indicates that genetics tend to play a stronger role in determining age-related deficits compared to lifestyle and environmental variables. (170-171)

Essay Questions

1.   Describe the imaginary audience and the personal fable, and state how they affect adolescent behavior. (148)

2.   Describe the cognitive changes that occur after age 65, and discuss the impact they have on elderly individuals. (170-173)

When You Have Finished!

Surf's Up!!

After you've read and reviewed, try these web sites for additional information about some of the topics covered in this chapter.

1. **National Eating Disorders Association** (http://www.nationaleatingdieorders.org)
   An association dedicated to understanding and spreading accurate information to the public about eating disorders. In addition, this site also attempts to support families and those affected with eating disorders by providing access to appropriate resources and treatment.

2. **National Institute on Aging** (http://www.nia.hih.gov)
   This site provides information on health and research related to aging. Of particular interest might be a section on some of the latest research and information on Alzheimer's disease.

3. **Senior Net** (http://www.seniornet.org)
   This site is dedicated to providing information and resources to older adults. Links include information on technology, culture, health, money and recreation.

4. **Campaign for Our Children** (http://www.cfoc.org/Home/)
   This organization is devoted to providing information to teens, their parents, and the general public about issues related to teen pregnancy. There is a wealth of information at the site and links to additional information, including an up-to-date count on the number of babies born to teenagers in the United States in this year.

5. **Adolescent Directory On Line** (http://education.indiana.edu/cas/adol/adol.html)
   This site is a service of the Center for Adolescent Studies at Indiana University. It provides a wealth of information related to issues of adolescence.

6. **Society for Research on Adolescence** (http://www.s-r-a.org/)
   An interdisciplinary and international organization devoted to the study and dissemination of information related to adolescents.

7. **Alzheimer's Association** (http://www.alz.org)
   This association is devoted to preventing, treating, and curing Alzheimer's disorder. There are a number of helpful educational resources here and up-to-date information on some of the latest breakthroughs in research about this disorder.

Cross Check: Adolescence and Adulthood

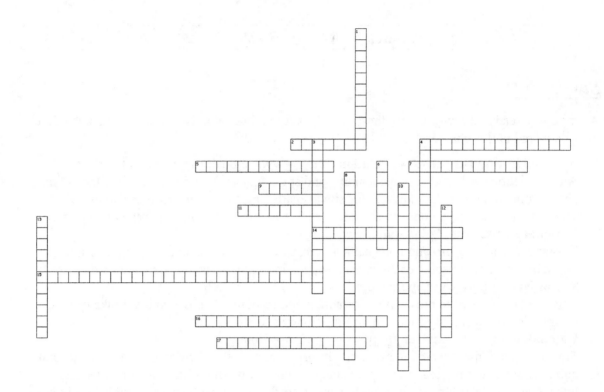

Across

2. Time where the reproductive system matures
4. A person's sense of being male or female
5. Cognitive distortion where person believes that they are special and unique
7. Having both stereotypically male and female characteristics
9. Prejudice toward the old
11. Impairment in mental functioning and global cognitive abilities
14. Feeling of membership in ethnic or cultural group
15. Sex characteristics that are genetically determined physical features
16. Theory that children and adolescents use gender as an organizing theme for thinking about self and the world
17. Average number of years a newborn can expect to live

Down

1. Study of psychological and physical aspects of death and dying
3. Eating disorder characterized by binging and purging
4. Exaggeration of traditional gender roles
6. Type of eating disorder characterized by food restriction
8. A cognitive distortion in which the person feels that they are always "on stage"
10. Disease that is chronic and progressive and results in functional impairments to cognitive abilities
12. Condition characterized by low bone mass and deterioration of bone tissue
13. Period extending from puberty to early adulthood

Chapter 6

Sensation and Perception

Before you read...

You have heard the old riddle...If a tree falls in the woods and no one is around, does it make a sound? Well, you will learn that this riddle encompasses the very topics covered in this chapter. More specifically, you will find that the tree does send off information into the environment; however, unless there is an organism there to receive it, there is no sound. You will also learn that your perception of how loud that sound is or how far away you think the tree is varies considerably based on a number of factors.

You will start your journey into sensation and perception by exploring some of the common aspects related to all of our sensory systems. Psychologists study perception primarily because what people sense and perceive determines how they interpret their environment. In this chapter, you will explore the different types of thresholds thought to be necessary for perception, including a discussion of the possibility of subliminal perception. You will also learn that we must choose to attend to selected stimuli in order for sensory information to make an impact on our perception of the environment. Finally, the topic of sensory restriction as a means of relaxing and altering such behaviors as smoking and insomnia will be explored.

In reviewing our sensory and perceptual systems, you will soon discover that we know more about some systems than we do about others. The first system you will explore is also the one we know the most about—the visual system. The structure and functions of the eye are discussed in detail. In addition, the electrochemical process of visual perception is explored.

In the next part of the chapter, you will explore the perception of form and substance. This discussion will include how we perceive form, depth, and faces. In addition, you will learn about visual illusions, which act to fool the visual system and our perception of the environment. Finally, you will be introduced to Gestalt psychology and the laws of perceptual organization.

The next sensory system that is explored is the auditory system. Like vision, our ability to hear is a key factor related to our ability to adapt to and cope with the environment around us. You will learn the basic components of sound and the structure of the ear, and you will come to understand how psychologists believe auditory information is translated into sound and meaning. In addition, you will learn about how the auditory system might be damaged and some of the current research that is attempting to correct some of this damage and restore hearing.

In the final two sections of the chapter, you will learn about five senses that psychologists know less about—taste, smell, vestibular, kinesthetic, and skin senses. Taste and smell are characterized as chemical senses, and the role of smell in communication is explored in animals and humans. In contrast, the skin senses of touch and pain are related to the complex transmission of nerve signals in the body, whereas kinesthetic and vestibular senses are a complex mix of skin and nervous system messages. To close the chapter, you will explore each of these sensory systems and come to understand how they operate and are interpreted by humans.

Learning Objectives

After reading this chapter, you should be able to:

1. Define and differentiate between sensation and perception and discuss the difference between top-down and bottom-up approaches to studying sensation and perception.
2. Explain the relationship between psychophysics, absolute thresholds, and difference thresholds.
3. Compare and contrast signal detection theory, the method of limits, and the method of constant stimuli as they relate to studying sensation and perception.
4. Discuss the role of selective attention in our perception and identify the limits of human beings with regard to their ability to attend to multiple stimuli.
5. Discuss the positive and negative effects of a restricted environment. Discuss what factors might influence the effects of such deprivation.
6. Identify and describe the parts of the eye, explain how each is related to the processing of visual stimuli, and trace light through the visual system to the brain.
7. Explain the role of receptive fields, what and where receptors are, and eye movement in visual perception.
8. Characterize the relationship between the psychological and physical properties of color. Specifically, compare and contrast trichromatic and opponent-process theories as they relate to color blindness.
9. Explain how our visual perception system and experience allow us to maintain a uniform view of the world by means of size and shape constancy.
10. Explain how monocular and binocular cues are associated with depth perception.
11. Characterize some of the common illusions we experience and examine how perception may be culturally dependent.
12. Explain the phenomena of agnosia and prosopagnosia and discuss what factors might cause these difficulties.
13. Discuss the Gestalt approach to conscious experience, describe five Gestalt laws of organization, and discuss some of the limitations of Gestalt theory.
14. Identify two physical and two psychological properties of sound.
15. List and describe the parts of the ear and explain how each part functions to process auditory stimuli.
16. Compare and contrast the place and frequency theories of hearing and evaluate how modern researchers utilize these theories together.
17. Discuss the two key concepts involved in sound localization, and define some of the common types of hearing impairments.
18. Identify the four basic tastes and describe the phenomenon called sensory adaptation.
19. Develop an understanding of olfaction in humans, and summarize the research comparing communication and smell in humans and animals.
20. Summarize the structure and function of the skin and its relationships to touch and tickling.
21. Examine the physical and psychological aspects related to pain, discuss factors involved in pain control and management, and explain the neuromatrix theory.
22. Explain the systems involved in balance and body control.

Key Terms

Sensation
Perception
Bottom-up Analysis
Top-down Analysis
Psychophysics
Absolute Threshold
Subliminal Perception
Signal Detection Theory
Selective Attention
Electromagnetic Radiation
Light
Retina
Myopic
Hyperopic
Photoreceptors
Rods
Cones
Transduction
Convergence
Dark Adaptation
Visual Cortex
Optic Chiasm
Receptive Fields
Saccades
Hue
Brightness
Saturation

Trichromatic Theory
Color Blindness
Opponent-Process Theory
Trichromats
Monochromats
Dichromats
Size Constancy
Shape Constancy
Monocular Depth Cues
Accommodation
Binocular Depth Cues
Retinal Disparity
Convergence
Illusion
Agnosia
Law of Pragnanz
Sound
Frequency
Pitch
Amplitude
Conduction Deafness
Sensorineural Deafness
Olfaction
Endorphins
Kinesthesia
Vestibular Senses

As you read...

How Are Stimulation and Perception Linked?

1. Sensation is the process of _____, whereas _____ refers to the process of organizing information so that it acquires meaning.

2. Provide one example each of sensation and perception.

3. Describe the difference(s) between bottom-up analysis and top-down analysis.

6-1   Psychophysics

1. Psychophysics focuses on the relationship between what two factors?

2. What are the differences between a threshold, an absolute threshold and a difference threshold?

3. List and describe three methods for studying perceptual thresholds.

4. Researchers using Signal Detection Theory have found that what four factors influence a person's perception?

5. When perception takes place below the threshold level of awareness, it is referred to as _____ perception.

6-1   Selective Attention

1. Define selective attention.

2. You are in a crowded room of people having a discussion with one individual. All of a sudden, you find your attention drawn to another person's conversation from across the room when you hear her mention your name. This phenomenon referred to as _____.

3. Perceptual psychologists focus on the _____ of a person's attention.

6-2	Restricted Environmental Stimulation

1. Define and give an example of restricted environmental stimulation.

2. Give examples of some positive and negative effects of sensory restriction.

3. What factors might influence whether people experience positive or negative effects of sensory restriction?

6-3	Inattentional Blindness

1. In a recent experiment, people who were attending to a scene with sports figures in it did not notice that a figure in a gorilla suit appeared and then disappeared. This would be an example of what phenomenon?

2. The more you pay attention to the _____ _____, the less likely you will be to notice the _____ _____.

How Do We See the World?

1. The stimulation from the environment that results in vision is _____ _____.

2. Which part of the electromagnetic spectrum is visible to humans?

6-4	The Structures of the Visual System

1. Identify and describe the parts of the eye and explain how each is related to the processing of visual stimuli.

2. Myopia refers to having trouble seeing things that are _____, whereas _____ refers to difficulty seeing objects that are _____.

3. What is macular degeneration and what is its most common cause?

4. Describe the layers of photoreceptors that are part of the retina and describe the function of each.

5. Light in the photoreceptor layer breaks down _____, which causes electrochemical changes in the rods and cones.

6. _____ or coding is the process by which stimuli are analyzed and converted into electrical impulses.

7. Describe how information gets from the rods and cones to the brain.

8. Describe the duplicity theory of vision.

9. When illumination levels change from high to low, the increase in light sensitivity that occurs is called _____ _____.

10. The point at which half of the optic nerve fibers from each eye cross over and connect to the other side of the brain is called the _____ _____.

6-5   The Electrochemical Basis of Visual Perception
---

1.   Receptor fields are _____.

2.   Define feature detectors and describe the 3 types of feature detectors.

3.   Simultaneous and coordinated processing of information in multiple locations in the brain is referred to as _____ _____.

4.   Are there gender differences in perception?

5.   Saccades are _____.

6.   Explain how eye movement relates to better perception.

6-6   Color Vision
---

1.   List and define the 3 psychological dimensions of color.

2.   The color of an object is referred to as _____, the _____ is how light or dark hue is, and the purity of the color is known as _____.

3.   Define color coding

4.   Describe the trichromatic theory of color vision.

5.   What phenomena does the trichromatic theory of vision fail to explain?

6.   Describe the opponent-process theory of color vision.

7. People possessing normal color vision are called _____, those who do not see any color are called _____, and those who can only distinguish two different colors are called _____.

How Do We Perceive Form and Substance?

1. Size constancy is _____.

2. List and describe the three things that might influence the perception of size constancy.

3. The ability of the visual perceptual system to recognize a shape despite changes in its orientation or the angle from which it is viewed is _____. Provide one example.

6-7   Depth Perception

1. Define *depth perception.*

2. Define the following monocular depth cues and provide one example for each.

Monocular Cue	Definition	Example
Motion parallax		
Kinetic depth effect		
Linear perspective		
Interposition		
Texture gradient		
Shadowing		
Atmospheric perspective		
Accommodation		

3. Depth cues that need two eyes to be used are called _____ depth cues.

Psychology

4. Name and describe the two binocular depth cues.

6-8   Illusions

1. Define *illusion*.

2. Describe each of the following illusions and give an explanation of why each is thought to occur.

   a) Müller-Lyer

   b) Explanation

   c) Ponzo

   d) Explanation

   e) Moon illusion

   f) Explanation

3. Describe how culture affects the perception of illusions.

6-9 Prosopagnosia: The Inability to Recognize Faces

1.   The inability to recognize a sensory stimulus that should be recognizable, despite having normal, intact perceptual systems is _____.

2.   Prosopagnosia is _____.

3.   Summarize the evidence that supports the notion that the brain contains specific facial detectors.

| 6-10 | **Gestalt Laws of Organization** |

1. Early Gestalt psychologists believed that people organize each complex visual field into _____ rather than _____.

2. The law of Pragnanz states that _____.

3. Match the following laws of organization to the appropriate description:

   proximity   similarity   continuity   common fate   closure

   a) _____ Items that move or change together are seen as a whole.
   b) _____ Parts of a figure that are left out will be filled in by the perceptual system.
   c) _____ Groups are formed by elements close to one another in space and time.
   d) _____ A string of items indicates where the next item will be found.
   e) _____ Similar items tend to be perceived in groups.

4. List some of the problems with Gestalt theories.

5. Identify the perceptual process that best explains why each of the following situations is perceived by the observer as described.

   monocular depth cue   binocular depth cue
   Gestalt laws organization   illusion

   a) _____ A basket of fruit and a bottle of wine are positioned in such a way that the basket blocks part of the image of the wine bottle; as a result the observer perceives the wine bottle as being closer.
   b) _____ As you move your new record album closer to your face so that you can read the song titles, a series of muscles attached to the crystalline lenses in your eyes change the shape of the lenses and keep the image on your retinas in focus.
   c) _____ As your lover moves closer to you to establish intimate eye contact, your eyes converge, moving toward one another and providing you with necessary depth cues.
   d) _____ An auditorium is filled with folding chairs that are either gray or blue. They are set up in sections by color beginning with ten rows of blue chairs, ten rows of gray chairs, another ten rows of blue chairs and so on. As an observer, you perceive the chairs in groups by the similarity of their color.

e) _____ As you look at your favorite painting you notice the darker objects seem to be farther away than the lighter objects.

f) _____ You look at two lines, one of which appears to be longer. When you measure the two lines you find that they are the same length. Yet, when you look at them again one of the lines still appears to be longer.

g) _____ The cowboy on a sign outside of "Joe's Place" appears to be waving at you because the light bulbs that make up the sign blink in a synchronized manner.

How Do We Perceive Sounds?

1. Define sound.

2. The three psychological aspects of sound are _____, _____, and _____.

3. The psychological experience that corresponds with the frequency of an auditory stimulus is _____.

4. High pitched tones usually have _____ frequencies.

5. Amplitude is _____.

6. The specific mixture of frequencies and amplitude that make up sound is called _____.

6-11   The Structure of the Ear

1. Audition is also known as _____.

2. List and describe the 3 major parts of the ear.

3. Where is the eardrum (tympanic membrane) located and what does it do?

4. List the parts of the middle ear.

5. The _____ is a spiral tube in the inner ear.

6. Different areas of the _____ _____ in the cochlea are stimulated by different frequencies.

7. _____ _____ initiate the electrical coding of sound waves.

8. Trace the route of nerve impulses in the brain's auditory system.

9. Match the following structures of the ear with the appropriate description:

    external ear   middle ear   inner ear.

   a) _____ The snail-like tube where pressure changes, received by the basilar membrane, stimulate hair cells and bring about the initial electrical coding in the nervous system of sound waves. This structure is also known as the cochlea.
   b) _____ The fleshy tissue on the outside of the head and the opening that leads to the eardrum.
   c) _____ The eardrum and tiny bones that amplify sound waves and stimulate the basilar membrane.

6-12   Theories of Hearing

1. Describe the two major classes of hearing theories.

2. Both the place theory and frequency theory of hearing have limitations. Describe them.

6-13   Sound Localization

1. Describe the 2 key factors that influence sound localization.

2. How do you localize sound when it is in front of you?

6-14	Hearing Impairments

1.   Conduction deafness is defined as _____.

2.   Deafness resulting from damage to the cochlea, the auditory nerve, or auditory processing areas is called _____.

3.   Exposure to very high intensity sound for prolonged periods can lead to _____.

4.   How is a person's hearing sensitivity assessed?

Which Senses Are the Least Understood?

1.   _____ _____ are the primary receptors for taste stimuli.

2.   You are born with a certain number of taste buds and these are the same ones that you have throughout your life. Is this statement true or false? Explain.

3.   List the 4 basic tastes.

4.   You start to eat some salted French fries and you find that you continue to salt them as you eat because the salty taste has "warn off." Explain why this might happen.

6-15	Smell

1.   The sense of smell is referred to as _____.

2.   Trace the path of smell from the environment to the brain. In doing so, define the various structures that process the information from the environment.

3. Smell experience depends on a sensory stimulus and _____ _____, including _____ _____.

4. Pheromones are _____.

5. Give 3 examples of how animals use pheromones to communicate and elicit behavior.

6. If you read any magazine, you will find numerous ads that claim to have a perfume or cologne that can invoke feelings of passion in the opposite sex. Based on the research examining human pheromones, should you buy these products? Explain.

What is the Relationship Between Touch and Pain?

1. List the 3 skin senses.

2. Information from the _____ _____ is ultimately sent to the _____ cortex.

6-16   Touch

1. List and describe the 3 layers of the skin.

2. The cells of the _____ are replaced approximately every 28 days.

3. Are the receptors for each of the skin senses similar or different? Explain.

4. Sometimes, a person who is tickled for an extended period of time reports that it starts to "hurt." Knowing what you do about the receptors for the skin senses, explain how these two messages might get confused.

5. Why can't people tickle themselves?

6-17   Pain
---

1.   What types of stimuli do psychologists use to study pain?

2.   Most psychologists believe that the receptors for pain are _____ _____ _____.

3.   Research indicates that pain is both physical and _____. Support this later factor by discussing how pain varies based on certain factors.

4.   Explain neuromatrix theory.

5.   List the 5 inputs that act on the neuromatrix programs.

6.   _____ are painkillers that are produced naturally in the brain and the pituitary gland.

7.   Acupuncture is _____.

8.   Traditional models of acupuncture suggest that it works by stimulating certain life-force meridians; however, research evidence indicates that _____.

9.   A friend of yours is suffering from chronic pain due to a back injury. They are wondering what they might do to cope with this pain and what factors might make it worse. Based on your knowledge, what would you tell them?

How Do We Keep Our Balance?

1.   Kinethesis is _____.

2.   Sensory cues that come from within the body are called _____ _____.

3.   Describe the vestibular sense.

Does Extrasensory Perception Exist?

1.   Telepathy is _____

2.   _____ is the ability to predict future events.

3.   You are listening to the news and hear an "expert" indicate that he is often aware that an event might occur before it actually does. Based on the research related to extrasensory perception, how would you respond to this statement?

After You Read, Practice Test #1

1. The relationship between a person's conscious experience of a stimulus and the physical properties of a stimulus is the focus of _____. (179)
   A. Transduction
   B. Perception
   C. Sensation
   D. Psychophysics

2. What is the name of the bulging, transparent, protective layer covering the front of the eye? (186)
   A. Pupil
   B. Lens
   C. Iris
   D. Cornea

3. The point at which half of the optic nerve fibers from each eye cross over and connect to the other side of the brain is called the _____.
   A. Visual cortex
   B. Auditory crossing
   C. Receptive mix
   D. Optic chiasm

4. Name the type of eye movements being made as you read this statement. (194)
   A. Saccadic
   B. Random
   C. Mergence
   D. Pursuit eye

5. The ability to make all colors by mixing three basic colors, red, blue, and green is part of the _____. (196)
   A. Opponent-process theory
   B. Law of Similarity
   C. Trichromatic theory
   D. Law of Proximity

6. The illusion in which two horizontal lines of the same length, bracketed by slanted lines, appear to be of different lengths is the _____. (202)
   A. Ponzo Illusion
   B. Moon Illusion
   C. Muller-Lyer Illusion
   D. None of the above

7. Cross-cultural research on the perception of illusions indicates that people whose culture does not include many straight lines or sharp corners will _____. (203-204)
    A.   Have more trouble seeing many illusions
    B.   Be fooled more easily by many illusions
    C.   Be unable to interpret the pictures at all
    D.   See the illusions exactly as Americans do

8. The cochlea is _____. (209)
    A.   Part of the middle ear
    B.   The fleshy tissue on the outside of the head that we usually refer to as the ear
    C.   A snaillike tube where hair cells are stimulated by a change in sound pressure
    D.   A and C

9. Sensorineural deafness results from damage to the _____. (211)
    A.   Ear drum
    B.   Ossicles
    C.   Tympanic membrane
    D.   Cochlea

10. Adult human skin is made up of _____ layer(s). (217)
    A.   3
    B.   2
    C.   4
    D.   1

After You Read, Practice Test #2

1. When an incoming stimulus is interpreted and acquires meaning, it is called _____. (178)
   A. Threshold
   B. Adaptation
   C. Sensation
   D. Perception

2. An absolute threshold is _____. (179)
   A. A statistically determined minimum level of stimulation needed to excite a perceptual system
   B. The smallest amount of change in a stimulus needed for most people to detect the change
   C. A relatively permanent change in the level of sensitivity in a sense organ due to experience
   D. The shortest amount of time a stimulus can exist before it will be detected by the perceptual system

3. The purposeful focusing of conscious awareness on a specific stimulus or event in the environment to the exclusion of other stimuli is _____. (181)
   A. Selective attention
   B. Appropriate assertion
   C. Restricted stimulation
   D. Attentional blindness

4. The photoreceptors for the visual system are contained in the _____. (187)
   A. Lens
   B. Retina
   C. Iris
   D. Cornea

5. The opponent process theory assumes that _____. (196)
   A. There are three types of receptors, each maximally sensitive to one group of wavelengths
   B. That three sets of receptors respond positively or negatively to different wavelengths
   C. Color coding occurs at the retina
   D. A and C

6. Which of the following objects best illustrates the property of color called "saturation?" (195)
   A. A pink carnation
   B. A blue sapphire
   C. A green olive
   D. A red brick

7. You perceive a book as having the same shape whether you see it from the side or from the front because of a perceptual process known as _____. (198)
   A. Similarity
   B. Accommodation
   C. Interposition
   D. Constancy

8. Which of the following statements is true? (209)
   A. Auditory cells are maximally sensitive to certain narrow ranges of frequencies
   B. Frequency theories seem to be much more accurate than place theories in providing an explanation for how we hear
   C. One Hertz (Hz) is equal to ten cycles per second
   D. Hair cells in the cochlea stimulate the basilar membrane

9. In the auditory system, transduction occurs at the _____. (209-210)
   A. Ear drum
   B. Cochlea
   C. Outer ear
   D. Ocicles

10. The first bite of Joe's soup seemed very salty. After eating continuously for several minutes, it seemed less salty. This is probably due to the phenomenon of _____. (214)
    A. Sensory overload
    B. Chemical deterioration
    C. Sensory adaptation
    D. Gustatory amnesia

After You Read, Practice Test #3

1. What is another name for nearsightedness? (186)
    A. Hypermetropic
    B. Myopic
    C. Prebyopic
    D. None of the above

2. The brain can process two sets of signals about a particular image and allows us to see form and depth because impulses cross to the opposite side of the brain when they reach the _____. (189)
    A. Optic chiasm
    B. Lateral geniculate nucleus
    C. Striate cortex
    D. None of the above

3. Hypercomplex cells in the visual system respond to what types of stimuli? (191)
    A. Lines of a specific length
    B. Shape and size of light
    C. Color
    D. Movement of light

4. A color with low saturation is _____. (195)
    A. Green
    B. Pink
    C. Blue
    D. Yellow

5. In the opponent-process theory of color, our experience of a color is controlled by _____. (196)
    A. Its position on three dimensions (red-green, blue-yellow, black-white)
    B. The relative activations of three different kinds of cones (red, green, and blue)
    C. The frequency of firing in the optic nerve, corresponding to the frequency of the light
    D. An automatic process that triggers the opposite color for any wavelength of light

6. Which of the following is the physical attribute of loudness? (208)
    A. Frequency
    B. Amplitude
    C. Pitch
    D. Tone

7. Taste receptors are _____ found on the tongue. (213)
   A. The papillae
   B. The "moats"
   C. The taste buds
   D. In the saliva

8. Which of the following is not one of the basic tastes? (213)
   A. Salty
   B. Sour
   C. Bitter
   D. Tart

9. When a police officer asks a suspected drunk driver "How many fingers do you see?" it is a test of vision. When the officer asks the driver to touch his finger to the tip of his nose with his eyes closed, which sense is being tested? (221)
   A. Kinesthesis
   B. Olfaction
   C. Gustation
   D. Orientation

10. An extrasensory process by which thought is transferred from one person to another without the use of normal communications is _____. (222)
    A. Transference
    B. Telepathy
    C. Clairvoyance
    D. Precognition

After You Read, Comprehensive Test

1. Sensation _____. (178)
    A. Allows us to experience and adapt to our environment
    B. Is a complex process of receiving stimuli from the environment
    C. Allows sensory input to acquire meaning
    D. Can only occur following perception

2. The theory of selective attention that states that all incoming information is analyzed, but only certain information is chosen to be passed on to higher levels for more complex processing, is called the _____. (181)
    A. Localization theory
    B. Filter theory
    C. Attenuation theory
    D. Threshold theory

3. The part of the eye that contains rods and cones is called the _____. (187)
    A. Retina
    B. Iris
    C. Cornea
    D. Bipolar layer

4. When a sense organ processes stimuli and converts them into electrical impulses, it is called. _____. (187)
    A. Lateralization
    B. Localization
    C. Papillation
    D. Transduction

5. The part of your eye in which you have mostly rods is _____. (188)
    A. The top half of your retina
    B. Your fovea
    C. The center of your retina
    D. The outer edge of your retina

6. We can discriminate between a circle and a triangle because each shape _____. (190-192)
    A. Is clearly different from any other shape
    B. Stimulates the cells of different receptive fields
    C. Passes through a different portion of the crystalline lens
    D. Is recognized by the primary visual cortex

7. When a person describes their car is red, they are describing the psychological dimension of hue. Which physical dimension corresponds to hue? (194)
    A. Wavelength
    B. Intensity
    C. Purity
    D. Saturation

8. Persons who are totally colorblind would be considered _____. (197)
    A. Monochromats
    B. Trichromats
    C. Dichromats
    D. Anomolous trichromats

9. An object that is moving appears more three-dimensional than one that is perfectly still. This is called the _____ effect. (200)
    A. Visual motion
    B. Shape constancy
    C. Optical localization
    D. Kinetic depth effect

10. Retinal disparity _____. (201)
    A. Is most likely to occur when objects are far away
    B. Is greatest when images on the retina are the farthest apart
    C. Keeps information on corresponding points on the retina
    D. Is a monocular depth cue

11. Elements close to one another in space or time will be perceived as groups in the Law of _____. (205)
    A. Common Fate Principles
    B. Similarity
    C. Proximity
    D. Continuity

12. The three major parts of the ear are the _____. (208)
    A. Hammer, anvil, and stirrup
    B. Timbre, pitch, and loudness detectors
    C. Rods, cones, and hair cells
    D. Outer ear, middle ear, and inner ear

13. Where are the true sensory receptors for sound located? (210)
    A. Cochlea
    B. Occipital lobe
    C. Eardrum
    D. Retina

14. The factor that seems to play the biggest role in conduction deafness is _____. (211)
     A. Life-long exposure to excessive noise
     B. Sudden, loud noises
     C. Aging
     D. Hardening of tympanic membrane

15. The _____ allows you to touch your finger to your nose with your eyes closed. (221)
     A. Sense of touch
     B. Vestibular sense
     C. Kinesthesis sense
     D. Optical alignment sense

True or False

1. The study of selective attention by psychologists is important because humans can generally attend to very view stimuli in the environment at one time. (181)

2. The benefits of restricted environmental stimulation are related to the person's perception of the benefits and purpose of such restriction. (184)

3. Researchers generally believe that humans derive more information through their auditory system (ears) compared to other sensory systems. (185)

4. When you walk from a dark room to a well-lit room, your visual system will undergo dark adaptation. (188)

5. The most specific receptor cells in the visual field are the complex cells, which respond to the movement of light. (191)

6. Motion parallax is a binocular depth cue. (199)

7. The two key factors that influence sound localization are interaural time differences and interaural intensity differences. (210)

8. All taste buds are sensitive to all taste stimuli in the environment. (213)

Essay Questions

1. Compare and contrast top-down and bottom-up analysis. (178)

2. Define prosopagnosia and what research about it has told us about the visual system. (204-205)

When You Have Finished!

Surf's Up!!

After you've read and reviewed, try these web sites for additional information about some of the topics covered in this chapter.

1. **Sensation and Perception Tutorials** (http://psych.hanover.edu/Krantz/sen_tut.html)
    A number of interactive and colorful tutorials on a variety of topics in sensation and perception.
2. **Seeing, Hearing, & Smelling the World** (http://www.hhmi.org/senses/)
    This interactive site allows you read more about the topics of sight, hearing and smelling. There are some great diagrams and key terms defined for you.
3. **The National Pain Foundation** (http://www.painconnection.org/)
    Devoted to patients and professionals and loaded with information about pain and pain management.
4. **Illusion Works** (http://psylux.psych.tu-dresden.de/i1/kaw/diverses%20Material/www.illusionworks.com/)
    Contains a number of great visual illusions and information on illusions!
5. **Color Matters** (http://www.colormatters.com/entercolormatters.html)
    A site devoted to color and how it is related to the brain, behavior, and emotions.
6. **Neurological Eye Stimulator** (http://cim.ucdavis.edu/Eyes/eyesim.htm)
    Follows the stimulation of the visual system.
7. **Motion Perception** (http://www.biols.susx.ac.uk/home/George_Mather/Motion/index.html)
    Some interesting and interactive visual demonstrations related to how we perceive movement.

Cross Check: Sensation and Perception

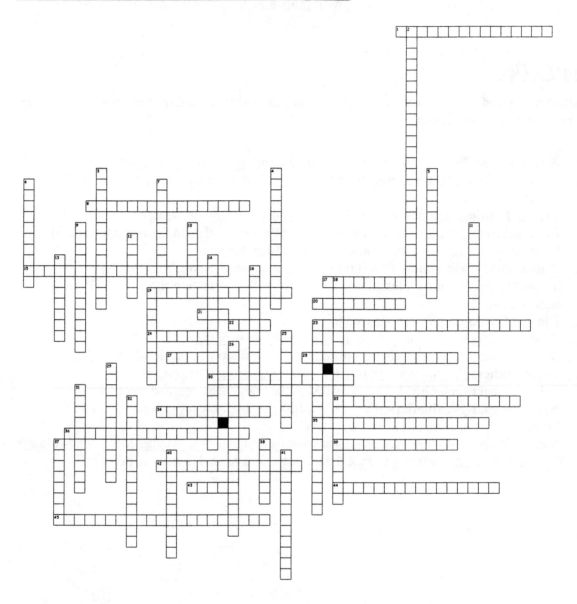

Across

1. Areas of the retina that produce a change in the firing of cells in the visual system
8. Analysis of the perceptual process that begins at the most fundamental level of sensation and works up to more complex perceptual tasks
15. Perception that occurs below the threshold of awareness
17. The synapsing of electrochemical signals from many rods or cones onto one bipolar cell
19. Ability of the visual perceptual system to recognize a shape despite changes in its orientation
20. The total energy of a sound wave that determines the loudness of the sound
21. The psychological property referred to as "color," determined by the wavelengths of reflected light
22. Rod-shaped receptors primarily responsible for vision at low levels of illumination
23. Deafness resulting from damage to the cochlea or the auditory nerve
24. An inability to recognize a sensory stimulus that should be recognizable
27. Experience that occurs when changes in air pressure stimulate the receptive organ for hearing
28. The sense of bodily orientation and postural adjustment
30. The rods and the cones
33. Deafness resulting from interference with the transmission of sound to the inner ear
34. The point at which half of the optic nerve fibers from each eye cross over and connect to the other side of the brain
35. The statistically determined minimum level of stimulation necessary to excite a perceptual system
36. Theory that proposed that all colors can be made by mixing red, green, and blue
39. People who can perceive all three basic colors and thus can distinguish any hue
42. The increase in sensitivity to light that occurs when illumination level changes from high to low
43. Corresponds with frequency of an auditory stimulus
44. The slight different between the visual images projected on the two retinas
45. Theory that holds that an observer's perception depends not only on the intensity of a stimulus but also on the observer's motivation

Down

2. The entire spectrum of waves initiated by the movement of charged particles
3. The Gestalt notion that when stimuli can be grouped together and seen as a whole, they will be
4. Subfield of psychology that focuses on the relationship between physical stimuli and people's conscious experiences of them
5. Receives and further processes visual information from the lateral geniculate nucleus; it is the most important are of the brain's occipital lobe

6. The lightness or darkness of a hue
7. Farsighted
9. The change in the shape of the lens of the eye that enables the observer to keep an object in focus on the retina when the object is moved
10. The small portion of the electromagnetic spectrum that is visible to the human eye
11. Analysis of perceptual phenomena that begins at the more complex level of the perceptual process
12. Nearsighted
13. A perception of a physical stimulus that differs from measurable reality
14. Cues for depth perception that do not depend on the use of both eyes
16. Process by which a perceptual system converts stimuli into electrical impulses
18. Theory, proposed by Herring, that there are six basic colors and color is coded by varying responses of three types of paired receptors
19. Process by which the sense organs' receptor cells are stimulated and relay initial information to the brain
23. The purposeful focusing of conscious awareness on a specific stimulus to the exclusion of other stimuli
25. The sense of smell
26. Cues for depth perception that require the use of both eyes
29. The awareness aroused by movements of the muscles, tendons, and joints
31. People who can distinguish only two of the three basic colors
32. The inability to perceive different hues
37. Rapid voluntary movements of the eyes
38. A multilayered network of neurons that line the back of the eyeball and generate signals in response to light
40. The depth and richness of a hue
41. People who cannot perceive any color

Created by Puzzlemaker at
DiscoverySchool.com

Chapter 7

Consciousness

Before you read...

Each day you likely experience various levels of awareness, ranging from being wide awake and aware to asleep and unaware of what is going on around you. In between these two regular states of consciousness, you might also experience other states of consciousness such as daydreaming, meditative states, or the effects of substance use. The current chapter explores all of these various states and discusses how psychologists have come to understand naturally occurring and artificially induced state of consciousness.

The chapter begins with a broad overview of what consciousness is and a discussion of some of the common theories about consciousness. Next, the most widely studied state or level of consciousness, sleep, is explored. In this section you will be introduced to normal variations in the sleep-wake cycle, the stages of sleep we go through during the night, and what positive and negative effects sleep has on our behavior. You will also learn about some of the common sleep problems and their causes.

Although you might not remember them all, research tells us that you likely dream three to four times a night! In the next section of the chapter, you will learn all about dreams, including what a dream is, the common content of dreams, and theories regarding why we dream. If you have ever wondered aloud what your dreams mean, you will find this section very interesting.

In the third section of this chapter, you will learn that consciousness can be controlled and modified by biofeedback, hypnosis, or meditation. Each of these methods has had some success in treating problems such as headaches, high blood pressure, stress-related illness, pain management, and memory loss. Read ahead and learn how and why! In addition, explore some of the common criticisms related to these methods.

The chapter concludes with a look at how conscious experience can be altered by artificial means. You will learn about how we live in a drug-using culture with numerous legal and illegal drugs readily available for all ages. In addition, you will come to understand the difference between dependence, tolerance, and withdrawal and how to differentiate between substance use and abuse. Finally, you will review various types of substances, their effects on human functioning, and their more general effects on society, and public safety.

Learning Objectives

1. Define consciousness and describe the continuum view of conscious awareness.
2. Describe and differentiate the mysterians, materialist, and evolutionary views and theories of consciousness.
3. Develop an understanding of circadian rhythms and discuss how they impact human behavior and functioning.
4. List the stages of the sleep cycle and discuss the various phenomena that one is likely to experience at each stage.
5. Explain how sleep deprivation impacts our functioning.
6. Discuss the major theories and research related to the question of why we sleep and what makes us sleep and wake.
7. List and describe the major sleep disorders.
8. Discuss the factors that might impact our dream content and differentiate between normal and lucid dreaming.
9. Compare and contrast the psychodynamic, cognitive, evolutionary, and physiological views of dreaming.
10. Describe biofeedback and its uses and critically evaluate its effectiveness in helping people manage physiological problems.
11. Describe the effects of hypnosis and discuss some of the alternative explanations and controversies that are associated with hypnosis.
12. Describe the two types of meditation and summarize their effects or uses.
13. Define and differentiate between tolerance, dependence, and withdrawal.
14. Identify the different types of psychoactive drugs and their influence on behavior and functioning.
15. State the three criteria for substance abuse and understand why people use and abuse drugs.

Key Terms

Consciousness
Circadian Rhythms
Suprachiasmatic Nucleus
Electroencephalogram (EEG)
Non-Rapid Eye Movement (NREM) sleep
Rapid Eye Movement (REM) sleep
Narcolepsy
Sleep Apnea
Insomnia
Night Terrors
Dream
Lucid Dream
Manifest Content
Latent Content
Collective Unconscious
Biofeedback
Hypnosis
Meditation
Posthypnotic Suggestion
Drug
Psychoactive Drug
Tolerance
Dependence
Blood-Brain Barrier
Sedative-Hypnotic
Sedatives
Depressants
Opiate
Stimulant
Psychedelic
Substance Abuse

As you read...

What is Consciousness?

1.   Consciousness is _____.

2.   What is the doctrine of dualism?

3.   Define materialism (reductionism).

4.   An _____ _____ of consciousness is a dramatically different state of consciousness that is different from ordinary awareness and responsiveness.

5.   Metacognition is _____.

7-1	**Theories of Consciousness**

1.   Describe a materialist's view of consciousness.

2.   Define consciousness from an evolutionary perspective.

3.   Subjective experiences and a person's awareness and feelings are referred to as _____.

4.   Define access.

5.   What is self-knowledge?

6.   Unlike sentience, _____ and _____ can be analyzed because they are cognitive activities.

7.   Describe a neuroscience view consciousness.

What Happens When We Sleep?

1.   Define circadian rhythms are internally generated patterns of body functions, including _____, _____, and _____, which vary over _____ and occur even in the _____ of normal cues about whether it is day or night.

2.   What factors affect and control circadian rhythms?

3.   What can be done to minimize the adjustment process when your circadian rhythms are thrown off?

7-2   Sleep Stages: REM and NREM Sleep

1.   An EEG is a device that is used to record _____ by placing electrodes _____.

2.   _____ is height of the waves and _____ is the number of waves per second.

3.   Define rapid eye movement (REM) sleep and differentiate it from non-rapid eye movement sleep (N-REM).

4.   Describe the 5 stages of sleep and the associated changes that occur at each stage.

5.   A person can dream in _____ stage (s) of sleep.

7-3   Sleep Deprivation
---

1.   Describe of the problems Randy Gardner had during his 11 days of sleep deprivation.

2.   In the United States _____ % of adults do not get enough sleep.

3.   Driving skills are impaired after only _____ hours of missed sleep.

4.   Describe the results of the study examining the effects of sleep deprivation on long-haul truckers.

5.   Define sleep debt.

7-4   Why Do We Sleep?
---

1.   Does sleep serve a restorative function? Explain.

2.   What does the evolutionary approach say about why we sleep?

3.   Describe the theories that focus on the importance of REM sleep.

7-5   Is There a Sleep Switch?
---

1.   How is the suprachiasmatic nucleus (SCN) involved in sleep?

2.   What is the ventrolateral preoptic area (VLPO), and how is it involved in sleep?

3.   Of the brain structures, the _____ appears to be most important to sleep and waking.

| 7-6 | **Sleep Disorders** |

1. _____ is characterized by sudden, uncontrollable episodes of sleep.

2. What problems are associated with the use of barbiturates as sleeping aids?

3. Night terrors are _____.

4. What is sleepwalking?

5. Match the following sleep disorders with the appropriate description.

   narcolepsy   sleep apnea   insomnia   night terrors

   a) _____ People with this disorder stop breathing for at least fifteen seconds up to as many as 100 times a night. During the day they are very sleepy, may have memory losses, work related accidents, and severe headaches.
   b) _____ This disorder is especially common in children between the ages of 3 and 8. The symptoms involve sitting up abruptly in a state of sheer fright, screaming, and breathing quickly.
   c) _____ This is a common disorder often caused by anxiety or depression where a person has a prolonged inability to fall asleep.
   d) _____ People with this disorder could have difficulty on the job or when driving a car because they suddenly and unexpectedly fall asleep.

What Are Dreams and What Do They Mean?

1. A dream is a state of consciousness that occurs during sleep, and it is usually accompanied by _____.

2. Approximately _____ percent of people woken from REM sleep report that they were dreaming.

3. Approximately 90 minutes after a person falls asleep, the first _____ period occurs.

7-7	**Content of Dreams**

1. What are some common events and themes reported when people dream?

2. According to brain imaging studies, what areas of the brain are active during REM sleep?

3. What are lucid dreams?

7-8	**Dream Theories**

1. Complete the missing parts of the following table.

Theory of Dreaming	Basic Orientation to Dreaming
Freudian	
	View dreams as continuations of waking thought processes reflecting people's everyday concerns.
Evolutionary	
	Views dreams as both an expression of unfulfilled needs and as a reflection of the collective unconscious.
Physiological View	

2. The actual content of the dream is called the _____ content, whereas the deeper, hidden meaning of the dream is called the _____ content.

3. In Jung's view, the archetype of the _____ represents a person's inner striving for unity. This archetype would be part of what storehouse of primitive ideas and images that are inherited from our ancestors?

4. What is the cognitive view on dreaming?

5. What does cross-cultural research show about dreams of children?

6. According to the activation-synthesis theory of dreaming, what is taking place when we dream?

7. Describe the research that supports a biological view of dreaming.

Is It Possible to Control Consciousness by Using Biofeedback, Hypnosis, or Meditation?

1. Biofeedback is a process through which people receive information about their physical functioning and use this feedback to _____.

2. What did Miller's research contribute to biofeedback?

3. List some disorders that biofeedback has been used to treat and describe their successfulness.

7-9   Hypnosis

1. Hypnosis is the state of consciousness during which a person's _____, _____, or _____ change because of _____.

2. Hypnotic suggestions always contain some sort of suggestion that _____.

3. What qualities does a good hypnotic subject have?

4. Define suggestibility.

5. The person's willingness to follow the instructions of the hypnotist is called suggestibility or _____ _____.

7-10   Meditation

---

1.   Meditation is _____.

2.   There are two types of meditation: _____ and _____.

3.   Research has indicated that meditation is effective at doing what?

How Do Drugs Alter Consciousness?

1.   What is the difference between a drug and a psychoactive drug?

2.   Define tolerance.

3.   _____ occurs when a person discontinues taking a drug they have developed a _____ for.

7-11   Psychoactive Drugs

---

1.   What is the blood-brain barrier?

2.   _____ _____ affect the brain's neural transmissions and chemicals to induce an altered state of consciousness.

3.   Define sedative-hypnotics (depressants).

4.   Describe the effects of alcohol.

5.   _____ are a class of drugs that reduce pain, calm, are addictive, and produce tolerance.

6.   Opiates are hypnotic drugs that have what types of effect?

7.   Stimulants are _____.

8.   List and describe 4 stimulants.

9.   Describe the effects of psychedelic drugs.

10.   What is MDMA?

11.   _____ is the active ingredient in marijuana (cannabis sativa).

12.   Describe how marijuana affects people.

7-12	Drug Use and Abuse

1.   Which two substances constitute the biggest drug problems in the United States?

2.   What is the difference between drug use and drug abuse?

3.   List the 3 things that indicate someone is a substance abuser.

Psychology

4.   Match the following terms to the appropriate definition.

          dependence   *tolerance*   *withdrawal symptoms*

      a)   _____ Reliance on regular use of a drug, without which the individual suffers a psychological and/or physiological reaction.

      b)   _____ A variety of physiological reactions that occur when a person who has developed a physiological dependence to a drug no longer takes the drug.

      c)   _____ A progressive insensitivity to repeated use of a drug in the same dose. A user must have increasingly greater amounts of the drug to achieve the desired high.

5.   Outline the genetic and evolutionary explanations of alcohol abuse.

After You Read, Practice Test #1

1. Consciousness refers to being both _____ and _____ to one's environment and mental
    processes. (228)
    A.   Alert; Afraid
    B.   Aware; Responsive
    C.   Committed; Alert
    D.   Responsive; Afraid

2. According to Daniel Dennett and the materialist view of consciousness, the brain _____.
    (230)
    A.   Creates multiple drafts of experience that are constantly being reanalyzed
    B.   Is busy deleting extraneous information and experience from storage
    C.   Operates out of the active and receptive modes proposed by Ornstein
    D.   All of the above

3. Circadian rhythms vary over a _____ hour period. (231)
    A.   12
    B.   24
    C.   48
    D.   8

4. Why has REM sleep been referred to as "paradoxical sleep?" (235)
    A.   It has little or no restorative value
    B.   There is a great deal of body movement
    C.   The EEG resembles that of an aware person
    D.   The sleeper is aware of environmental stimuli

5. A sleep disorder in which an individual stops breathing for several seconds during sleep is
    called _____. (239)
    A.   Apnea
    B.   Night terrors
    C.   Hypersomnia
    D.   Somnambulism

6. When you tell another person about a dream you have had, Freud would say you are
    reporting the _____ of your dream (243)
    A.   Superficial aspect
    B.   Manifest content
    C.   Ulterior theme
    D.   Latent content

Psychology

7. In Jung's theory of dreams, the storehouse of ideas and images inherited from our ancestors is called the _____. (245)
    A. Latent content
    B. Manifest content
    C. Mandala archetype
    D. Collective unconscious

8. When an individual requires progressively more and more of a drug to get the same effect, that individual has developed a _____ to a drug. (253)
    A. Tolerance
    B. Antipathy
    C. Immunity
    D. Insensitivity

9. A major psychological effect of alcohol is that it acts as a _____. (254)
    A. Stimulant and makes us overactive
    B. Depressant, and reduces our inhibitions
    C. Tranquilizer, and makes us feel fearful
    D. Aggressor, and makes us more violent

10. Which of the following has been used to provide an explanation for substance use and abuse? (259-261)
    A. Societal factors
    B. Individual family situations
    C. Genetic heritage and medical problems
    D. All of the above

After You Read, Practice Test #2

1. The doctrine of dualism, which states that the mind and body are separable, is a concept linked to _____. (228)
    A. Sigmund Freud
    B. William James
    C. Rene Descartes
    D. Arnold Lazarus

2. Circadian rhythms control each of the following, except_____. (231)
    A. Yawning
    B. Bodily rhythms
    C. Body temperature
    D. Sleep patterns

3. NREM sleep consists of _____ stages. (233)
    A. One
    B. Three
    C. Five
    D. Four

4. What do researchers use to study changes in brain wave activity during sleep? (233)
    A. Electroencephalogram
    B. Positron oscilloscope
    C. Electromyogram
    D. Electro-sleep monitor

5. Each of the following theories regarding why we sleep have been postulated, except _____. (237-238)
    A. Evolutionary
    B. Cognitive
    C. Restorative
    D. Circadian

6. Night terrors are a sleep disorder that mainly affects children and that involves _____. (239)
    A. Frequently experiencing vivid, powerful bad dreams
    B. Intense feelings of terror not associated with any dreams
    C. The desire to sleep with the parents to avoid "monsters"
    D. Being afraid to fall asleep for fear of not waking up again

7. Cross-cultural studies of dream content indicate that _____. (245)
    A. A person's environment played no role in dream content
    B. Dreams incorporated basic cultural views of the purpose of dreaming
    C. A person's environment was more important than their cultural view
    D. A person's cultural view was more important than his or her environment

Psychology

8. Meditation is a state of consciousness that is characterized by _____. (252)
    A. Concentration and deep relaxation
    B. Lack of awareness of one's environment
    C. Giving control to another person.
    D. Information about bodily processes

9. A drug that alters a person's behavior, thoughts, or emotions through its effects on the nervous system is called a(n) _____ drug. (253)
    A. Addictive
    B. Abusive
    C. Neurological
    D. Psychoactive

10. Which of the following drugs alters consciousness, affects moods, thoughts, memory and perception, and is considered a psychedelic? (256)
    A. Cocaine
    B. Crack
    C. Marijuana
    D. Crank

After You Read, Practice Test #3

1. John B. Watson and other early behaviorists did not believe that consciousness was an appropriate subject for psychologists to study because ____. (228)
   A. It invalidates research done with animals
   B. It is not observable and measurable
   C. The elements of consciousness had not been identified
   D. Individual differences in consciousness are too large

2. From an evolutionary perspective of consciousness, access is ____. (230)
   A. The ability to recognize the uniqueness of experiences
   B. The awareness of a pattern in the rhythms of one's life
   C. The awareness of subjective experience
   D. The ability to report on the end products of thought

3. Subjective experience and awareness is called ____. (230)
   A. Emotion
   B. Access
   C. Sentience
   D. Self-knowledge

4. What stage of sleep has over 50% delta waves? (234)
   A. REM
   B. Stage 2
   C. Stage 3
   D. Stage 4

5. Research suggests that sleep deprivation has which of the following effects? (236-237)
   A. Increases test scores on multiple choice examinations
   B. Decreases motor performance and memory
   C. Decreases sex drive
   D. Increases coordination and concentration

6. Insomnia is defined as ____. (239)
   A. The inability to sleep and breathe at the same time
   B. Falling asleep suddenly and unexpectedly during the day
   C. A prolonged inability to fall asleep or stay asleep
   D. Sudden feelings of terror at night when not dreaming

7. The following is NOT mentioned in the cognitive view of dream theory? (245)
   A. Dreams are connected to reality
   B. Dreams reflect issues with which a person is dealing
   C. Dreams have meaning
   D. Dreams have a deep hidden meaning

8.   Biofeedback is a technique that allows individuals to _____. (249)
    A.   Gain control over the content of their dreams
    B.   Alter the patterns of their sleep cycles
    C.   Interpret the true meanings of their dreams
    D.   Control some of the body's involuntary responses

9.   Which of the following drugs produce the most marked shifts in consciousness? (256)
    A.   Cocaine
    B.   Stimulants
    C.   The opiates
    D.   The hallucinogens

10. Approximately what percentage of 18-25 year olds have used marijuana? (258)
    A.   50
    B.   25
    C.   2
    D.   10

After You Read, Comprehensive Practice Test

1. The beginning of the concept of dualism is most closely associated with _____. (228)
   A. Stephen Pinket
   B. John Watson
   C. Sigmund Freud
   D. Rene Descartes

2. When a person is conscious of, or thinks about, their own thought processes, it is called _____. (228)
   A. Consciousness
   B. Altered consciousness
   C. Metacognition
   D. Self consciousness

3. Jet lag and irregular work shifts are problems for individuals and society because they contribute to _____. (232)
   A. Increasing separation of human society from the natural world
   B. Disruptions of the circadian rhythms, leading to reduced efficiency
   C. Feelings of powerlessness, isolation, and disorientation
   D. Poor nutrition as a result of grabbing irregular meals

4. During REM dreams, a person experiences _____. (234)
   A. A relaxed brain state and rapid body movements
   B. Powerful feelings of fear and terror
   C. Sleep spindles and K complexes
   D. Vivid visual imagery and a lack of body movements

5. The proportion of REM to NREM sleep is greatest for _____. (235)
   A. Adolescents
   B. Newborns
   C. Elderly people
   D. Young children

6. A function of the ventrolateral preoptic area of the hypothalamus may be that of a _____. (238)
   A. Anxiety interpretation center
   B. Hunger center controlled by visual stimuli
   C. Sleep switch
   D. Sexual orientation center

7. A dream in which a person is aware that she is dreaming while the dream is being experienced is called a _____. (242)
   A. NREM dream
   B. Lucid dream
   C. Hypnogogic
   D. Spiritual

8. What aspect of dreams did Freud emphasize? (243)
   A. The use of symbolism
   B. The role of environmental stimuli in dream content
   C. Their relationship to physiological variables
   D. Their function in the organization of memory

9. According to the activation-synthesis theory of dreams, a dream is the result of _____. (246)
   A. Unacceptable impulses buried in the unconscious
   B. Ideas and images we inherited from our ancestors
   C. Trying to make sense of random brain activity
   D. An attempt to initiate processing of cognitive information

10. Sharon is learning to relax her heart in order to lower her blood pressure. This method of monitoring and controlling involuntary activity is called _____. (249)
    A. Meditation
    B. Hypnotic induction
    C. Biofeedback
    D. Medication

11. For which disorders have biofeedback procedures been most frequently used? (249)
    A. Digestive
    B. Hereditary
    C. Stress-related
    D. Mental

12. According to research on hypnosis, memories discussed under hypnosis are likely _____. (251)
    A. Recreations of early experiences versus memories of them
    B. Highly accurate
    C. Indirectly influenced by whether the memories are negative or positive
    D. Unreliable except for the case of recovered sexual abuse memories

13. When we say a person has gained a tolerance to a drug, we mean that the person _____. (253)
    A. Can take a drug without suffering from any negative side effects
    B. Can take a minimum amount of a drug without experiencing withdrawal symptoms
    C. No longer experiences the desired effect from that particular amount of a drug
    D. Has become addicted to a drug

14. Alcohol is classified as a _____ drug. (254)
    A. Sedative-hypnotic
    B. Narcotic
    C. Psychostimulant
    D. Psychedelic

15. Ecstasy was designed from _____. (256)
    A. LSD
    B. Methamphetamine
    C. Cocaine
    D. Methatrexate

True or False

1. Most psychologists believe that consciousness exists on a continuum ranging from alert attention to drug-induced states. (229)

2. A materialist view of consciousness suggests that consciousness developed as a means of helping people adapt and survive within the environment. (230)

3. There are five stages of sleep. (233-234)

4. Research indicates that there are certain brain areas that act to turn on and turn off our desire to sleep. (238)

5. People dream every night and perhaps several times a night. (242)

6. Carl Jung suggested that dreams contain both a manifest and latent content. (244-245)

7. In order for a drug to alter behavioral and cognitive processes, it must first cross the blood-brain barrier. (253)

8. Illegal drug use tends to be more widespread among adolescents and young adults. (258)

Essay Questions

1. Why do we need sleep? (237)

2. Define substance abuse and list 3 things that indicate a person is a substance abuser. (259)

When You Have Finished!

Surf's Up!!

After you've read and reviewed, try these web sites for additional information about some of the topics covered in this chapter.

1. **International Association for the Study of Dreams**
   (http://www.asdreams.org/index.htm)
   > This association is all about the applied investigation of dreams and dreaming. You can learn about dreams, chat online about dreams and follow links to all sorts of information about dreams and dreaming.

2. **Hypnosis.com** (http://www.hypnosis.com/)
   > The website of the American Board of Hypnotherapy, this site contains information on how to do hypnosis and other information and links to information about hypnotherapy.

3. **National Sleep Foundation** (http://www.sleepfoundation.org)
   > A website that is full of information about sleep! It includes information on the stages of sleep, sleep disorders and problem, and even tools and test to examine your own sleep patterns.

4. **Association for Applied Psychophysiology and Biofeedback**. (http://www.aapd.org/)
   > This organization is concerned with all aspects of the mind-body connection and the site has information on disorders, treatment, meetings, and education.

5. **National Institute of Drug Abuse Club Drugs Website**. (http://www.clubdrugs.org/)
   > A website developed to provide accurate and up-to-date information on club drugs such as ecstasy.

6. **The Dreams Foundation.** (http://www.dreams.ca/)
   > Information on the application of dreams, how to improve the recall of your dreams, lucid dreaming and the science associated with dreaming.

Cross Check: Consciousness

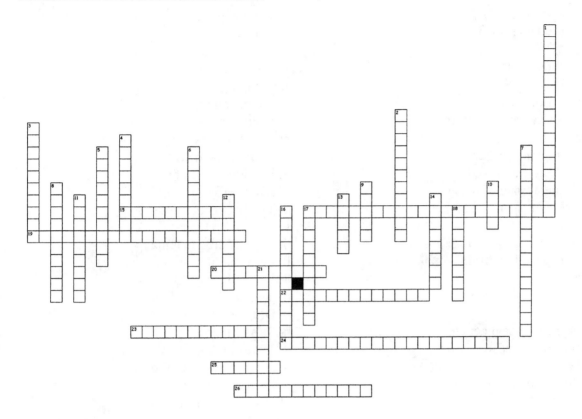

Across

15. Characterized by uncontrollable episodes of sleep
17. Structure in hypothalamus involved in sleep-wake cycles
19. All sleep except REM sleep
20. Symptoms that come when drug is removed
22. General state of being aware and responsive to the environment
23. High levels of arousal 60-90 minutes after falling asleep
24. A way to record brain waves
25. Type of dream content Freud considered symbolic and hidden
26. Suggestion made during hypnosis

Created by Puzzlemaker at DiscoverySchool.com

Down

1. Internal pattern of bodily functions
2. Process of receiving information about functioning to learn to alter that functioning
3. State of consciousness characterized by deep relaxation and detachment
4. Needing more of drug to get same effect
5. Type of unconscious supported by Jung
6. Type of drug that may bring on hallucinations
7. Stage of sleep related to dreaming
8. Drug becomes part of body's functioning
9. Type of dream in which dreamer is aware of dreaming while it is happening
10. Chemical that alters perception
11. Drug that relaxes and calms the person
12. Altered state of consciousness due to suggestions made by another
13. State of consciousness during sleep that is accompanied by vivid images
14. Type of dream content Freud considered overt
16. Overuse or reliance on a drug
17. Restricted airflow during sleep
18. Problems going to sleep
21. Drugs that depress the body's responses

Chapter 8

Learning

Before you read...

You have likely spent a lot of time thinking about learning (and actually learning!), but you have also likely never really thought about what learning means or how it really happens. In this chapter, you will learn how psychologists have defined the learning process from three distinct, yet interrelated ways: classical conditioning, operant conditioning, and observational learning. In addition, you will lean about the biological components of learning and how psychologists are tracing learning to the basic levels of communication within the nervous system.

The chapter begins with a discussion of Pavlov's accidental discovery of the process of classical conditioning. In this section, you will discover the power of association and predictability in learning. In addition, you will come to understand some of the key variables associated with the classically conditioned response. Finally, you will come to understand how classical conditioning has been applied to some everyday experiences and problems.

"As a result of..." This phrase summarizes what B. F. Skinner thought about learning. In the second half of this chapter, you will learn about Skinner's theory of operant conditioning, which suggested that behaviors are acquired and maintained as a result of the consequence that follows the behavior. Put simply, this theory states that behaviors will increase when reinforced and decrease when punishment is the consequence. Like classical conditioning, operant conditioning is influenced by many variables, such as the nature of reinforcers, schedules of reinforcement and stimulus discrimination and generalization. You will also again visit the real world application of this type of learning!

The third major theory of learning that you will encounter is that of observational or social-cognitive learning theories. These theories arose out of the observation that all learning could not be explained by associations or consequences. Here you will learn about how we sometimes learn things by just watching other people engaging in certain behaviors. In addition, you will come to understand about more cognitively based learning such as insight, latent learning, and cognitive maps.

Finally, you will revisit a common theme that runs throughout the text, namely how evolution and biology affect other psychological processes. Specifically, you will explore the seeming contradiction between evolution and learning. You will also find out how learning and reinforcement affects the brain and the neurotransmitters that control the pleasure we experience after getting rewarded.

Learning Objectives

After reading this chapter, you should be able to:

1. Define learning and discuss the four important concepts in the definition.
2. Describe classical conditioning and define the key terms and procedures associated with classical conditioning.
3. Explain how classical conditioning is used to elicit behavioral and emotional responses in humans.
4. Discuss higher order conditioning and list two factors that determine the extent of conditioning.
5. Explain the importance of strength, timing, frequency, and predictability in classical conditioning.
6. Describe how classically conditioned responses undergo extinction, spontaneous recovery, generalization and discrimination.
7. Discuss how the process of classical conditioning has been applied to daily human life.
8. Define operant conditioning and discuss two American psychologists who contributed greatly to our understanding of this type of learning.
9. Define reinforcement, compare and contrast positive and negative reinforcement, and differentiate between primary and secondary reinforcers.
10. Explain the importance of shaping to operant conditioning and discuss how a Skinner box can be used to shape behavior.
11. Define and differentiate between positive and negative punishment and explain the effect of punishment on behavior.
12. Discuss how to use punishment effectively, and list the limitations of punishment.
13. Explain how strength, timing, and frequency of consequences affect operant conditioning and state how schedules of reinforcement can be used in practical ways.
14. Describe how operantly conditioned responses undergo extinction, spontaneous recovery, generalization and discrimination.
15. Discuss the application of operant conditioning to real life by discussing the concepts of superstition, intrinsic and extrinsic motivation, and behavioral self-regulation.
16. Define social learning theory and discuss the impact of modeling on human behavior.
17. Explain the key processes involved in observational learning.
18. Explain the process of consolidation.
19. Distinguish between insight, latent learning, and cognitive maps and describe how these concepts are related to learning.
20. Describe evolutionary theories and how they conceptualize learning.
21. State which parts and processes of the brain have been associated with learning, and discuss what changes occur as the result of learning.

Key Terms

Learning
Conditioning
Reflex
Classical Conditioning
Unconditioned Stimulus
Unconditioned Response
Conditioned Stimulus
Conditioned Response
Higher-Order Conditioning
Extinction
Spontaneous Recovery
Stimulus Generalization
Stimulus Discrimination
Operant Conditioning
Reinforcer
Positive Reinforcement
Negative Reinforcement
Primary Reinforcer
Secondary Reinforcer
Skinner Box
Shaping
Punishment
Primary Punisher
Secondary Punisher
Learned Helplessness
Schedule of Reinforcement
Fixed-Interval Schedule
Variable-Interval Schedule
Fixed-Ratio Schedule
Variable-Ratio Schedule
Extinction
Superstitious Behavior
Social Learning Theory
Modeling
Insight
Latent Learning
Cognitive Maps

As you read...

What is Learning?

1.   Learning is _____.

2.   List and describe the 3 important concepts related to the definition of learning.

What Type of Learning is Pavlovian, or Classical Conditioning?

1.   A systematic procedure through which associations and responses to specific stimuli are learned is _____.

2.   What is the difference between a stimulus and a response?

3.   Provide one example of a stimulus and one example of a response.

4.   A reflex is _____.

5.   Whereas reflexes are _____, conditioned behaviors are _____.

8-1   Terms and Procedures

1.   Classical conditioning is a procedure in which _____.

2.   What is another name for classical conditioning?

3.   The stimulus that normally produces an involuntary response is called the _____ stimulus.

4. What is a conditioned stimulus and response?

5. The bell in Pavlov's experiment that caused the dogs to salivate as a result of learning was the _____ stimulus.

6. The process of repeating trials to get the neutral stimulus to yield a conditioned response is called the _____ process.

7. Identify the stimuli and responses that are involved in each of the following examples of classically conditioned behavior:

   unconditioned stimulus (UCS)   *unconditioned response (UCR)*
   conditioned response (CR)   *neutral stimulus that becomes the conditioned stimulus (NS/CS)*

   On several occasions Sybil's teacher gave her permission to draw on the blackboard. On each occasion, just as Sybil picked up the chalk, the recess bell that hung directly above where she was standing blasted a loud ring and startled her. Now whenever Sybil is asked to write on the blackboard, she feels apprehensive about having to touch the chalk.

   UCS

   UCR

   NS/CS

   CR

   When Jake first adopted his pet cat, Tiger, he was able to use his electric can opener without any interference. However, after using the can opener many times just before giving Tiger his canned food, Jake finds that when he tries to use the appliance Tiger makes a nuisance of himself by standing underfoot and making anticipatory eating responses.

   UCS

   UCR

   NS/CS

   CR

8-2   Classical Conditioning in Humans
---

1.   Describe Marquis' classical conditioning of infants.

2.   How are the startle response and the eye puff be used to demonstrate learning?

3.   Describe the conditioning of Albert and who conditioned him.

8-3   Higher Order Conditioning
---

1.   Higher order conditioning is the process _____.

2.   What 2 factors determine the extent of higher-order conditioning?

3.   Give an example of higher order conditioning.

What Are the Key Variables in Classical Conditioning?

1.   How does the timing of the unconditioned stimulus impact conditioning?

2.   How does the frequency of pairings impact conditioning?

3.   The likelihood that the occurrence of the unconditioned stimulus can be anticipated is defined as _____.

4.   Describe how extinction works.

5. Psychologists say a behavior has been _____ when the conditioned stimulus no longer elicits the conditioned response.

6. Define spontaneous recovery.

7. Stimulus generalization is _____. Provide an example.

8. The more _____ two stimuli are, the more likely stimulus generalization is to occur.

9. Stimulus discrimination is _____.

10. Describe the Garcia Effect.

11. Another name for the Garcia Effect is _____ _____ _____.

12. Which two aspects of Garcia's research were surprising to learning researchers?

| 8-4 | Learning and Chemotherapy |

Pretend that you know someone who will soon be going through chemotherapy. Based on the research of Bernstein and what you know about classical conditioning, what would you recommend to them to reduce the possibility that they would experience a conditioned taste aversion?

13. Discuss how the immune system can be influenced by learning.

What Type of Learning is Operant Conditioning?

1.   Operant conditioning is _____.

2.   Operant conditioning is also known as _____ _____.

3.   What are the key differences between classical and operant conditioning?

4.   What are instrumental behaviors?

5.   Instrumental conditioning was introduced by _____, whereas _____ _____ was introduced by B. F. Skinner.

6.   Both Thorndike and Skinner acknowledged what about behavior?

8-5   Reinforcement: A Consequence That Strengthens a Response

1.   Any event that increases the probability of a recurrence of the response that came before it is a _____.

2.   Define positive reinforcement.

3.   Define negative reinforcement.

4.   What is the difference between escape conditioning and avoidance conditioning?

5.   Money would be an example of a _____ reinforcer, whereas food would be an example of a _____ reinforcer.

6.   Define the two types of reinforcers listed in the question above.

8-6   The Skinner Box and Shaping

1.   What is a Skinner box?

2.   Shaping is _____.

3.   You want get your cat to walk across the room, jump up on a couch, and scratch a spot on the wall. Using what you know about shaping, how would you do this?

8-7   Punishment: A Consequence that Weakens a Response

1.   Define punishment and state how it is different from reinforcement.

2.   What are primary and secondary punishers?

3.   What are the limitations of punishment?

4.   Describe learned helplessness.

5.   In each of the four boxes in the table above, draw an arrow pointing either up (for increase) or down (for decrease) to indicate how the behavior will be affected by the consequence.

	Desired stimulus	Noxious stimulus
Stimulus is presented after a particular behavior	Positive reinforcement	Punishment
Stimulus is removed after a particular behavior	Punishment	Negative reinforcement

Psychology

6.   Define the following types of punishment and punishers; give an example of each.

A) Punishment _____

Example

B) Removal of a pleasant stimulus _____

Example

C) Primary punisher _____

Example

D) Secondary punisher _____

Example

7.   The combination of _____ of bad behaviors and _____ of desired behaviors is the most effective way to control behavior.

What Are the Key Variables in Operant Conditioning?

1.   How does the strength of consequences impact operant conditioning?

2.   The shorter the time interval between the _____ _____ and the _____ the greater the likelihood that the behavior will be learned.

3.   What is a schedule of reinforcement?

4.   Describe the following types of reinforcement schedules and give an example of each.

Fixed-interval _____

Example

Variable interval _____

Example
Fixed-ratio _____

Example

Variable-ratio _____

Example

5. The most efficient combination of the schedules of reinforcement would be to start with a _____ schedule, followed by a _____ schedule, and finishing with a _____ schedule.

6. How do stimulus generalization and discrimination differ in operant conditioning?

7. Extinction is _____.

8. Resistance to extinction is a measure of how long it takes before _____.

9. How is spontaneous recovery in operant conditioning affected by the number of rest periods?

8-8 **Operant Conditioning in Daily Life**

1. How do superstitions develop based on operant behavior?

2. Define and provide an example of intrinsically motivated behavior.

3. Define extrinsically motivated behaviors.

4. How do behavioral regulation theorists view behavior?

5. What 3 things must people do to regulate themselves?

Can Learning Occur Through Observation?

1.   Observational learning theory is also known as _____ _____ _____, and it was originally developed by whom?

2.   Modeling is _____.

3.   Describe the results of Bandura's research with regard to the learning of aggression.

4.   List and describe the four key processes involved in observational learning.

5.   Identify the type of learning process that would be involved in establishing the italicized behaviors in each of the following situations.

   classical   *operant*   *observational*
   conditioning   *conditioning*   *learning*

   a) _____ On several occasions during lightening storms, when Terry switched on the kitchen light she received a shock that caused severe pain. Now, even when the sky is clear, she feels *frightened as she touches the kitchen light switch.*

   b) _____ Randy used an aerosol product to soothe his painful sunburn. The product eliminated the pain and now whenever Randy is sunburned, *he uses the product.*

   c) _____ Lee's cat Belle purrs when its scalp is scratched. When Lee gets home from work she usually does two things in this sequence: she plays Beethoven's Ninth Symphony on her stereo, and she scratches Belle's head while she listens. One day Lee played the Ninth Symphony but she did not have time to scratch the cat's head. She noticed with surprise that when the music began, *Belle began to purr.*

   d) _____ Daryl, who has never eaten a Chinese meal before, watched his friends eat for several minutes and then he too *positioned his chopsticks in his hand* and began to eat.

8-9	Observational Learning in Daily Life

1.   Although observational learning occurs in many aspects of daily life, it is particularly important in _____ and in _____ .

2.   Define how household chores are related to observational learning.

3.   Parents, _____, and _____ are all influential in modeling gender role information.

4.   Research suggests that children begin to learn through observation at what age?

8-10	Other Types of Cognitive Learning

1.   When you discover a relationship among a series of events that you did not recognize before, _____ has taken place.

2.   Describe Köhler's research with chimpanzees.

3.   Insight requires no direct _____ or further training.

4.   Define latent learning.

5.   Based on his research with rats and mazes, Tolman argued that _____ .

6.   Cognitive maps are _____ .

7.   Allen suggests that cognitive maps are formed how?

Psychology

What is the Biological Basis for Learning?

1. Evolutionary theory leads to the identification of factors that can be described as _____ _____, whereas learning theory focuses on more _____ _____ of behavior.

2. Pinker argues that humans are not "blank slates." Describe his argument to support this statement.

3. The neurotransmitter _____ appears to be important to reinforcement in the brain.

4. Describe the research that supports the role of dopamine in learning.

5. A reverberating circuit is _____

6. The more stimulation a reverberating circuit receives, the _____.

7. The transformation of a temporary neural circuit into a more permanent circuit is known as _____.

8. List the changes that take place in the brain when learning occurs.

After You Read, Practice Test #1

1. Conditioning is defined in your text as _____. (266)
   A. Modifying reflexive behavior
   B. Being prepared to respond to stimuli
   C. Being able to tell the difference between stimuli
   D. A systematic procedure through which new responses to stimuli are learned

2. Pavlov's dogs were trained to salivate in response to a bell. After repeatedly pairing the bell with a light, the dogs begin to salivate in response to the light. This is an example of _____. (270)
   A. Extinction
   B. Higher-order conditioning
   C. Stimulus generalization
   D. Acquisition process

3. Whether or not conditioning takes place depends on the predictability of the association between the _____. (272)
   A. NS and CS
   B. UCS and CS
   C. UCS and CR
   D. NS and UCR

4. The process by which an organism learns to respond only to a specific stimulus and not to other similar stimuli is called _____. (274)
   A. Stimulus generalization
   B. Extinction
   C. Classical conditioning
   D. Stimulus discrimination

5. Punishment and negative reinforcement are _____. (281)
   A. Different terms for the same concept
   B. Different in terms of their effect on behavior
   C. Same because both reduce behaviors
   D. Same because both increase emotions

6. A dental insurance company will reimburse claims for regular checkups only if at least six months have passed since the last checkup. This is an example of a _____ schedule of reinforcement. (288-289)
   A. Fixed ratio
   B. Variable ratio
   C. Fixed interval
   D. Variable interval

7.   On which of the following schedules would a salesman be given a bonus for every fifth item sold? (288-289)
     A.   Variable ratio
     B.   Variable interval
     C.   Fixed ratio
     D.   Fixed interval

8.   On several occasions Julie found and bought her favorite dresses at Cecilia's Discount Clothing store. Now, whenever she does shopping for clothes, she heads for the nearest discount store. Julie's habit of shopping at any discount store illustrates _____. (290)
     A.   Higher-order conditioning.
     B.   Latent learning.
     C.   Generalization.
     D.   Discrimination.

9.   The idea that learning occurs in the absence of direct reinforcement and is not necessarily demonstrated through observable behavior is called _____. (299)
     A.   Generative learning
     B.   Insight
     C.   Cooperative learning
     D.   Latent learning

10.   When provided with hypothalamic stimulation, rats will _____. (302)
      A.   Attack members of their own species
      B.   Fall asleep
      C.   Stop responding
      D.   Frequently choose brain stimulation over food

After You Read, Practice Test #2

1. In classical conditioning, the stimulus that is neutral prior to conditioning is referred to as _____. (267)
   A. Unconditioned stimulus
   B. Unconditioned response
   C. Conditioned stimulus
   D. Conditioned response

2. A conditioned stimulus that has ceased to produce conditioned reactions is presented at a later time and again evokes those responses. This process is known as _____. (273)
   A. Spontaneous recovery
   B. Acquisition
   C. Stimulus generalization
   D. Extinction

3. The Garcia effect is _____. (276-277)
   A. Organisms learning to avoid foods that make them sick
   B. Pairing pills with nausea such that an aversion is produced in animals
   C. Cancer patients avoiding certain foods following their chemotherapy
   D. All of the above

4. Select an example of a primary reinforcer. (282)
   A. Books
   B. Food
   C. Money
   D. Praise

5. Which is an example of a secondary reinforcer? (282)
   A. Food
   B. Praise
   C. Termination of pain
   D. Spanking

6. Name the procedure in which subjects are given reinforcers for performing behaviors that get closer and closer to some target behavior. (283)
   A. Tracing
   B. Observational learning
   C. Shaping
   D. Flooding

7. Punishment can be administered in two ways _____. (283)
   A. Delivering a pleasant stimulus or removing an unpleasant stimulus
   B. Delivering an unpleasant stimulus or removing a pleasant stimulus
   C. Through classical conditioning or operant conditioning principles
   D. Either before or after the behavior that is being conditioned

8. Ratio schedules of consequences are based on _____. (289)
    A. Time passing between responses
    B. Time passing between a response and a consequence
    C. The frequency of responses (i.e., work output)
    D. The number of consequences that are given for the response

9. Which behaviors would be repeated for their own sake? (293)
    A. Latently learned
    B. Extrinsically motivated
    C. Secondary reinforced
    D. Intrinsically motivated

10. The transformation of a temporary neural circuit into a more permanent circuit is known as _____. (302)

    A. Reverberating circuit
    B. Consolidation
    C. Plasticity
    D. Cognitive map

After You Read, Practice Test #3

1. Karen's father had several accidents while she was a passenger in his car. By the time she was eighteen, riding in a car as a passenger was so frightening for Karen that she could not go anywhere if someone else was going to drive. In this case, the unconditioned stimulus was _____. (267)
    A.   The accidents
    B.   Fear
    C.   The car
    D.   Her father

2. Randy taps her foot and gets involved in the tune whenever she hears a country song. However, if the music is not country, she does not even know it's playing. Randy's response to country music illustrates _____. (274)
    A.   Formation of a conditioned stimulus
    B.   Instrumental conditioning
    C.   Stimulus discrimination
    D.   Stimulus generalization

3. Antabuse is a drug that reacts with alcohol to cause nausea and vomiting. This drug is used to treat alcoholism by making the person who ingests alcohol feel extremely nauseous when they drink. As a result, the person becomes nauseous when even thinking about alcohol. This would be an example of _____. (276-277)
    A.   Stimulus generalization
    B.   Conditioned taste aversions
    C.   Negative reinforcement
    D.   Higher-order conditioning

4. Psychologists call behavior that receives feedback in the form of a reinforcing or punishing consequence _____ behavior. (280)
    A.   Respondent
    B.   Classical
    C.   Operant
    D.   Involuntary

5. Which of the following psychologists identified the concept of instrumental conditioning? (280)
    A.   Skinner
    B.   Pavlov
    C.   Bandura
    D.   Thorndike

6. The presentation of a rewarding or pleasant stimulus after some behavior in order to increase the likelihood of the behavior is called _____. (281)
    A. Positive reinforcement
    B. Negative reinforcement
    C. Stimulus discrimination
    D. Stimulus generalization

7. Maritta bought her weekly lottery ticket at a different store than usual one week, and that was the week she won a respectable prize. She now prefers to buy her tickets at that store. This is an example of _____. (292)
    A. Stimulus generalization
    B. Superstitious behavior.
    C. An unconditioned response
    D. A conditioned response

8. A rat is being trained to press a lever. The rat is given a food pellet after pressing the lever five times. The rat is on a _____ schedule of reinforcement. (288-289)
    A. Fixed interval
    B. Variable interval
    C. Fixed ratio
    D. Variable ratio

9. A hospital-based program for helping heart attack patients follow their new lifestyle requirements has the patients chart their own behaviors, observe their progress, and reward their achievements with rewards of their choice. This program uses principles of _____. (293)
    A. Classical conditioning
    B. Spontaneous recovery
    C. Continuous reinforcement
    D. Behavioral regulation

10. Research by Bandura and others on how children respond to witnessing aggressive actions, for instance on TV, shows that watching aggression will make children act more aggressively _____. (295)
    A. In almost every case that was tested
    B. Only under the most unusual conditions
    C. Unless the observed aggressive person is punished
    D. If parents and teachers put too much emphasis on it

After You Read, Comprehensive Self Test

1. Psychologists define learning as _____. (266)
   A. A process that increases the intelligence and creativity of an individual
   B. The acquisition of new knowledge
   C. The ability to think rationally
   D. A relatively permanent change in behavior that occurs as a result of experience

2. In Pavlov's classical conditioning experiment the _____ acted as an unconditioned stimulus. (267-268)
   A. Food
   B. Bell
   C. Dog trainer
   D. Salivation

3. A conditioned stimulus was repeatedly paired with an unconditioned stimulus. When the trainer presented the conditioned stimulus alone, the subject responded with a(an) _____. (268)
   A. Unconditioned stimulus
   B. Conditioned stimulus
   C. Unconditioned response
   D. Conditioned response

4. According to Watson and Raynor, which of the following can human beings sometimes acquire through classical conditioning? (270)
   A. Intense disgust
   B. Parental instincts
   C. Strong fears
   D. New skills

5. Extinction is the term used to describe _____. (272)
   A. A process where the unconditioned stimulus is no longer paired with the conditioned stimulus
   B. A conditioned response that is no longer elicited by the conditioned stimulus
   C. A situation where the reinforcer is withheld
   D. All of the above

6. When the conditioned stimulus is repeatedly presented without the unconditioned stimulus, in order to reduce the probability of the conditioned response occurring, it is called _____. (272)
   A. Spontaneous recovery
   B. Operant conditioning
   C. Extinction
   D. Stimulus discrimination

7. The Garcia taste-aversion effect is a type of classical conditioning that contradicts the traditional principle that _____. (276)
    A.   Understanding the situation is important for conditioning
    B.   Conditioning only works with very short time intervals
    C.   Stimuli must be paired over and over for conditioning
    D.   Conditioning has no real effect on important behaviors

8. The Richardsons are trying to get their son to study more. To try to get their son to study more, they give him money for every test that he does well on in school. This is an example of _____. (281)
    A.   Positive reinforcement
    B.   Negative reinforcement
    C.   Positive punishment
    D.   Negative punishment

9. A device that allows researchers to control when an organism will receive reinforcement or punishment is called a _____. (283)
    A.   Cumulative recorder
    B.   Skinner box
    C.   Maze
    D.   Differential apparatus

10. In order for a consequence to act as a reinforcer, the organism must _____. (282)
    A.   Know that it has made the correct response
    B.   Feel positive about the response it has made
    C.   Understand the value of the consequence
    D.   Need or want the consequence

11. If using punishment to discipline a particular behavior, a parent should _____. (286)
    A.   Positively reinforce desired behaviors that are incompatible with the undesired behavior
    B.   Use a very mild punisher
    C.   Punish the behavior on a variable-interval schedule
    D.   All of the above

12. Research on schedules of reinforcement suggests that when reinforcement is linked to _____ people work harder to achieve. (290)
    A.   Interval
    B.   Time
    C.   Output
    D.   Frequency

13. When an organism receives a reinforcer for correctly discriminating between two stimuli, it illustrates _____. (290)
    A. Stimulus generalization
    B. Stimulus discrimination
    C. Classical conditioning
    D. Primary reinforcement

14. A fitness program that requires the participants to chart their own nutrition, exercise and aerobic activity is using the principles of _____. (293)
    A. Self stimulation
    B. Negative reinforcement
    C. Observational learning
    D. Behavioral self regulation

15. Which of the following are key processes to observational learning? (296)
    A. Attention
    B. Representation
    C. Motivation
    D. All of the above

True or False

1. Classical conditioning can occur outside of conscious awareness. (269)

2. Research shows that when the unconditioned stimulus is strong and constantly elicits the reflexive response, conditioning to the neutral stimulus is less likely to occur. (271)

3. One of the ways that irrational fears may develop is because of stimulus generalization. (274)

4. The effectiveness of reinforcers may change with a person's age and experiences and may depend on how often the person has been reinforced. (282)

5. One of the most effective ways to use punishment is to pair it with reinforcement. (286)

6. In order for people to learn aggressive behavior, they must see it being reinforced. (295)

7. Latent learning refers to learning that was once reinforced, but that is not currently being reinforced in the environment. (299)

8. The neurotransmitter that has been implicated in learning is serotonin. (302)

Psychology

Essay Questions

1. Describe how principles of classical conditioning can be used to impact the immune system. (277)

2. Describe how neurons are affected by learning. (302)

When You Have Finished!

Surf's Up!!

After you've read and reviewed, try these web sites for additional information about some of the topics covered in this chapter.

1. **B. F. Skinner Foundation** (http://www.bfskinner.org/)
   This foundation is devoted to the understanding of human behavior using the science of behaviorism proposed by Skinner. Among the many things at this site are the woks of Skinner, information on the analysis of behavior, and video and audio clips.

2. **Association for Behavioral and Cognitive Therapies** (http://www.aabt.org/)
   This association is dedicated to supporting and providing resources for the application of behavioral and cognitive science to the treatment of psychological disorders.

3. **The Psi Café: A Psychology Resource Site, Albert Bandura**
   (http://www.psy.pdx.edu/PsiCafe/KeyTheorists/Bandura.htm)
   This site is part of a larger site that is devoted to providing resources about psychology. On this page, you will find useful background information about Bandura and many links that cover diverse topics related to Bandura and Social Learning Theory.

4. **An Animal Trainer's Introduction to Operant and Classical Conditioning**
   (http://www.wagntrain.com/OC/)
   Devoted to resources and information about behavioral psychology applied to training animals.

5. **Association for Behavior Analysis** (http://www.abainternational.org/)
   Home of the international organization devoted to developing, enhancing, and supporting behavioral analysis through research, education, and training.

6. **Teaching Children with Autism & Schedules of Reinforcement**
   (http://www.polyxo.com/discretetrial/schedules.html)
   This page provides a nice and simple overview of schedules of reinforcement. The website itself is an interesting look at how applied behavioral analysis is being applied to the treatment of autism.

7. **Positive Reinforcement: A Self-Instructional Exercise**
   (http://psych.athabascau.ca/html/prtut/reinpair.htm)
   An interesting discussion about positive reinforcement filled with different examples and illustrations regarding the application of positive reinforcement. A great review page as you are studying and learning about behavioral applications!

Cross Check: Learning

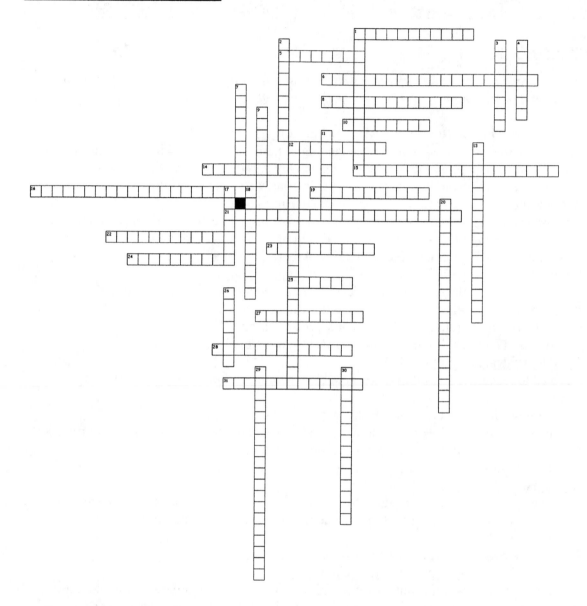

Across

1. Stimulus that comes to produce a response based on pairing with another stimulus
5. Permanent change that occurs as result of experience
6. Developed by Albert Bandura
8. Schedule of reinforcement in which a reinforcer is delivered after a predetermined but variable number of responses has occurred
10. Type of response that is involuntary
12. Type of reinforcer that is learned
14. Schedule of reinforcement in which a reinforcer is delivered after a specified number of responses has occurred
15. Recurrence of an extinguished conditioned response
16. Behavior learned through its coincidental association with reinforcement
19. Type of conditioning that is most complex
21. Generalization of a response to a new, similar stimulus
22. Procedure through which associations and responses are learned
23. Box that contains a responding mechanism and device for delivering consequences
24. Process for reducing the likelihood of behavior recurring again
25. Automatic response that occurs without learning
27. Procedure that gradually reduces the probability that a conditioned response will occur
28. Stimulus that normally produces an involuntary response

Created by Puzzlemaker at DiscoverySchool.com

31. Schedule of reinforcement in which a reinforcer is delivered after a specified interval of time

Down

1. Mental representations that enable people to navigate their environment
2. Type of conditioning that involves the association of a neutral stimulus to a non-neutral stimulus
3. Process of learning by watching others
4. Type of conditioning originally developed by Skinner
7. Type of reinforcement that works by removing negative stimuli in environment
9. Type of reinforcer that naturally occurs
11. Type of reinforcement that increases likelihood that a response will recur
12. Learning to respond only to specific stimuli
13. Schedule of reinforcement in which a reinforcer is delivered after predetermined but varying amounts of time
17. Process of finding a solution to a problem by thinking about it in a new way
18. Event that increases probability of recurrence of behavior that preceded it
20. Type of response that is elicited by conditioned stimulus
26. Process of gradually reinforcing behaviors that approximate the desired behavior
29. Reaction of a person that feels powerless to control punishment or negative consequences
30. Learning that occurs in the absence of direct reinforcement and not demonstrated through behavior

Chapter 9

Memory

Before you read...

Quick! What did you have for dinner last night? Who was the last United States President? What city were you born in? The answers to all of these questions are dependant on your ability to remember certain things about your environment. In this chapter, you will learn all about the fascinating area of memory and some of the factors that are related to our ability to encode information, place it in storage, and retrieve it when needed. The chapter begins with a basic overview of memory and a discussion of the first step in memory formation: encoding. In this section, you will discover why focusing your attention and getting information into your memory in the first place is such an important first step in the memory process.

In the second part of the chapter, you will explore the different types of memory storage: sensory memory, short-term storage, and long-term memory. Sensory and short-term memories tend to be very brief and fleeting, whereas long-term memories tend to be more permanent and resistant to retrieval errors. You will also learn about the various types of long-term memories, including procedural, declarative, episodic, and semantic memories. In addition, you will learn that memories are formed both through conscious effort and without conscious awareness. Finally, in this section you will explore the neurological bases of memory and come to understand some of the basic biochemical processes involved in forming memories.

What good would a storage space be if you did not have the key to access what was inside? This is exactly the topic of the next section of this chapter, which explores influences on memory retrieval. Within this section, you will examine a variety of topics that have been studied over the years. These include the accuracy of recall and methods to improve recall, encoding specificity, primacy and recency effects, imagery techniques, and flashbulb memories. In addition to these topics, you will also explore the effects of culture and gender on memory processes.

In the final part of the chapter, you will explore stress and health. Oops. Actually, you will learn about forgetting. As this opening indicates, we are all subject to forgetting things at times. In this part of the chapter, you will learn about both what helps people to not forget and what factors might interfere with remembering. You will also learn about some of the extreme deficits of memory such as amnesia and Alzheimer's disorders. As you will see, difficulties in recalling important information can have a significant impact on one's life and daily functioning.

The process of discovery in this chapter has many applications to your own life. As a student, a primary aspect related to your goals is to encode, retain, and be able to use and recall information you are studying. As you read this chapter, pay attention to the various tips that are sprinkled throughout the chapter that might help you to improve your own life and functioning.

Learning Objectives

After reading this chapter, you should be able to:

1. Detail how encoding, storage, and retrieval are involved in memory processes, and explain how attention and encoding are interrelated.
2. Describe the levels of processing approach and the neuroscience approach to memory and encoding.
3. Explain the process of encoding that take place in sensory memory, and discuss the capacity and limits of sensory memory.
4. Compare and contrast short-term and sensory memory, state how short term storage can be enhanced through different types of rehearsal, and discuss the duration and capacity limitations in short term memory.
5. State how short-term and working memory are different and characterize the functions of working memory.
6. Describe the encoding and storage processes characteristic of long-term memory and distinguish between the different types of long-term memories.
7. Describe the role of practice on memory.
8. Explain how the consolidation process may explain both memory and learning, and state what is known about the location of memories.
9. Define and differentiate between retrieval, recall, recognition, and relearning.
10. Outline the factors that are related to retrieval success and failure, and specifically discuss the role of state-dependent learning.
11. Explain the primacy and recency effects and how imagery can be used as an important perceptual memory aid.
12. Define flashbulb memories and summarize the research examining the validity of this type of memory.
13. Discuss the impact of culture and gender on memory.
14. Describe how memory is lost through decay and interference, and differentiate between proactive interference, retroactive interference, and interference in attention.
15. Examine the contradictory research findings concerning the accuracy of eyewitness testimony.
16. Examine the debate between clinical psychologists and memory researchers on the issue of motivated forgetting.
17. Define and differentiate between anterograde and retrograde amnesia.

Key Terms

Memory
Encoding
Levels-of-Processing Approach
Encoding Specificity Principle
Transfer-Appropriate Processing
Storage
Sensory Memory
Memory Span
Chunks
Rehearsal
Maintenance Rehearsal
Elaborative Rehearsal
Short-Term Memory
Working Memory
Long-Term Memory
Procedural Memory
Declarative Memory
Episodic Memory
Semantic Memory
Explicit Memory
Implicit Memory
Consolidation

Long-term Potentiation
Retrieval
Recall
Recognition
Relearning
State-Dependent Learning
Factorial Research Design
Interaction Effect
Primacy Effect
Recency Effect
Serial Position Curve
Imagery
Flashbulb Memory
Schema
Decay
Interference
Proactive Interference
Retroactive Interference
Repression
Amnesia
Retrograde Amnesia
Anterograde Amnesia

As you read...

How Does the Memory Process Begin?

1.　Memory is _____.

2.　Psychologists often use the _____ _____ model to explain the way that memory works. Explain this model.

3.　Memory involves three key processes. Name and briefly describe each and provide one example at each stage of processing.

9-1　Encoding

1.　What is encoding?

2.　At the first stage of memory, the information that is encoded will be of what type?

3.　_____ refers to the process of directing mental focus to some features of the environment and not to others. How is this concept important to encoding?

9-2　Levels of Processing

1.　Explain the levels of processing approach.

2.　According to the levels of processing approach, how information is originally processed influences what two other factors associated with memory?

3.　Deeper processing is better for long term retention. Explain why this statement is true using the levels of processing approach.

4.   Transfer-appropriate processing is _____.

5.   Describe the encoding specificity principle.

6.   The process of encoding is affected by both the demands of _____ and the _____ provided.

7.   Describe confirmation bias and give an example.

9-3	Neuroscience and Encoding

1.   According to Tulving's research, how are the left and right prefrontal cortexes involved in memory?

2.   What has fMRI research shown about the role of the temporal lobes in encoding and retrieval?

3.   Research indicates that your brain becomes more active when it is processing information at a deeper level versus a shallow level. Does this support or refute the levels of processing model? Explain.

What Are the Types of Memory Storage?

1.   The process of maintaining or keeping information available is _____, whereas the place the information is held is _____.

2.   List the 3 stages of the stage-model for memory storage.

9-4	**Sensory Memory**

1.   Define sensory memory.

2.   Sensory memory is sometimes referred to as the _____ _____.

3.   If you are talking to someone and they introduce themselves, you are likely to forget their name very quickly if they (or you) continue to talk. How does Sperling's studies on sensory memory explain this?

4.   A visual representation is called a(n)_____, and a auditory (sound) representation is called a(n) _____.

5.   In order for sensory information to be remembered, what must happen?

9-5	**Short-Term Storage**

1.   Short-term memory is defined as _____.

2.   Another name for short-term memory is _____ _____.

3.   How are short-term storage and working memory similar and different?

4.   How long is information available in short-term storage?

5.   What is the memory span?

6. If you wanted to remember the colors of the rainbow, you might have done so by remembering the name Roy G. Biv. Explain how this help your memory using the concept of chunking.

7. _____ is the process of repeatedly verbalizing, thinking about or otherwise acting on transforming information in order to keep it in short-term memory.

8. List, define, and provide an example of the 2 types of rehearsal.

9. There are believed to be four subsystems in the working memory. For each of them, list the definition and provide an example.

   a. Phonological loop

      Example

   b. Visual-Spatial Scratchpad

      Example

   c. Episodic Buffer

      Example

   d. Executive Mechanism

      Example

9-6	**Long-Term Storage**

1. Long-term memory is the storage mechanism that keeps a relatively permanent record of information from which _____.

2. Using the file cabinet analogy, discuss some of the ways that memories can be lost once they are placed in long term storage. Provide a real life example of each.

3. How long do long term memories last, and what is the capacity of long-term memory?

4. Who was the first president of the United States? Your knowledge of the answer to this question (George Washington) is an example of what type of memory?

5. The necessary memory to operate a car, wash dishes, or swim involves _____ memory.

6. Define and differentiate between declarative and procedural memory.

7. Episodic memory is _____.

8. One particular type of episodic memory _____ _____, is defined as memories about ourselves.

9. Define semantic memory.

10. Compare and contrast explicit and implicit memories.

11. You friend is convinced that "cramming" for a test is the best way to study. Based on what you know about practice and memory, convince her that she is wrong.

9-7	**Neuroscience and Storage**

1. Describe the different areas of the brain that become active during different working memory tasks.

2. As a result of the research with H.M., researchers began looking at the _____ and its role in memory. Explain why this was.

3. The process of changing a temporary memory to a permanent one is called _____.

Psychology

4.   Long-term potentiation is _____.

5.   Where is long-term memory stored in the brain?

What Influences Memory Retrieval?

1.   The process by which stored information is recovered from memory is _____.

2.   Define and differentiate between recall and recognition.

3.   List and provide an example of the 3 types of recall tasks.

4.   How might you measure the process of relearning?

9-8   Retrieval Success and Failures: Encoding Specificity

1.   Forgotten information is not gone, just _____.

2.   Describe the encoding specificity principal.

3.   You drink a lot of caffeinated soda while you study, yet your classes are often early in the morning and you do not like to drink soda early in the day. The fact that you often have trouble recalling information that you studied because you are not ingesting caffeine before the test supports which type of learning? Explain.

4.   Give an explanation for state-dependent learning.

| 9-9 | **What Facilitates Retrieval?** |

1. You just met a new group of people and are introduced to them one by one. According to the primacy effect, you are likely to remember whose name?

2. The primacy effect is defined as _____.

3. Words at the end of a list are easily recalled. This is explained in the _____ effect.

4. What is the von Restorff effect and why is it an "exception" to the serial position cureve?

5. _____ is the creation or recreation of a mental picture of a sensory or perceptual experience.

6. How is imagery used as a memory aid and why might this aid be effective?

| 9-10 | **Flashbulb Memories** |

1. A flashbulb memory is _____.

2. Your friend believes that flashbulb memories are more accurate and remembered longer than other memories. Using the research from your text, argue against this position.

3. How are flashbulb memories created?

4. Is the process outlined in question #3 different than that of other memories? Explain.

9-11	**Gender and Memory**

1. Are there gender differences in memory? Explain.

2. Gender _____ might have a bigger impact on memory than gender itself.

3. Explain the research which supports the role of gender stereotypes in memory differences between men and women.

9-12	**Culture and Memories**

1. Culture influences what information becomes encoded into long-term memory or how it is encoded. Describe the research that supports this claim.

2. Describe the differences in memories between individuals in a collectivist versus an individualist culture.

What Causes People to Forget?

1. Ebbinghaus' early research on forgetting found that when lists were _____, his learning was nearly perfect after one or two trials. However, when they were longer, what happened?

2. Summarize what Ebbinghaus' research said about forgetting and relearning.

3. List and describe the 3 changes people make to information they are trying to remember according to Barlett's research.

4. A _____ is a conceptual framework that organizes information and allows a person to make sense of the world.

9-13	Key Causes of Forgetting

1. _____ is the loss of information from memory as the result of disuse and the passage of time.

2. Interference is _____.

3. Define and distinguish between proactive and retroactive interference.

4. You have two final exams coming up at the end of the week and they are scheduled on the same day. Design a plan that applies the concepts of proactive and retroactive interference and limits the amount of interference studying for one exam might have on studying for the other exam.

5. _____ is due to interference in attention and is an encoding problem.

6. How does divided attention affect encoding and retrieval?

9-14	Special Types of Forgetting

1. You and your friend are arguing the merits of a case that has currently made the headlines. You friend is arguing that they "know for sure" the person is guilty because there was an eyewitness to the crime. Based on your knowledge of memory and eyewitness testimony, argue against your friend's belief.

2. Describe how the following factors might influence eyewitness testimony.
   a) Prolonged attempts to remember details of an event.

   b) Confidence in what someone saw.

   c) The time it take someone to identify culprits in a crime.

3. Define motivated forgetting and provide an example.

4. _____ refers to the burying of traumatic events in the unconscious, where they remain but are inaccessible to conscious memory. It is different from motivated forgetting because _____.

5. Can false memories be created?

6. Everyone can create false memories. Describe the research that supports this statement.

9-15	**Neuroscience and Forgetting: Studies of Amnesia**

1. Amnesia is_____.

2. Retrograde amnesia refers to the inability to remember events the preceded the brain injury, whereas _____ amnesia refers to _____.

3. Identify the concept that explains why remembering or forgetting occurs in each of the following situations.

    decay   *retrograde amnesia*
    retroactive inhibition   *anterograde amnesia*
    proactive inhibition   *primacy effect*
    motivated forgetting   *recency effect*

    a) _____ Joyce could not remember her grandfather's version of the family's traditional Thanksgiving blessing after having recited a different one at a church social gathering.

    b) _____ When Sam arrived at the company party he was introduced to twelve other guests. Sam can remember the names of the first three people he met.

    c) _____ As a result of a serious head injury Jennifer suffered some brain damage. She remembers things like her name, where she grew up, and what she was doing before the accident. However, she cannot remember who her doctor is, what she ate for breakfast, or that her mother visited her yesterday.

d) _____ For years, as a child, Dale dialed his friend Leon's phone number from memory. Ten years later while visiting his hometown, Dale decided to phone Leon's parents to see if they could help him get in touch with his old friend. When Dale went to dial the number he realized that he could not remember it.

e) _____ Doug studied his psychology vocabulary words and then his sociology vocabulary words. His accuracy in recalling the sociology vocabulary words was poor.

f) _____ Somehow Claire lost her grocery list on the way to the store. Although she had read over the list just before leaving home, when she began to shop she realized that all she could remember were the last few items on the list.

g) _____ When David was five years old he lost his puppy, which upset him very much. When his mother related the story later she said she thought it strange that he did not remember the event, because the puppy had been so important to him and the loss was so traumatic. David's mother suggested that perhaps he did not want to remember.

h) _____ While climbing a mountain Frank fell and received a serious blow to his head. When he regained consciousness, he did not know who he was, where he came from, or when he was born.

Psychology

After You Read, Practice Test #1

1. _____ refers to the process of directing mental effort to some features of the environment and not to others (309)
   A. Recall
   B. Storage
   C. Encoding
   D. Attention

2. According to the levels of processing theory, when the level of processing becomes more complex, a memory code _____. (310)
   A. Will be more deeply incorporated into memory stores
   B. Is likely to suffer from retrograde forgetting
   C. Will not be encoded into memory stores
   D. Is easily forgotten because it is too difficult

3. Which of the following is not a subsystem of working memory? (315-316)
   A. Episodic buffer
   B. Meaning control system
   C. Executive mechanism
   D. Visual-spatial scratch pad

4. _____ memory is the memory store for specific events or facts. (317)
   A. Declarative
   B. Restorative
   C. Procedural
   D. Consolidated

5. Implicit memory tasks indirectly test _____. (318)
   A. Knowledge acquired through study
   B. Unconsciously remembered knowledge
   C. Emotional memory traces
   D. A person's personal retrieval strategies

6. Hebb argues that _____ serves as the basis of short-term memory and permits coding of information into long-term memory. (320)
   A. Coding
   B. Consolidation
   C. Neural activity
   D. Circuits

7. Which of the following is required when material must be recalled in a specific order? (323)
   A. Structured recall
   B. Serial recall
   C. Fixed recall
   D. Free recall

8. An example of state dependent learning would be _____. (324)
   A. Learning information while sober and recalling while intoxicated
   B. Learning and recalling information while sober
   C. Learning the items in one setting and recalling them in another
   D. Learning information while intoxicated and recalling while sober

9. Retroactive inhibition is _____. (333)
   A. Retrieval failure
   B. The decrease in accurate recall of an item as a result of later presentation of other items
   C. The increase in accurate recall of an item as a result of later presentation of other items
   D. The decrease in accurate recall as a result of previous events interfering with a to-be remembered one

10. Burying unpleasant ideas in the unconscious because one wants to forget them is called _____. (336)
    A. Motivated forgetting
    B. Amnesia
    C. Retrograde amnesia
    D. Anterograde amnesia

After You Read, Practice Test #2

1.   The information-processing approach to the study of memory assumes that _____. (308)
     A.   Memories are neither altered nor lost after they are stored in long-term memory
     B.   There are separate stages in memory
     C.   Specific areas of the brain store specific types of information
     D.   Recognition and recall memory are served by different but related systems

2.   The sensory register provides _____. (312)
     A.   Coding and storage for about 30 seconds
     B.   Coding and permanent storage
     C.   Initial encoding of information and brief, temporary storage
     D.   Encoding, storage, and retrieval

3.   Which type of memory can be described as lasting only briefly, and serves the function as a place where information can be manipulated. (313)
     A.   Sensory
     B.   Short-term memory
     C.   Working memory
     D.   Long-term memory

4.   The function of the "central executive mechanism" in Baddeley's conception of working memory is most accurately described as _____. (316)
     A.   Monitoring the content of the sensory registers
     B.   Seeing that information does not get lost or discarded
     C.   Retaining information by maintenance rehearsal
     D.   Controlling the flow and processing of information

5.   Your grandmother tells you detailed stories from her childhood. She is relating information that is stored in her _____ memory. (317)
     A.   Procedural
     B.   Sensory
     C.   Episodic
     D.   Semantic

6.   When material can be remembered in any order, _____ it is called. (323)
     A.   Serial recall
     B.   Free recall
     C.   Fixed recall
     D.   Recognition

7. To aid in the retrieval of information, research regarding the _____ suggests that you should study the same way you will be tested. That is, if you will be tested using an essay format, you should study by developing essay answers to possible questions. (324)
   A. Parallel distributed process
   B. Encoding specificity principle
   C. Metacognitive appeal principle
   D. Transfer-appropriate processing principle

8. Even though it is years since Phil witnessed a fatal auto accident, he still remembers every detail very vividly. This is an example of a(n) _____. (329)
   A. Implicit memory
   B. Procedural memory
   C. Semantic memory
   D. Flashbulb memory

9. Recall of words at the end of a list is an example of _____. (326)
   A. Recency effect
   B. Extraordinary memory
   C. Primacy effect
   D. Rehearsal of information

10. The loss of memory due to the passage of time or disuse is referred to as _____. (332)
    A. Attenuation
    B. Decay
    C. Time loss
    D. Deterioration

After You Read, Practice Test #3

1.   _____ involves the organization of sensory information so that the nervous system can process it. (309)
   A.   Storage
   B.   Recall
   C.   Attention
   D.   Encoding

2.   Janet sees Carol frequently on campus and speaks to her. When she saw Carol in the department store, she couldn't remember her name. Her forgetting the name is best explained by _____. (310)
   A.   The decay theory of forgetting
   B.   State-dependant learning theory
   C.   The encoding specificity hypothesis
   D.   Freud's idea of motivated forgetting

3.   When one is unable to accesses memories only seconds after exposure, it can be said that these _____ never made it into _____. (313)
   A.   Flashbulb memories; long-term storage
   B.   Flashbulb memories; short-term storage
   C.   Sensory memories; long-term storage
   D.   Sensory memories; short-term storage

4.   What is the storage mechanism for visual sensory memory called? (313)
   A.   Mantra storage
   B.   Echoic storage
   C.   Iconic storage
   D.   None of the above

5.   Information can be held in short-term memory for about _____. (314)
   A.   2-3 minutes
   B.   11/2 minutes
   C.   20-30 seconds
   D.   5-10 seconds

6.   What type of memory stores the ability to type? (317)
   A.   Declarative
   B.   Procedural
   C.   Representational
   D.   Propositiona

7. Explicit memory tasks usually require subjects to _____. (318)
    A.   Use creative strategies to solve problems
    B.   Perform complex tasks without the benefit of direct instructions
    C.   Use recall and recognition strategies to identify information that is not deliberately learned
    D.   Use recall and recognition strategies to identify previously studied material

8. Which type of practice seems to be most effective? (319)
    A.   Massed practice
    B.   A mix of massed and spaced practice
    C.   Practice that involves multiple sensory mechanisms
    D.   Spaced practice

9. _____ interference refers to a decrease in accurate recall of information as a result of the effects of previously learned or presented information. (333)
    A.   Retroactive
    B.   Reactive
    C.   Proactive
    D.   Interactive

10. People who suffer from anterograde amnesia will have the most difficulty remembering (338)
    A.   Something they think very hard about
    B.   Something that produces strong emotions
    C.   Something that happened many years ago
    D.   Something that happened an hour ago

After You Read, Comprehensive Self Test

1. Even though something is learned it may not always be remembered because _____. (308)
   A. Learning is a relatively permanent change
   B. Learning and memory are two separate processes
   C. Memory is the ability to remember past events, information, or skills
   D. A and C

2. How is information retained in memory? (309)
   A. Storage
   B. Reminiscence
   C. Retrieval
   D. Encoding

3. A chunk _____. (314)
   A. Can be a letter, a group of words and numbers, or sentences organized in a familiar way
   B. Is a manageable and meaningful unit of information
   C. A brief and limited number of items that can be easily reproduced after presentation
   D. A and B

4. When studying for a test, you may learn definitions by repeating them over and over. This process is known as _____. (314)
   A. Consolidation
   B. Indexing
   C. Rehearsal
   D. Categorization

5. Procedural memory _____. (317)
   A. Is memory for specific facts
   B. Is storage for the perceptual, motor, and cognitive skills necessary to complete a task
   C. Covers specific events, objects, and situations
   D. Covers the memory of ideas, rules, and general concepts about the world

6. Your ability to do well on these exam questions relies on _____. (318)
   A. Short-term memory
   B. Maintenance memory
   C. Semantic memory
   D. Episodic memory

7. The hippocampus region of the brain is responsible for _____. (320)
   A. Remembering old information, but not new information
   B. The ability to remember remote events
   C. The transfer of new information to permanent memory
   D. The ability to remember new information, but not old information

8. _____ is the process by which stored information is recovered from memory (323)
   A. Encoding
   B. Retrieval
   C. Storage
   D. Declaration

9. Subjects remember items they memorize at the beginning of a list better than they do items in the middle of the list illustrates the _____. (326)
   A. Massed practice effect
   B. Motivated forgetting
   C. Primacy effect
   D. Recency effect

10. Jeff could only remember the names of the last two people he met at the reception. This is an example of _____. (326)
   A. The recency effect
   B. Chunking
   C. The initialization principle
   D. The primacy effect

11. Paivio and other researchers argue that imagery, verbal coding mechanisms, and semantic memory operate together to _____. (328)
   A. Code information.
   B. Retrieve information
   C. Form conceptual memory
   D. Both A and B

12. Relearning a skill or information easily is an example of _____. (332)
   A. Recall
   B. Retrieval
   C. Savings method
   D. Retention

13. Decay theory suggests that we fail to remember things due to _____. (332-333)
   A. Interference and crowding
   B. Proactive and retroactive inhibition
   C. Rate and mode of stimulus presentation
   D. The failure to use information over time

14. _____ is a suggested cause of forgetting involving the suppression of one bit of information by another received earlier or later or the confusion of two pieces of information. (333)
    A.   Interference
    B.   Decay
    C.   Representation
    D.   Memory tracing

15. Hans was in an auto accident, and for a long time he couldn't remember anything that happened for a day or two leading up to the accident. This is an example of _____. (338)
    A.   Anterograde amnesia
    B.   Retrograde amnesia
    C.   Proactive interference
    D.   Retroactive interference

True or False

1.   Psychologists now recognize that memory is a step-by-step linear process versus a simultaneous, parallel process. (308)

2.   Sensory memories generally last between 15-30 seconds. (313)

3.   Both implicit and explicit memories may be formed without conscious awareness. (319)

4.   Studying for your upcoming test for one and a half hours a day for a week instead of 10 hours over the course of a weekend is likely to earn you a better grade on your test. (319)

5.   If you are given a cue for retrieval that relates to some aspect of the originally stored information, retrieval will be faster. (324)

6.   The primacy effect refers to the increased likelihood of remembering a term in a list of terms that has some meaning or personal relevance to you. (326)

7.   Gender differences in memory tend to be small to non-existent unless gender stereotypes are evoked in the environment. (330)

8.   Research indicates that eyewitnesses tend to be very accurate, both in experimental studies and in the recalling of actual crimes. (335)

Essay Questions

1.   Define and differentiate between declarative, procedural, episodic and semantic types of long-term memory. (316-319)

2.   Describe the research on practice by Baddeley and Longman (1978) and what it indicates about the impact of the timing of practice. (319)

When You Have Finished!

Surf's Up!!

After you've read and reviewed, try these web sites for additional information about some of the topics covered in this chapter.

1. **Memory Loss and the Brain** (http://www.memorylossonline.com/index.htm)
   A newsletter of the memory disorders project at Rutgers University, this site has a load of information on memory loss caused by various factors.
2. **Committee for the Scientific Investigation of Claims of the Paranormal**
   (http://www.csicop.org/si/9511/eyewitness.html)
   This site contains many different articles related to scientifically investigating common beliefs and reports. This particular section of the site contains a look at eyewitness testimony in support of the paranormal.
3. **The Memory Exhibition** (http://www.exploratorium.edu/memory/)
   This site is devoted to the exploration of memory and various topics related to memory. There are online exhibits, games, pictures of the brain structures associated with memory, and articles and lectures presented by memory researchers.
4. **Tips for Improving Your Memory** (http://www.mindtools.com/memory.html)
   You will find a lot of different tips and techniques at this site which are aimed at helping you improve your skills. Topics include how to improve memory for exams and how to remember people's names, among many others.
5. **The Recovered Memory Project**
   (http://www.brown.edu/Departments/Taubman_Center/Recovmem/)
   This project is aimed at providing information about recovered memory and contains a database of 96 corroborated case of recovered memory. It also addresses critics of the project and of recovered memories in general. There is also information and links for individual who might have recovered memories.
6. **Alzheimer's Disease Education and Referral Center** (http://www.alzheimers.org/)
   Sponsored by the National Institute on Aging, this site contains information and resources about Alzheimer's disease.

Cross Check: Memory

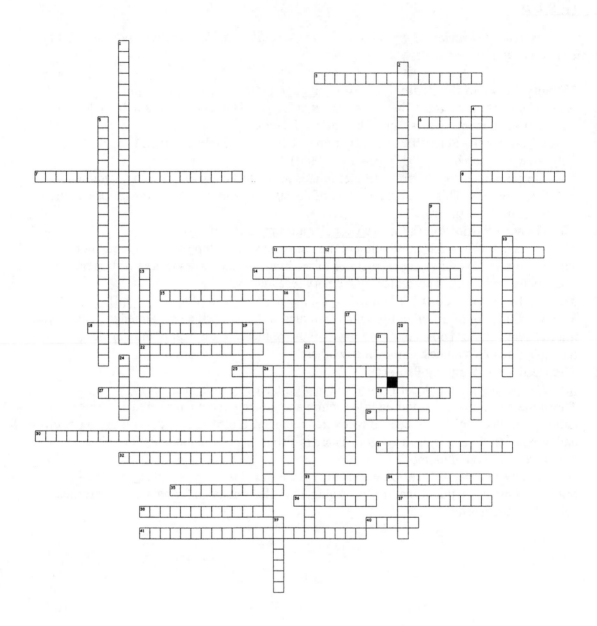

Across

3. Memory for skills
6. The creation of a mental picture of a perceptual experience
7. Rehearsal involving repetition and analysis in which a stimulus may be linked to other information and further processed
8. The number of items that a person can reproduce from short-term memory
11. Theory of memory that suggests the brain encodes and processes stimuli in different ways
14. An increase in responsiveness of a neuron after it has been stimulated
15. Memory for specific personal events tagged with information about time
18. Memory for specific information
22. The suppression of one bit of information by another that is received either earlier or later
25. An effect of the combination of two variables that is separate from the influence of either variable
27. A detailed memory for circumstances at the time of some dramatic event
28. Inability to remember information, usually because of physiological trauma
29. Manageable and meaningful units of information
30. A decrease in accurate recall of information as a result of the effects of previously learned information
31. The storage mechanism that temporarily holds current information for immediate use
32. The more accurate recall of items presented at the beginning of a series
33. The ability to recall past events, images, ideas, or previously learned information
34. The burying of traumatic events in the unconscious
35. A method of measuring memory in which participants select previously presented information from other unfamiliar information
36. The process by which stored information is recovered from memory
37. The process of repeatedly verbalizing or thinking about information in order to keep that information active in memory
38. The mechanism that performs initial encoding of sensory stimuli
40. Loss of information from memory as a result of disuse and the passage of time
41. The tendency to recall information learned while in a particular emotional state

Down

1. Effectiveness of a specific retrieval cue depends on how well it matches with the originally encoded information
2. A type of experimental design that includes two independent variables with conditions arranged so that participants are subject to all possible combinations of the variables
4. Processing of information that is similar for both encoding and retrieval of information
5. A decrease in accurate recall of information as a result of the subsequent presentation of different information

9. Memory a person is not aware of processing

10. The process of changing a temporary memory to a permanent one

12. Memory for ideas, rules, and words about the world

13. A method of assessing memory by measuring how long it takes participants to relearn material

16. Inability to remember events that preceded a blow to the head

17. The storage mechanism that keeps a relatively permanent record of information

19. The more accurate recall of items presented at the end of a series

20. Repetitive review of information with little or no interpretation

21. A conceptual framework that organizes information and allows a person to make sense of the world

23. Inability to remember events that occur after brain damage

24. A method of measuring memory in which participants have to retrieve previously presented information by reproducing it

26. Conscious memory that a person is aware of

39. Maintaining or keeping information readily available

Created by Puzzlemaker at
DiscoverySchool.com

Chapter 10

Cognitive Psychology

Before you read...

Cognitive psychology is a broad area that incorporates all aspects related to human thinking. Cognitive psychologists are interested in a variety of thought-oriented issues, many of which overlap with other topics in psychology. In this chapter, the focus is on thought and language. Specific areas of thought that will be explored include concept formation, problem solving, decision-making, and artificial intelligence. In relation to language, both acquisition and the structure of language will be explored.

The chapter begins by exploring how humans form concepts, solve problems, and make decisions. Cognitive psychologists are interested in the thinking process and in exploring what allows people to make accurate and good decisions. You will have the opportunity to review information on how people introduce creativity into their decision making and how people tend to make significant errors when estimating probability. In addition, you will be introduced to some helpful information on how to avoid barriers to sound decision-making and how to become a better critical thinker in your day-to-day life. Finally, you will learn about how culture and evolution come to impact an individual's reasoning and decision-making abilities.

In the middle of the chapter, you will be introduced to a fascinating and rapidly developing area in psychology called artificial intelligence. You will learn how psychologists and other scientists are working to develop computers that think and make decisions in ways that are similar to human beings. You will also learn why computer model cannot, as of yet, completely mimic human thought and some of similarities and differences between human beings and computers.

In the last two sections, you will be introduced to the study of language structure and function. As you know, people come from diverse cultures and experience life in many different contexts, but all societies have some form of language. The study of psycholinguistics and the major areas of phonology (the study of the sounds of language), semantics (the study of the meaning of language), and syntax (the study of the relationships of words) are examined. You will also be exposed to the nature versus nurture debate of language acquisition, and you will be briefly introduced to the learning and biological theories of language acquisition. The chapter closes with an examination of communication (but not language; be careful, there is a difference!) in other species such as chimpanzees, dolphins, and whales.

Learning Objectives

After reading this chapter, you should be able to:

1.   Describe the field of cognitive psychology and summarize the key processes and phenomena that are emphasized within the field.
2.   Define a concept, explain how people form concepts, and discuss some of the methods researchers use to study concepts.
3.   Explain the process of problem solving, and describe how psychologists can help people become better problem solvers through the use of heuristics and algorithms.
4.   Examine how functional fixedness and metal set can interfere with effective problem-solving.
5.   List the six tips that can allow you to become a better critical thinker.
6.   Review the important attributes and stages of creative problem solving and compare and contrast convergent and divergent thinking and brainstorming.
7.   Distinguish between the terms *reasoning* and *decision making* and develop an understanding of how logic is involved in each.
8.   Explain the psychological factors that are involved in estimating the probability of specific behaviors and events.
9.   Describe the five common barriers to sound decision-making.
10. Review the ways in which culture and evolution impact reasoning and decision-making.
11. Explain how psychologists use computer simulations to mimic human information processing.
12. Describe how the concept of neural networks is being used to understand and generate models that mimic the processing of information in the human brain.
13. Define language and discuss the key components of language.
14. Discuss how gender, thoughts, and culture influence language.
15. Distinguish between linguistics and psycholinguistics and relate each of these areas of study to the acquisition of language.
16. Describe what is learned through research in phonology, semantics, and syntax.
17. Differentiate between learning and biological theories of language acquisition, especially as they relate to learning readiness.
18. Discuss the research on language acquisition in chimpanzees, dolphins, and whales, and explain how chimp language differs from human language.

Key Terms

Cognitive Psychology
Concept
Prototype
Problem Solving
Algorithm
Heuristics
Subgoal Analysis
Means-Ends Analysis
Backward Search
Functional Fixedness
Mental Set
Creativity
Convergent Thinking
Divergent Thinking
Brainstorming
Reasoning
Logic
Decision Making
Gambler's Fallacy
Belief in Small Numbers
Availability Heuristic
Overconfidence Phenomenon
Confirmation Bias
Belief Perseverance
Artificial Intelligence
Information Processing Approach
Pragmatics
Language
Androgyny
Linguistics
Psycholinguistics
Phonology
Phoneme
Morpheme
Lexicon
Semantics
Telegraphic Speech
Syntax
Grammar
Lateralization

As you read...

What is Cognitive Psychology?

1.   Cognitive psychology is _____.

2.   How is cognitive psychology similar and different from behavioral psychology?

3.   Another term for cognition is _____.

How Do We Form Concepts and Solve Problem?

1.   _____ are the mental categories people use to classify events or objects according to their common properties or features.

2.   What would an exemplar of the concept "automobile" be?

3.   Concept formation is the study of _____.

4.   The process of organizing things into categories is _____.

5.   Describe the basic design of a laboratory study of concept formation.

6.   What are positive and negative instances?

7.   A prototype is _____.

8.   How is a prototype different than an exemplar? Could they possibly be the same things?

10-1	Problem Solving

1.   Define problem solving.

2.   Define the four stages of problem solving listed below.

STAGE 1   STAGE 2   STAGE 3   STAGE 4

3.   An algorithm, when performed correctly, _____ a correct solution. Explain why.

4.   What is the problem with developing an algorithm for every potential problem?

5.   _____ are sets of strategies that serve as flexible guidelines for discovery-oriented problem solving.

6.   List and describe the 3 main heuristic procedures.

10-2	Barriers to Problem Solving

1.   Describe functional fixedness.

2.   What two factors limit the function of objects in people's minds?

3.   A mental set is a _____.

Psychology

4.   Provide an example of a mental set.

| 10-3   Avoid Barriers: Be a Critical Thinker |

1.   List and describe the 6 tips that can make you a better critical thinker.

| 10-4   **Creative Problem Solving** |

1.   Creativity is the ability to _____.

2.   Define and differentiate between an original, novel, and appropriate response.

3.   What factors might make people more creative in their thinking, or who is more likely to be creative?

4.   Compare and contrast convergent and divergent thinking.

5.   In _____, all possible solutions are considered without any initial judgments of worth.

6.   You are working with a group to solve a particular problem. The group leader suggests that you start with one person's suggestion, evaluate it thoroughly, and then go on to the next potential solution. Knowing what you do about brainstorming, suggest and alternative approach and state why it might be preferred.

7.   Explain the investment theory of creativity.

How Do We Reason and Make Decisions?

1. Reasoning is _____.

2. _____ is a system of reasoning used to make inferences and reach valid conclusions.

3. Describe decision-making.

4. What is the difference between decision-making and problem solving?

10-5   Uncertainty: Estimating Probabilities

1. What is an educated guess?

2. Define probability and list some of the factors that might influence probability judgments.

3. _____ and _____ are especially useful for teaching students scientific concepts.

10-6   Barriers to Sound Decision Making

1. What is the gambler's fallacy?

2. How does belief in small numbers contribute to poor decision-making?

3. Define the availability heuristic.

Psychology

4.   The overconfidence phenomenon is _____.

5.   The tendency of people to discount information that does not fit with their pre-existing views is called _____.

6.   Discuss how the confirmation bias and belief perseverance lead to poor decisions.

| 10-7   Culture and Reasoning |

1.   Characterize the differences between Chinese and European Americans as they relate to reasoning and decision-making.

| 10-8   Evolution and Reasoning |

1.   How do the evolutionary psychologists view cognition?

2.   Evolutionary psychologists criticize traditional psychological research on problem solving for what reason?

| How Does Artificial Intelligence Reveal About Cognition? |

1.   Artificial intelligence is _____.

2.   Why do researchers use the game of chess to study artificial intelligence?

3.   What can humans do that computers cannot with regard to problem solving?

10-9	Neural Networks

1.   A _____ _____, or center, is what mediates and organizes information from various brain locations.

2.   What is blindsight?

3.   Define parallel distributed processing.

4.   Artificial neural networks are _____

What is the Structure of Language?

1.   Language is _____.

2.   What does human language allow us to do that no animals can?

3.   Some psychologists claim that language is a social tool. Explain what they mean by this.

10-10	Language and Gender Stereotypes

1.   How are men and woman described differently?

2.   Describe the differences between male's and female's use of language.

3.   _____ refers to behavior and attitudes that incorporate qualities traditionally considered masculine as well as those traditionally considered feminine.

10-11   Thought, Culture, and Language

1.   Language may _____ thought but language does not _____ thought.

2.   How does culture and language affect a person's responses to questions?

3.   What is the impact of being bilingual on children's language development?

10-12   Linguistics

1.   Linguistics is _____ .

2.   The study of how language is acquired, perceived, understood and produced is _____ .

10-13   Language Structure

1.   List and describe the 3 major components of language.

2.   What is semantics?

3.   The way groups of words come together to form language is called _____ .

4.   The function of a language is called _____ .

5.   Match the following terms with the appropriate definition.

> *Psycholinguistics*   *syntax*
> *Grammar*   *phonemes*
> *Phonology*   *morpheme*
> *Semantics*

a) _____ The study of the basic units of sound found in a language.
b) _____ The basic unit of meaning in a language; a word or meaningful part of a word.
c) _____ The basic units of sound in a language.
d) _____ The study of how language is acquired, perceived, understood, and produced.
e) _____ The linguistic description of how a language functions.
f) _____ The relation between groups of words and how those words are arranged in phrases and sentences.
g) _____ The study of meanings of words and sentences, and the analysis of how thought is generated by the placement of words in a particular context.

10-14   The Biological and Evolutionary Basis of Language

1.   What did Noam Chomsky suggest about language?

2.   Describe the research supporting Chomsky's theory of language.

How Do We Acquire Language?

1.   Describe Brown's research.

2.   What is naturalistic observation?

3.   What conclusions about language can be drawn from Brown's research?

10-15 Learning Theories
---

1.   Describe the learning approach to language acquisition.

2.   Learning theories of language development use both operant conditioning and observational learning theories to describe how language develops. Explain how these terms are used and provide an example of each.

10-16 Biological Theories
---

1.   Explain how the concept of an inborn language acquisition device (LAD) is used to explain why language develops.

2.   List and describe the 3 types of evidence that support the role of nature in language development.

3.   _____ refers to the localization of a particular brain function primarily in one area.

10-17 Do Chimpanzees Use Language?
---

1.   Describe the language of Washoe, Sarah, Lana, and Nim.

2.   How is language different with chimpanzees than with humans?

10-18 Do Dolphins or Whales Use Language?
---

1.   What did Janik's research demonstrate about dolphin language and communication?

2.   What does Miller and Bain's research indicate about whales and language?

3.   Do dolphins and whales have language?

10-19 Social Interaction Theories: A Little Bit of Each

1.   How is language both innate and reinforced?

2.   How does context affect language?

3.   What are the keys to understanding language acquisition?

After You Read, Practice Test #1

1. A mental category of objects or events that are grouped together because they have some common properties is a(n) _____. (345)
   A. Image
   B. Heuristic
   C. Mental set
   D. Concept

2. The problem-solving heuristic that involves breaking a problem down into several smaller steps is called _____. (348)
   A. Algorithmic analysis
   B. Backward analysis
   C. Subgoal analysis
   D. Linkage analysis

3. A team of programmers is working to develop a new software system. Which of them is demonstrating mental set? (349-350)
   A. One who develops a new technique for graphical displays
   B. One who figures out a new formula for a certain calculation
   C. One who uses a program he has used many times before
   D. One who brings ideas from Eastern philosophy to the project

4. Brainstorming: (351-352)
   A. Decreases functional fixedness
   B. Promotes creativity
   C. Produces a higher quality of ideas
   D. All of the above

5. Pensacola will probably have a bad hurricane this year because there has not been one since hurricane Erin several years ago. This statement is an example of _____. (354)
   A. Syllogistic thinking
   B. Belief in small numbers
   C. Gambler's fallacy
   D. Critical thinking

6. The following can be said about the human brain in comparison to the computer: (359)
   A. The two are not at all compatible
   B. It has about the same options and ways for processing information
   C. It has fewer options for information processing
   D. It has more options and strategies for information processing

7. The view that many different processes are taking place in many different areas of the brain all at the same time is called _____. (361)
   A.   Parallel distributed processing
   B.   Multiple resource processing
   C.   Independent convergent processing
   D.   Conditional interlinked processing

8. What are the basic units of sound that compose the words in a language? (366)
   A.   Phonemes
   B.   Morphemes
   C.   Graphemes
   D.   Phones

9. If language is based on biology _____. (372)
   A.   Many aspects should be evident early in life
   B.   Regardless of culture or language, all children should develop in a similar way
   C.   The role of learning should be permanent
   D.   A and B

10. Lana, the chimpanzee, learned to communicate _____. (374)
   A.   With geometric forms and a computer
   B.   By using sign language
   C.   By humming phonetic sounds
   D.   By arranging symbols on a magnetized board

After You Read, Practice Test #2

1. If a child is shown examples from a set of figures (triangle, square, and circle) that are large, middle-sized and small, and told that the large square is an example of the concept, the experimenter is using _____ of the concept. (346)
    A.   A positive instance
    B.   A negative instance
    C.   A discriminate
    D.   The rule

2. Suppose this weekend you have to take your clothes to the laundry, because everything you own is dirty, but you also want to see a movie, and you don't have enough money to do both. In the terminology of a cognitive psychology, your ability to figure out what to do will depend on your capacity for _____. (347)
    A.   Hypothesis testing
    B.   Problem solving
    C.   Syllogistic reasoning
    D.   Linguistic determinism

3. Mike is planting his garden by looking at a landscaper's drawing of what the finished plants will be like, and buying those plants each year that he can afford and that will get him closest to the drawings. Mike is primarily using which problem-solving heuristic? (348)
    A.   Functional analysis
    B.   Hypothetical analysis
    C.   Subgoal analysis
    D.   Means-end analysis

4. When leaders are accused of lacking creative solutions to problems, they may find it a good idea to try _____. (351-352)
    A.   Means-end analysis
    B.   Computer simulation
    C.   Brainstorming
    D.   Functional fixedness

5. Cognitive psychologists define reasoning as a process by which we _____. (353)
    A.   Evaluate situations to reach a conclusion
    B.   Decide which member of a category is most "typical"
    C.   Express our ideas to other people
    D.   Understand how to define a new concept

6. When people tend to cling to beliefs despite contradictory evidence, psychologists term it_____. (355)
    A. Confirmation bias
    B. Prejudicial bias
    C. Overconfidence
    D. Judgmental

7. Computer programs that are able to perform some types of human activities are said to involve _____. (359)
    A. Heuristic algorithms
    B. Linguistic processes
    C. Brain stimulations
    D. Artificial intelligence

8. In what aspect of language would a psycholinguist most likely be interested? (366)
    A. Phonology
    B. Evolution
    C. Origins
    D. Acquisition

9. Learning theories for the acquisition of language would agree with the importance of which of the following statements _____ ? (372)
    A. The language we speak depends on what verbal skills are reinforced
    B. Children must be carefully taught to speak to be healthy
    C. Humans have an inborn ability to learn and use language
    D. No other animals can use a real language in any way

10. All of the following are true about children's use of language except _____. (376)
    A. Children are born with a predisposition for language
    B. Language acquisition in children is purely biologically-based
    C. Children are reinforced for their language behavior
    D. Language is innate in children

After You Read, Practice Test #3

1. When do humans begin to develop concepts? (345)
   A. Late childhood
   B. Infancy
   C. Early adolescence
   D. Early childhood

2. What is the first stage in problem solving? (347)
   A. Implementing your strategy
   B. Gathering data
   C. Assessing the complexity of the problem
   D. Generating solutions

3. Select the major disadvantage of using heuristics to solve problems. (347-348)
   A. No solution is guaranteed.
   B. They are time consuming and inefficient.
   C. They involve so much effort.
   D. All of the above

4. Problem-solving processes that focus on finding a single best solution involve_____ thinking; processes that focus on expanding the range of possible solutions involve _____ thinking. (351)
   A. Functional; hypothetical
   B. Hypothetical; functional
   C. Divergent; convergent
   D. Convergent; divergent

5. Carlos is going through his college catalogue, trying to select an elective to fulfill his course requirements for next semester. Which cognitive process is Carlos engaged in? (353)
   A. Hypothesis testing
   B. Decision making
   C. Concept formation
   D. Linguistic acquisition

6. The tendency to judge the probability of an event by how easy it is to think of examples of it is called _____. (355)
   A. Availability heuristic
   B. Overconfidence
   C. Gambler's fallacy
   D. Belief in small numbers

7. A stroke patient knows that an object has a rod and a reel but cannot identify it as a fishing rod. What key zone does Domasio believe has been corrupted? (360-361)
   A. Divergence
   B. Semantic
   C. Convergence
   D. Parallel

8. A person who is concerned with what the word love means in the sentence, "I love roses," is concerned with _____. (368)
   A. Grammar
   B. Semantics
   C. Syntax
   D. Phonology

9. A language acquisition device (LAD) is _____. (372)
   A. A mechanical device that enhances spoken word for hard of hearing infants
   B. A procedure that all infants must go through in the acquisition of language
   C. An innate, unique capacity to acquire and develop language
   D. A technique used by the Gardner's to train Washoe to use sign language

10. One important difference between the language abilities of chimps and humans is that children will often _____. (375)
    A. Spontaneously point to and name objects
    B. Repeat the same word over and over
    C. Use language to get something that they want
    D. Use words in surprising ways

After You Read, Comprehensive Self Test

1. The study of how we acquire, transform, store, retrieve and use knowledge is _____.
    (344)
    A. Classical conditioning
    B. Cognitive psychology
    C. Intelligence testing
    D. Generativity

2. A prototype of a concept is a member of the concept that _____. (346)
    A. Specifies exactly what members must be like
    B. Is one of the best examples of the concept
    C. Gives correct and incorrect properties of the concept
    D. Applies to artificial concepts, but not fuzzy concepts

3. The procedure for solving a problem by implementing a set of rules over and over again
    until the solution is found is called _____. (347)
    A. Logical-reasoning
    B. Heuristic
    C. Algorithm
    D. Problem-solving

4. In problem solving, functional fixedness refers to _____. (349)
    A. The ability to fix a problem in your mind and think about it
    B. The failure to realize objects can be used in unusual ways
    C. A tendency to focus on fixing things, even when they work
    D. Arranging it so that a solution seems to work, even if it doesn't

5. Functional fixedness decreases when _____. (349)
    A. An object has no name or label to describe it
    B. An object has no specific function
    C. A person has had previous experience with an object
    D. All of the above

6. Errors in probability judgments may be attributed to _____. (354)
    A. Ethical systems or religious beliefs
    B. Ignoring key pieces of data
    C. An individual's political view
    D. All of the above

7. Computers have been programmed to simulate human thought processes like _____. (359-360)
   A. Information processing
   B. Ingenuity
   C. Creativity
   D. A & C

8. When a part of a neural network is destroyed or removed, the usual result is that the network will _____. (361)
   A. Continue functioning but make some mistakes
   B. Stop functioning but repair itself automatically
   C. Make more and more mistakes until it is useless
   D. Stop functioning completely until it is replaced

9. Language and thought are____. (365)
   A. Related, but separate processes
   B. Both influenced by one's experience with the environment
   C. Both influenced by genetic factors
   D. All of the above

10. A phoneme is the basic unit of _____ in a language. (366)
    A. Sound
    B. Meaning
    C. Inflection
    D. Grammar

11. Name the smallest units of speech that contain meaning. (366)
    A. Semantics
    B. Morphemes
    C. Cognates
    D. Phonemes

12. Syntax is _____. (368-369)
    A. The analysis of the meaning of individual words
    B. The study of language
    C. The study of how words and word groups combine to form phrases, sentences, clauses
    D. The underlying patterns of words that help convey meaning

13. In psycholinguistics, grammar is a description of _____. (369)
    A. All the sounds used to speak a language
    B. How the language functions to generate sentences
    C. The meanings of all the words in the language
    D. How children will learn the language in infancy

14. Which of the following cannot be explained by learning theories of language acquisition? (372)
     A.   Why children are able to generate sentences they have not heard or used before
     B.   How reinforcement is used to teach language
     C.   Why children over generalize the concepts expressed in words
     D.   Why children imitate adults and other children in their speech

15. The key to understanding language acquisition is to _____. (376)
     A.   Consider the structure of language
     B.   Analyze the way a child learns language
     C.   Study the context in which language is learned and used
     D.   Concentrate on the biological basis for language

True or False

1. An algorithm, if performed correctly, guarantees a correct solution. (347)

2. The rationale behind brainstorming is that people will generate more high quality ideas if they are not first criticized by other in the group who are trying to solve a problem (352)

3. People in the real world are less likely to make accurate judgments than are people who are asked to make judgments in the laboratory. (354)

4. Reasoning and decision making tends to be similar across eastern and western cultural traditions. (356)

5. Scientists have been able to demonstrate imagination in computers. (360)

6. In typical descriptions of men and women, men are more often described using active, positive words whereas women are described using passive and negative terms. (364)

7. Research indicates that children who are raised in a bilingual home often experience difficulty in acquiring reading skills. (365)

8. One of the things chimps do similarly to humans is to generate spontaneous speech. (375)

Essay Questions

1. Describe the 3 qualities of ideas that indicate creativity and how each helps with problem solving. (351)

2. How do culture and language interact? What research do we have that demonstrates this interaction? (365)

When You Have Finished!

Surf's Up!!

After you've read and reviewed, try these web sites for additional information about some of the topics covered in this chapter.

1. **American Association of Artificial Intelligence** (http://www.aaai.org/)
   This site contains information about developments in artificial intelligence and aims to increase understanding about this interesting topic.
2. **Primate Use of Language** (http://www.pigeon.psy.tufts.edu/psych26/language.htm)
   Contains information on language use and development by primates, containing an interesting link to a transcript of a discussion with Koko the gorilla.
3. **The Cognitive Psychology Tutor** (http://teach.psy.uga.edu/CogPsychTutor/default.htm)
   Contains an online quiz related to cognitive psychology where you can get feedback regarding why your answer is right or wrong.
4. **Creativity Web** (http://members.optusnet.com.au/~charles57/Creative/index2.html)
   Feeling stuck and need some tips to get out of it? This site has a lot of information about creativity and how to improve your creativity skills.
5. **Critical Thinking and Problem Solving Skills**
   (http://falcon.jmu.edu/~ramseyil/critical.htm)
   This site is devoted to providing information about these two important cognitive skills.

Cross Check: Cognitive Psychology

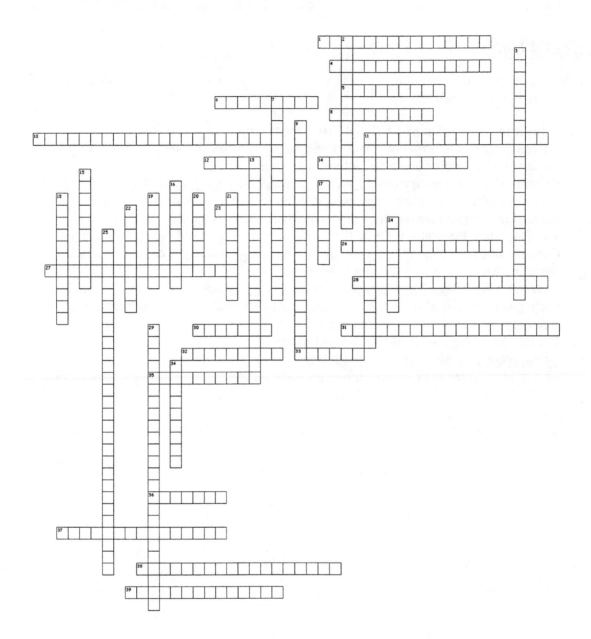

Across

1. The belief that the chances of an event's occurring increase if the event has not recently occurred
4. Heuristic procedure in which a problem solver works back from the goal to the current position in order to analyze the problem and reduce the steps needed to get to the goal
5. The analysis of the meaning of language, especially of individual words, the relationships among them, and their significance within particular contexts
6. An idealized pattern of an object that is stored in memory and used to decide whether similar objects are members of the same class of items
8. Behavior and attitudes that incorporate qualities traditionally considered masculine as well as those considered feminine
10. The branch of computer science concerned with making a device behave like a human being
11. The tendency of people to discount information that does not fit with their pre-existing views
12. The system of principles of reasoning that is used to reach valid conclusions
14. A problem solving technique that involves considering all possible solutions without any initial judgments
23. Assessing and choosing among alternatives
26. The localization of a particular brain function primarily in one hemisphere
27. The study of how language is acquired, perceived, understood, and produced
28. In problem solving, the process of widening the range of possibilities and expanding the options for solutions
30. The entire set of morphemes in a language
31. The inability to see that an object can have a function other than its usual one
32. The study of the patterns and distribution of speech sounds in a language and the commonly accepted rules for their pronunciation
33. The way words and groups of words can be combined to form phrases, clauses, and sentences
35. The ability to generate high quality ideas that are original
36. A basic unit of sound that combines with others to compose the words in a language
37. Heuristic procedure in which a problem is broken down into similar steps, each of which has a subgoal
38. To keep accepting something is true even in the face of conflicting data
39. The behavior of individuals when confronted with a situation that requires insight of some unknown elements

Down

2. Heuristic procedure in which the problem solver compares the current situation with a desired goal to determine the most efficient way to get from one to the other
3. The tendency to judge the probability of an event by how easy it is to think of examples of it
7. A condensed form of speech used by young children, consisting of almost all nouns and verbs
9. The willingness to draw conclusions from a small sample and to assume that such a sample is representative
11. In problem solving, the process of narrowing down choices to arrive at a suitable solution

13. The study of the related phenomena of perception, learning, memory, and thought with an emphasis on how people attend to acquire, transform, store, and retrieve knowledge

15. Sets of strategies that serve as flexible guidelines for discovery oriented problem solving

16. The study of how the social context in which words are used affects their meaning

17. The linguistic description of how a language functions, especially the rules and patterns used for generating appropriate sentences

18. The study of language, including speech sounds, meaning, and grammar

19. A system of symbols that conveys meaning, along with a set of rules for combining the symbols to generate an infinite number of messages

20. A mental category people use to classify events or objects according to their common features

21. A tendency to approach situations the same way because that way worked in the past

22. A procedure for solving a problem by implementing a set of rules over and over again until the solution is found

24. A basic unit of meaning in language

25. A model of human memory that proposes that information is processed and stored in three stages, moving in a sequential manner from one stage to the next

29. The tendency of individuals who are highly committed to their ideas to be more certain than correct and, when challenged, to be even more rigid

34. The purposeful process by which a person generates logical and coherent ideas, evaluates situations, and reaches conclusions

Created by <u>Puzzlemaker</u> at
DiscoverySchool.com

Chapter 11

Intelligence

Before you read...

Are you intelligent? When answering this question, did you think about your past experience in traditional academic situations? If you are like most people (and even many psychologists), you likely did. However, intelligence is thought of as a broader concept that allows us to effectively adapt to and cope with our environment.

In the first part of the chapter, you will briefly trace the origins and history of intelligence testing. You will see that intelligence testing was indeed initially developed in order to predict academic performance. This is likely why most modern intelligence tests still rely heavily on tasks and items that closely resemble common activities in academic situations.

In the second part of the chapter, you will examine the broader question of what intelligence is. Although you will learn a common definition, you will learn that this definition is hardly all encompassing or agreed upon by all psychologists. As part of this controversy, you will also explore some alternative definitions of intelligence that focus on emotional and social aspects of our functioning.

In the next part of the chapter, you will be introduced to some of the basic concepts involved in test developing. You will see that developing a test is a long and complicated process. Proper test development involves standardization, the establishment of test norms, and the provision of reliability and validity evidence for the test. To highlight the concept of validity, you will examine some common controversies associated with the validity (or meaning) of intelligence tests.

You may have heard some things about the causes of intelligence, and you likely have your own ideas about this topic. In the next section of the chapter, you will explore some of these issues and look at factors that contribute to intelligence. You might find some common answers to questions you have, such as the impact of race, culture, and gender on intelligence.

The chapter concludes with a look at giftedness and mental retardation. In exploring these issues, you will learn how they are defined and assessed in psychological and educational settings. In addition, you will explore how children that fall into extreme groups are treated in the school system. Finally, you will look at the impact that legislation and educationally policy has had on groups at the extreme ends of the intelligence spectrum.

Learning Objectives

After reading this chapter, you should be able to:

1. Describe and differentiate between Binet and Wechsler's tests of intelligence.
2. Describe the development of the Stanford-Binet Intelligence Scale and define the concepts of mental and chronological age.
3. Define intelligence.
4. Describe and differentiate between factor theories, biological theories, and the theories of Vygotsky, Gardner, and Sternberg as they relate to defining intelligence.
5. Explain the theory of emotional intelligence and differentiate it from more traditional models of intelligence.
6. Compare and contrast achievement and aptitude tests.
7. Describe how the terms *norms, representative sample*, and *the normal curve* are related and important to testing.
8. Explain how and why psychologists develop standardized tests and describe the types of scores that are obtained from these tests.
9. Examine how psychologists ensure that diagnostic tests are reliable and valid and discuss the debate concerning the validity of intelligence testing and the importance of interpretation.
10. Describe the research related to evolutionary and genetic contributions to intelligence.
11. Evaluate the research on test bias to explain why intelligence needs to be considered in a cultural context and how intelligence testing could be changed as a result.
12. Describe how biological and environmental factors might interact to influence the development of intelligence.
13. Define giftedness and the three factors that should be considered in evaluating giftedness.
14. Characterize mental retardation and describe the four levels of support required for people with intellectual disabilities.
15. Describe how the Individuals with Disability Education Act has influenced educational practices within the United States.

Key Terms

Mental Age
Intelligence Quotient
Intelligence Tests
Intelligence
Factor Analysis
Emotional Intelligence
Achievement Tests
Aptitude Tests
Standardization
Norms
Representative Sample
Normal Curve
Raw Score
Standard Score
Percentile Score
Deviation IQ
Reliability
Validity
Content Validity
Predictive Validity
Halo Effect
Stereotype Threat
Self-Fulfilling Prophecy
Heritability
Mental Retardation
Inclusion

Psychology

As you read...

What Are the Origins and History of Psychological Testing?

1. The first intelligence test was developed by _____ for what purpose?

2. Briefly describe the history of the Stanford-Binet Intelligence test.

3. On the original versions of the Stanford-Binet, IQ was calculated by dividing _____ by _____. Define each of these concepts.

4. The Stanford-Binet has generally been a good predictor of _____.

5. Intelligence tests are tests designed to measure _____ rather than _____.

11-1   **The Wechsler Scales**

1. One of the original purposes of the Wechsler Scales was to differentiate _____ skills from _____ skills.

2. Describe the difference between performance and verbal skills and list the Wechsler subscales that correspond to these broad areas.

3. What are the 3 different Wechsler tests, and state to who are they administered?

4. Test items on the Wechsler scales are grouped by _____.

11-2   **Group Intelligence Tests**

1. Why and when were group intelligence tests developed?

244

What is Intelligence?

1. Outline some of the agreements or disagreements in regard to the definition of intelligence.

2. Intelligence is _____.

3. Factor theories of intelligence are developed using a procedure called _____ _____. Define this technique.

4. Describe the two-factor theory of intelligence.

5. _____ is responsible for developing the two-factor theory of intelligence.

6. Who developed the factor theory of intelligence, and how is it different than the two factor theory of intelligence?

7. Describe Vygotsky's view of intelligence.

8. Explain the two observations about human brain functioning that support a biological view of human intelligence.

9. Complete the table below related to the 7 primary intelligences of Gardner's model of intelligence.

Type of Intelligence	Exemplar	Core Components
Linguistic		
Logical-mathematical		
Musical		
Spatial		
Bodily-kinesthetic		
Interpersonal		
Intrapersonal		

10. According to Sternberg's theory, successful intelligence is _____.

11. Define and provide an example of the three components of successful intelligence as defined by Sternberg.

     a. Analytic Dimension

        Example

     b. Practical Dimension

        Example

     c. Creative Dimension

        Example

11-3 Emotions- A Different Kind of Intelligence?

1. The concept of emotional intelligence was originally developed by _____.

2. Emotional intelligence is ____.

3. What are the four aspects of emotional intelligence described by Goleman?

4. How does Mayer, Salovey and Caruso's (2000) view of emotional intelligence differ from Goleman's?

5. Match the following theorists with the appropriate explanation of their theories of intelligence.

Wechsler　　　　　Gardner　　　　　Sternberg

Spearman　　　　　Thurnstone　　　　　Vygotsky

   a) _____ argued that intelligence is not a product, but a process.

   b) _____ Believed intelligence consists of general factors (affecting all performance) and specific factors (affecting specific tasks)

   c) _____ sees intellectual development in a social context.

   d) _____ Has criticized most widely used intelligence tests stating that they are too narrow and don't account for intelligence in the everyday world; believes in multiple types of intelligence.

   e) _____ Criticizes IQ tests as being too heavy on linguistic and mathematical skills.

   f) _____ Described seven factors of intelligence such as word fluency, number facility, perceptual speed, reasoning, and spatial visualization.

How Do Psychologists Develop Tests?

1. An aptitude test is designed to measure _____, whereas a (n) _____ test is designed to measure how well students have learned specific content.

2. A test is _____.

3. You just developed a new intelligence test and distributed it to a large, representative sample of individuals. The scores and percentile ranks that are achieved on this test would be considered what?

Psychology

4.   What is the purpose of standardization?

5.   A _____ _____ refers to a sample of individuals who match the larger population for which a test is designed with regard to key variables such as socioeconomic status and age.

6.   Draw a normal distribution and state what it means to say that sores on an intelligence test should be normally distributed.

7.   Match the following terms to the appropriate definitions.

Standardization   normal curve   percentile score

Norms   raw score   deviation IQ

representative sample   standard score   intelligence quotient

   a) _____ A large group of individuals who match the target population (the group for whom the test is being designed) with regard to important variables such as socioeconomic status and age.
   b) _____ Necessary for standardization, these scores and corresponding percentile ranks are obtained by administering the test to the individuals in the representative sample. When the test is released for general use, the scores of those who take the test will be compared to these scores.
   c) _____The process of developing a uniform procedure for administering and scoring the test. The test is given to a large sample of people who are matched with regard to important variables so that norms can be determined for the basis of comparison. In addition, time limits for testing and specific guidelines for test administration are established.
   d) _____ The number of correct answers an individual receives on the test. To be meaningful this score must be converted, taking into account the individual's age, sex, and grade level.
   e) _____ A bell-shaped curve that provides a graphic illustration of representative test scores. The data are arranged so that those with low scores fall on the left side of the curve; those with middle range scores fall in the middle of the curve (most people achieve scores in the middle ranges); and those with high scores fall on the right side of the curve.
   f) _____ A standard score that indicates what percentage of people in the population under consideration would achieve a lower score.
   g) _____ A simple formula to measure intelligence calculated by dividing a person's mental age by the person's chronological age and multiplying the result by 100.

h) _____ A standard score that has the same mean and standard deviation at all ages. Thus, a child of nine and a child of sixteen, each with an IQ of 115, occupy the same position (they have the same percentile score) relative to others who have taken the same IQ test.

i) _____ A score that expresses an individual's position relative to the mean based on the standard deviation. It is often derived by converting a raw score to one that can be interpreted on the basis of a population variable such as age or grade. Two examples of this type of score are a percentile score and a deviation IQ.

11-4 Reliability

1. Reliability is _____.

2. You take a test of your scholastic ability one week and you score in the 50th percentile. If you take the same test one week later (without studying for it) and score in the 75th percentile, what would you say about this test's reliability?

3. The example of reliability listed in question #2 would be an example of what type of reliability?

4. List and describe the three ways to assess the reliability of a test.

11-5 Validity

1. Define validity.

2. The extent to which a test measures the quality it is supposed to measure is referred to as _____ _____.

3. The scholastic aptitude test (SAT) has been shown to be a good predictor of college student's grade point average and graduation from college. This would be evidence of what type of validity for the SAT?

4. Outline the five criticisms regarding the validity of intelligence tests.

5.   The _____ _____ is dangerous for teachers because this effect causes one to judge a person's performance more favorably because of other favorable characteristics.

6.   Describe the research studies that support the existence of stereotype threat.

How Do Biological and Environmental Factors Contribute to Intelligence?

1.   The evolution of ____ ____ ____ is the focus of intelligence for evolutionary psychologists.

2.   Why are general factors of intelligence less important to evolutionary psychologists than other psychologists?

3.   Heritability is _____.

4.   What does it mean when a trait is 50% heritable?

5.   Describe the two types of research methods that have been used to study the heritability of intelligence, and outline the results of this research.

11-6   Environmental and Cultural Factors in Intelligence

1.   The accusation that intelligence tests are culturally biased is based on what assertion?

2.   When is a test item or subscale considered to be culturally biased?

3.   What evidence is there that intelligence tests are culturally biased?

4. What conclusion about culture and intelligence is clear?

5. List the environmental factors that have been shown to influence intelligence and explain their influence on intelligence scores.

| 11-7 | The Interaction of Biological and Environmental Factors |

1. Are there gender differences in intelligence scores? Explain.

2. Are there gender differences in cognitive abilities?

3. One of the potential reasons for differences in cognitive abilities is _____.

4. If you were/are a parent, what might you do within your family to reduce the likelihood of there being gender differences in your children?

5. Describe the relationship between socioeconomic status and intelligence.

6. Research has indicated that intelligence scores have increased, on average, by about _____ points over the past 30 years. Describe how the interaction between biology and environment might account for this change.

What Is the Impact of Having an Exceptional IQ?

1. According to the Gifted and Talented Children's Act of 1978, giftedness is _____.

2. List and describe Renzulli's (2002) 3 key factors for determining giftedness.

3.   What types of programs exist for gifted students?

11-8   Intellectual Disability

1.   Mental retardation is _____.

2.   Approximately what percentage of the population is labeled as intellectually disabled?

3.   Outline some of the causes of mental retardation.

4.   Complete the following table regarding the type of support required for individuals with intellectual disabilities.

Level of Support	Description	Examples of Areas Where Assistance May Be Needed
Intermittent		
Limited		
Extensive		
Pervasive		

11-9   Special Education: The IDEA

1.   What is the IDEA, and what are its basic assumptions?

2.   How has the IDEA changed the life of people with disabilities?

3.   Mainstreaming is _____.

4.   Describe the benefits of inclusion to people with disabilities.

After You Read, Practice Test #1

1.   When Simon and Binet developed their first intelligence test their goal was to _____. (382)
     A.   Determine the cause of intelligence.
     B.   Determine the future of children with high intelligence.
     C.   Separate children of normal intelligence from those who showed signs of retarded intellectual development.
     D.   All of the above

2.   Which of these intelligence theorists developed the two-factor theory of intelligence? (387)
     A.   Sternberg
     B.   Spearman
     C.   Binet
     D.   Wechsler

3.   Vygotsky said that a child's private speech _____. (388)
     A.   Interfered with the development of logical intellectual abilities
     B.   Was the basis for understanding the world
     C.   Must be verbalized before a child can apply it to practical situations
     D.   Is unrelated to people's ability to use their capabilities in the environment

4.   A theory of intelligence that emphasizes a person's overall ability to achieve success in life was developed by _____. (391)
     A.   John Watson
     B.   Arthur Jensen
     C.   David Weschler
     D.   Robert Sternberg

5.   According to Sternberg's theory of intelligence, someone who has common sense is high in which kind of intelligence? (391)
     A.   Analytic
     B.   Practical
     C.   Creative
     D.   Successful

6.   The scores and corresponding percentile ranks of a large and representative sample of individuals from the population for which a test was designed are called _____. (394)
     A.   Standards
     B.   Norms
     C.   Comparatives
     D.   Raw score equivalents

7. Which term describes an intelligence test that consistently produces the same score on different occasions? (395)
    A.   Normal
    B.   Reliable
    C.   Valid
    D.   Standardized

8. Giving someone two different versions of the same test on two different occasions and comparing the scores is a _____ measure of reliability (396)
    A.   Content
    B.   Alternate-form
    C.   Split-half
    D.   Test-retest

9. Which of the following is not a criticism of the validity of intelligence tests? (396-397)
    A.   Scores on the tests are affected by the test takers expectations
    B.   There is no clear definition of what intelligence is
    C.   Test items tend to reflect prior learning versus innate ability
    D.   Many of the tests are only available in the English language

10. Mental retardation is characterized by _____. (408)
    A.   Deficits in intellectual functioning
    B.   Adaptive deficits and poor intellectual functioning
    C.   Lack of language development and poor intellectual skills
    D.   Lack of adaptive behavior

After You Read, Practice Test #2

1. According to the Stanford-Binet Intelligence Scale, IQ is based on a child's _____. (382-383)
    A. Mental age
    B. Chronological age
    C. Both a and b
    D. Neither

2. In Binet's original measurement of intelligence, the age level at which a child is functioning intellectually is the child's _____. (382)
    A. Chronological age
    B. Mental age
    C. Intelligence level
    D. General adaptation

3. According to a widely accepted definition of intelligence, the most important thing is that it _____. (387)
    A. Is inherited genetically from our parents
    B. Controls how much information we can retain
    C. Determines who will benefit from education
    D. Deals with our ability to adapt to our environment

4. In Sternberg's theory of successful intelligence, the ability to use one's capabilities in a specific situation is_____ intelligence; while the ability to decide what information needs to be processed and how is _____ intelligence. (391-392)
    A. Practical; analytic
    B. Practical; creative
    C. Analytic; creative
    D. Creative; analytic

5. Heather's teacher informed her that 92 percent of her classmates scored lower than she did on an intelligence test. The number 92 represents _____. (395)
    A. An intelligence quotient
    B. A standard deviation
    C. A percentile score
    D. A raw score

6. When measurements of a variable come out with most of the scores in the middle, and fewer as you go higher and lower, we ay that the scores are _____. (395)
    A. Normally distributed
    B. Analytically arranged
    C. Statistically reliable
    D. Computationally independent

7. A standard intelligence test score whose mean and standard deviation remain constant for all ages is called a _____. (395)
    A. Raw score
    B. Mental age
    C. Deviation IQ
    D. Variability score

8. The genetically determined proportion of a trait's variation among individuals in a population is _____. (401)
    A. Genotype
    B. Heritability
    C. Phenotype
    D. Genetics

9. Based on research on IQ tests in many different cultures, the author strongly concludes that _____. (403)
    A. There is a genetic component to our intelligence levels
    B. All current IQ tests exhibit systematic ethnic and cultural bias
    C. IQ tests measure a person's adaptability to his or her culture
    D. A person's intelligence is fixed at birth and can't be changed

10. _____ refers to the integration of children with special needs into regular classroom settings. (411)
    A. Special education
    B. Inclusion
    C. IDEA program
    D. Appropriation

After You Read, Practice Test #3

1. Who was responsible for the first intelligence test designed to test adults? (383)
    A. Binet
    B. Stanford
    C. Kaufman
    D. Wechsler

2. _____ intelligence refers to the ability to both perceive and express emotions in accurate and adaptive ways. (392)
    A. Creative
    B. Functional
    C. Real-life
    D. Emotional

3. A group of people taken from a larger population who match the population on all important variables is said to be a _____. (394)
    A. Social norm
    B. Representative sample
    C. Control group
    D. Correlation coefficient

4. What is standardization used to determine? (394)
    A. Achievement
    B. Test norms
    C. Reliability
    D. Validity

5. A test intended to measure musical ability should contain items that measure only this ability. In other words, the test should measure what it was intended to measure. This is called _____. (396)
    A. Content validity
    B. Predictive validity
    C. Face validity
    D. Construct validity

6. Critics claim that IQ tests cannot really measure intelligence, because psychologists have not even decided on a definition of what intelligence is. Defenders of IQ tests point out that these tests _____. (396-397)
    A. Are able to predict scholastic ability well
    B. Tend to be culturally fair
    C. Yield reliable results over time
    D. Are not influenced by expectations of the test taker

7. Intelligence test scores_____. (405)
    A.   Begin to gradually decrease beginning around age 40
    B.   Generally reach their peak when a child learns to talk
    C.   Have tended to get higher over the last 30 years
    D.   Are significantly higher for males compared to females

8. According to Renzulli's definition of giftedness, three key factors should be considered. Which of the following is not one of those factors? (407)
    A.   Problem solving ability
    B.   Ability
    C.   Task commitment
    D.   Creativity

9. Approximately what percentage of children are affected by mental retardation? (409)
    A.   20%
    B.   50%
    C.   15%
    D.   1%

10. When a child is placed in a mainstreaming educational system, the child typically _____. (411)
    A.   Is integrated into a regular classroom as much as possible
    B.   Is placed in school with other children who are mentally retarded
    C.   Is labeled according to his or her mental age level and level of retardation
    D.   Has only one teacher and learns on a one-to-one basis

After You Read, Comprehensive Self Test

1. Intelligence tests are designed to measure _____ versus specific learned content. (383)
    A. Learned adaptive skills
    B. Emotional maturity
    C. Problem solving
    D. General mental ability

2. The overall capacity to act purposefully, to think rationally, and to act in the environment is _____. (387)
    A. Adaptability
    B. Intelligence
    C. Social adaptability
    D. Motivation

3. Which view of intelligence uses correlations between items to uncover common underlying abilities? (387)
    A. Jensen's two-level theory
    B. Gardener's multiple intelligences
    C. Factor theories
    D. Wechsler's theory

4. Gardner and Hatch would say that a person who is sensitive to the sounds, rhythms, and meaning of words has a _____ type of intelligence and might choose to be a poet. (390)
    A. Musical
    B. Spatial
    C. Interpersonal
    D. Linguistic

5. Which of the following is not a dimension in Sternberg's theory of intelligence? (390-391)
    A. Analytic
    B. Practical
    C. Emotional
    D. Creative

6. According to Goleman, the key to getting ahead in life is _____. (392)
    A. Logical and linguistic abilities
    B. Intelligence in a cultural context
    C. Intellectual skills
    D. Emotional intelligence

Psychology

7. The Stanford-Binet Intelligence Scale was responsible for coining the term intelligence
   _____, which was defined as a child's mental age divided by their chronological age. (383)
   A. Indicator
   B. Scale
   C. Quotient
   D. Level

8. _____ tests are designed to measure the ability to learn specific types of material. (394)
   A. Achievement
   B. Intelligence
   C. Aptitude
   D. Projective

9. The first thing a psychologist must decide about a test is _____. (394)
   A. The mental age of the test subject.
   B. What the test is supposed to measure.
   C. The population for whom a test will be designed.
   D. A uniform procedure for administering and scoring the test

10. If a test is administered twice to the same person, and the scores are similar to one another,
    that test can be said to have high ____ reliability. (395)
    A. Predictive
    B. Test-retest
    C. Alternate form
    D. Content

11. The SAT is a standardized test of knowledge, skills, and reasoning ability for college
    applicants. If students who score well on this test are in fact more successful at college than
    those with low scores, then this test has high _____. (396)
    A. Predictive validity
    B. Retest reliability
    C. Normal distributions
    D. Cultural fairness

12. When one particular or outstanding characteristic about an individual is allowed to
    influence evaluations, this is called a _____. (397)
    A. Singular advantage.
    B. Blooming effect.
    C. Corona significance.
    D. Halo effect

13. Which set of percentages most accurately describes the relationship between heredity and environment in determining intelligence? (402)
    A.   10% heredity: 90% environment
    B.   50% heredity: 50% environment
    C.   75% heredity: 25% environment
    D.   90% heredity: 10% environment

14. A diagnosis of mental retardation requires _____. (408)
    A.   Intellectual and behavioral deficits
    B.   Difficulty adapting to the environment
    C.   Symptoms of hyperactivity
    D.   Both A and B are correct

15. The passage of Public Law 94-142 states that all school-age children are provided with appropriate and free public education. For those with mental retardation, this means _____. (409-410)
    A.   Special schools must be created for mentally retarded children
    B.   Mainstreaming must occur when possible
    C.   Mentally retarded children must be included in the social aspect of schooling
    D.   They must not be tested any more than normal children

True or False

1.   The Stanford Binet was originally developed to identify students that needed special educational attention. (382)

2.   The Wechsler Scales of intelligence were the first developed to be used with adults. (383)

3.   To date, there is no one agreed upon definition of intelligence. (387)

4.   According to Goleman's theory of emotional intelligence, intelligence is composed of five separate aspects. (392)

5.   According to stereotype threat, the fear that one's performance on a task will confirm a negative stereotype about one's group is likely to change their performance on a test. (397)

6.   Research indicates that the correlation between IQ scores for identical twins tends to be lower than the correlation between brothers and sisters reared together. (402)

7.   Women's IQ scores tend to be significantly below men's, especially in Western cultures. (404)

8.   The IDEA act requires the evaluation of a child by a multidisciplinary team that is able to evaluate their overall functioning versus only one aspect of functioning. (410)

Essay Questions

1. Define reliability and validity and state why they are important. (395-397)

2. Describe factors that may lead to mental retardation. (409)

262

When You Have Finished!

Surf's Up!!

After you've read and reviewed, try these web sites for additional information about some of the topics covered in this chapter.

1. **Human Intelligence** (http://www.indiana.edu/~intell/index.shtml)
   This site contains information about current and historical figures in intelligence, information about some of the controversies in intelligence testing, and other resources of interest to intelligence.
2. **Educational Testing Services** (http://www.ets.org)
   One of the leading administrators and developers of tests, including the SAT and GRE. In addition to information about these tests, you will find information about testing controversies and issues.
3. **American Association on Mental Retardation** (http://www.aamr.org/)
   Devoted to advocacy and education about mental retardation.
4. **Gifted Development Center** (http://www.gifteddevelopment.com/index.htm)
   This site is dedicated to the study of giftedness and exceptional development, and there are a number of interesting resources available.
5. **Finding Psychological Tests** (http://www.apa.org/science/faq-findtests.html)
   This is a link to a helpful handout prepared by the American Psychological Association that discusses how you might find a test that you are interested in knowing more about or using.
6. **Howard Gardner's Multiple Intelligence Theory, A Tutorial**
   (http://www.infed.org/thinkers/gardner.htm)
   An interesting and in depth overview of the multiple intelligence model and how it is being put into use in some school systems.

Cross Check: Intelligence

Across

8. A sample of individuals who match the larger population for which a test is designed
10. A disability defined by significant limitations in both intellectual functioning and adaptive skills
11. A score that expresses an individual's position relative to those of other test takers
12. The process of developing uniform procedures for administering and scoring a test
14. A score indicating what percentage of the population taking a test obtained a lower score
15. The age at which children of average ability are able to perform various tasks on an intelligence test
16. A situation in which personal expectations unintentionally influence people's behavior
18. The ability of a test to measure the knowledge it is intended to measure, determined through a detailed examination of the contents of the test items
19. A standard IQ test score whose mean and standard deviation remain constant for all ages
21. A test score that is not converted or transformed in any way
22. Tests designed to measure how well students have learned specific content
23. Tests designed to measure general mental abilities rather than specific learned content
24. The overall capacity of an individual to act purposefully, to think rationally, and to deal effectively with the environment
25. Psychological tests designed to measure the ability to learn specific types of material
26. The fear that one's performance on a task will confirm a negative stereotype about one's group

Down

1. The ability of a test to predict a person's future achievement with at least some degree of accuracy
2. A child's mental age divided by the child's chronological age and multiplied by 100
3. A bell shaped graphic representation of normally distributed data showing what percentage of the population falls under each part of the curve
4. The genetically determined proportion of a trait's variation among individuals in a population
5. The integration of children in the classroom
6. The tendency for one noticeable characteristic of an individual to influence the evaluation of other characteristics
7. The ability of a test to measure only what it is supposed to measure
9. The ability to both perceive and express emotions in accurate and adaptive ways
13. The ability of a test to yield very similar scores for the same individual over repeated testings
17. A statistical procedure designed to discover the independent factors in any set of data
20. The scores and corresponding percentile ranks of a large and representative sample of individuals from the population for which a test was designed

Created by Puzzlemaker at
DiscoverySchool.com

Chapter 12

Motivation and Emotion

Before you read...

Many people are interested in psychology because it allows them to answer very specific questions about why people think and behave the way they do. To answer these questions, we must try to understand the interacting forces behind specific thoughts and behaviors and accept that no one theory or explanation will fit all situations or all people. This chapter attempts to address these very complex questions by examining two key forces in human behavior, motivation and emotion.

The chapter begins by exploring motivation as a general construct and providing an overview of the various theories that continue to impact psychologists thinking about human motivation. A number of specific theories of motivation are discussed, including evolutionary, drive, arousal, cognitive, and humanistic theories. In exploring these theories, you will be introduced to some of the key theorists associated with the theory, the key focus and ideas involved in the theory, and a discussion of how behavior is viewed from within each theory. These theories might provide you with a way of thinking why you engage in some of the thoughts and behaviors you do, and it might be challenging to think about the theories based on their strengths and limitations in explaining some of your own behavior!

In the next section of the chapter, three specific motivators are introduced, and the impact of these motivations impact human behavior is explored. The first motivating force that is discussed is hunger. In this section, biological, cultural, and psychological factors related to eating behavior and obesity is explored. The second motivating force that is discussed is sex. Here, you will learn about factors that influence sexual behavior, the various stages of the human sexual response cycle, and how sexual attitudes and behaviors have changed over the years. In addition, some of the controversy regarding sexual orientation and the "nature-nurture" debate regarding are discussed. Finally, you will explore what psychologists call the social needs of affiliation and achievement. The interested reader might find answers to the question of why some people appear more socially active and open, while others seem more reclusive and focused on achievement.

In the third part of the chapter might inspire positive feelings such as joy and excitement, and wonder (but hopefully not boredom and anger!). Why? Well, it is all about those fascinating things we call our emotions. In this section, you are introduced to a basic definition of emotion that considers the physiological, behavioral, and feeling aspect. In addition, various theories of emotion such as the evolutionary, physiological, and cognitive models are discussed. For each theory, you will be introduced to the key theorists involved and you will be challenged to compare how each conceives of the role of physiology, cognition, and the situation when discussing emotion

The chapter concludes with a brief discussion of how emotions affect behavior. This question is addressed from the perspective of how both gender and culture might influence emotion and emotional expression. The chapter closes with an intriguing discussion of how and if we can actually control our emotions and emotional expression.

Learning Objectives

After reading this chapter, you should be able to:

1. Define motivation and describe the four basic components of motivation.
2. Explain the evolutionary theory of motivation and discuss how motivation and emotion might contribute to human survival and reproduction.
3. Outline drive theory and discuss how animals and human beings strive to maintain homeostasis and the types of conflicts that humans tend to deal with.
4. Specify how arousal and sensory stimulation needs differ from other biological needs and describe how various levels of arousal and anxiety affect performance.
5. Discuss expectancy theories and explain their relation to social needs.
6. Describe the cognitive theory of motivation and compare and contrast the roles of intrinsic and extrinsic motivation within this theory.
7. Outline Abraham Maslow's theory of motivation and define self-actualization.
8. Identify and explain the physiological, environmental, and cultural determinants of hunger.
9. Compare the physiological and psychological explanations of obesity and overeating.
10. Discuss how hormones, sights, sounds, smells, and fantasies may initiate sex drive in humans and animals.
11. Outline the human sexual response cycle, and compare and contrast the findings of the Kinsey studies and the Lauman studies as they relate to human sexual behavior.
12. Define the need for achievement and affiliation, describe how tests are used to describe individual differences in these needs, and discuss their importance based on research findings.
13. Define emotion and discuss the three key elements of emotion.
14. Describe the physiological theories of emotion and compare and contrast the James-Lange and Cannon-Bard physiological theories of emotion.
15. Summarize the evolutionary theory of emotion.
16. Describe the cognitive theories of emotion outlined by Schachter-Singer and Lazarus.
17. Review the interactions between culture, gender and emotion and discuss whether humans can control their emotions.

Key Terms

Motivation
Instinct
Drive Theory
Drive
Need
Motive
Homeostasis
Conflict
Approach-Approach Conflict
Avoidance-Avoidance Conflict
Approach-Avoidance Conflict
Arousal
Cognitive Theories
Expectancy Theories
Social Need
Extrinsic Motivation
Intrinsic Motivation
Overjustification Effect
Flow
Humanistic Theory
Self-Actualization
Excitement Phase
Vasocongestion
Plateau Phase
Orgasm Phase
Resolution Phase
Survey
Representative Sample
Need for Achievement
Need for Affiliation
Self-Efficacy
Social Support
Display Rules
Emotion
Appraisal

As you read...

What is Motivation?

1.   Motivation refers to an _____ condition that initiates, activates, or _____ an organism's _____.

2.   List and describe the 4 basic parts of motivation.

12-1   Theories of Motivation

1.   An _____ is a fixed behavioral pattern that occurs in all members of a species and appears without learning or practice.

2.   What is the evolutionary view of motivation and emotion?

3.   Explain the relationships between drive and need in drive theories of motivation.

4.   Homeostasis is _____. Provide one example of behavior that is motivated toward maintaining homeostasis.

5.   The goal that satisfies a need is often referred to as _____.

6.   Match the appropriate type of conflict to the example provided

Approach-Approach   Avoidance-Avoidance   Approach-Avoidance

   a.   _____ You were just offered two good jobs, both with comparable salaries and benefit packages.
   b.   _____ You really like the person you are dating, but when you take him home to meet your parents, they do not like the person.
   c.   _____You have the choice of studying for two exams in classes that you do not like.

7.   Define arousal and state how it is related to motivation.

8.   The basic human and animal phenomenon or observation that seves as the basis for arousal theory is that _____.

9.   According to the Yerkes-Dodson principle, performance will be optimal when what conditions are present?

10.   How are cognitive theories different from arousal theories regarding their view of behavior?

11.   According to expectancy theories, what would make you most likely to study for a test?

12.   You help rebuild houses in your local community after a natural disaster because it makes you feel good, whereas Gerard helps to build these houses because she is paid to do so. What type of motivation is driving you? Gerard?

13.   A_____ need is important to establishing and maintaining relationships with others.

14.   Based on your knowledge of the overjustification effect, should parents pay their children to study if the child likes to study? Explain why or why not.

15.   Humanistic theory emphasizes the _____ of life rather than _____.

16.   Fill in the following levels of Maslow's hierarchy.

Level 5	
Level 4	
Level 3	
Level 2	
Level 1	

17.   How would you know if you had reached the self-actualization level?

18.   Complete the following table.

Theory	Theorist	Focus of Theory	Key Idea	View of Behavior
	Cosmides & Tooby		Instincts apply even more to humans than other animals	
Drive	Hull			Largely Mechanistic
	Miller	Conflict among motivations		
	Hebb		Performance depends on the level of arousal	
Cognitive		Achievement motivation	Humans learn the need to achieve	
	Deci	Intrinsic motivation		
Humanistic			Self-Actualization	

How Does Motivation Affect Behavior?

1.   A set point is _____.

2.   What are the 2 necessary components related to homeostatic weight control?

3.   List and describe the hormones important to maintaining weight balance.

4.   The _____ is one of the main brain structures that influences and controls our eating behavior.

5.   Describe the environmental, cultural, and personal factors that might influence eating.

6.   The rate of clinical obesity in the U.S. is _____, whereas _____ are overweight.

7.   From an evolutionary perspective, people from what type of evolutionary history are likely to be overweight? Why?

8.   List and describe 2 inherited traits that can lead to obesity.

9.   List the 4 key factors that contribute to overeating.

12-2   Sexual Behavior: Physiology Plus Thought

1.   How is the sexual need different from the need for food?

2.   How do hormones such as androgen and estrogen influence sexual desire and characteristics?

3. How are sights, sounds, and fantasy involved in sex drive?

4. Identify the appropriate phase in the sexual response cycle.

   Excitement   Plateau   Orgasm   Resolution

   a) _____ The stage of the sexual response cycle in which both men and women are preparing for orgasm.
   b) _____ The stage of the sexual response cycle in which the body naturally returns to its resting or normal state.
   c) _____ The stage of the sexual response cycle in which there are initial increases in heart rate, blood pressure, and respiration.
   d) _____ The stage of the sexual response cycle in which the autonomic nervous system activity reaches its peak, and muscle contractions occur throughout the body in spasms.

5. In what areas are men and women similar and different from one another regarding sexuality?

6. How have people's views and behaviors changed over time regarding sexuality? How are these views and behaviors influenced by culture and age?

7. List and describe the 3 sexual orientations.

8. What evidence does research provide for biological and environmental determinates of sexual orientation?

12-3 Social Needs

1. The need for _____ directs a person's need to excel and succeed, whereas the need for _____ directs the desire to establish and maintain relationships.

2.   How is achievement motivation different in Asian and Western cultures?

3.   Describe how achievement motives might be measured.

4.   High _____ _____ is the belief that one can successfully engage in and execute a specific behavior. Discuss how this is related to the need for achievement.

5.   Social support refers to _____.

6.   What factors have been associated with a need for affiliation?

What is Emotion?

1.   Emotion is _____.

2.   What are the 3 key elements of emotion?

12-4   Theories of Emotion

1.   Compare and contrast the James-Lange and Cannon-Bard theories of emotion.

2.   What is the facial feedback hypothesis?

3.   According to an evolutionary view of emotion, how might our emotions have contributed to our survival?

4.   Schachter and Singer placed a greater emphasis on the _____ in which that emotion occurred, and stated that this factor is important in the _____ of the situation.

5.   Describe Schachter and Singer's 1962 experiments.

6.   Identify the theory that most adequately explains why the particular emotion in the following situations is experienced.

> *LeDoux's Emotional Brain*   *Cannon-Bard*
> *James-Lange*   *Schachter-Singer*

a)   _____ Barry lacks his usual energy level, does not have any appetite though he has not eaten for some time, and has trouble concentrating and going to sleep. Based on this feedback from his body, Barry is aware that he is *depressed*.

b)   _____ While discussing a pay raise with her boss, Tanya feels an awkward and odd feeling inside but is not certain what she is feeling or why. When she recounts the conversation, she realizes that her boss had subtly accused her of being lazy on the job. Based on this information she told herself she is feeling *embarrassed*.

c)   _____ .While walking to class Samantha hears what appears to be either firecrackers or maybe gunshots coming from the next hallway. She begins to feel herself sweat and she is confused. She decides to stay where she is and hope the incident will not involve her.

d)   _____ Olga sits in her hot tub and as her muscles begin to relax, she begins to feel *peacefully content*.

7.   Like Schachter and Singer, Lazarus' theory of emotion placed a great deal of emphasis on the role of _____, and specifically the person's _____ of the significance of a situation or event.

How Does Emotion Affect Behavior?

1.   How do cultural factors influence the ability to interpret the emotions of others?

2.   How are emotions viewed differently in individualist versus collectivist cultures?

3.   Describe the gender stereotypes about emotion.

4.   How are display rules related to the emotional experiences of men and women?

12-5	Can We Control Emotions?

1. Of the physiological, feelings, and behaviors related to emotions, which is the hardest to control and why?

2. How can we change our emotional reaction(s)?

3. Often, we can change our emotions by changing our thoughts and behaviors. How can you use this knowledge and apply it the next time you are feeling some negative emotion?

4. Sometimes we do things that we regret when we are sad or experiencing some other negative emotion. Describe why this might be based on Tice's (2001) research on impulse control.

After You Read, Practice Test #1

1. Which of the following statements about motivation is incorrect? (416)
    A. It is usually external to the individual
    B. It tends to be involved in the initiation and maintenance of behavior
    C. It is goal directed
    D. It is considered the link between internal states and external behavior

2. That organisms are motivated by instinct is a statement of _____. (417)
    A. Drive theory.
    B. Evolutionary theory
    C. Drive theory
    D. Cognitive theory

3. Maggie is considering leaving her abusive husband. Leaving would bring her physical security, but she has no job skills to support herself. Maggie is faced with a(n) _____ conflict (419)
    A. Approach-approach
    B. Avoidance-avoidance
    C. Approach-avoidance
    D. Double approach-avoidance

4. According to arousal theory, optimal performance occurs when arousal is matched with _____. (420)
    A. Previous experience
    B. The requirements of the task
    C. The motivation of the individual
    D. Rewards available in the environment

5. Maslow's humanistic theory of motivation _____. (423)
    A. Rejects drive theories
    B. Is an expectancy theory
    C. Is a unique theory that has nothing in common with the other theories
    D. Incorporates the best elements of drive, expectancy, and cognitive theories

6. What part of the brain regulates eating behavior? (426)
    A. Hypothalamus
    B. Amygdala
    C. Superior colliculus
    D. Reticular formation

7. At the age of 40, Dmitri suffered an injury that resulted in the complete removal of both of his testes. The most likely result of this removal on Dmitri's sexual activity is _____. (430)
   A.   He will no longer become sexually aroused
   B.   He will likely evidence a decreased interest in interest and performance
   C.   He will no longer feel pleasure with this orgasm
   D.   There will be no major change in his sexual activity

8. Name the stage of the sexual response cycle in which the body returns to its normal state. (431)
   A.   Post-orgasmic
   B.   Plateau
   C.   Recovery
   D.   Resolution

9. For adults who show a high need for achievement, a typical pattern of their childhood experiences is that (436)
   A.   A need for achievement developed in high school
   B.   They got lower than average grades in elementary school
   C.   Their parents praised them for their achievements
   D.   They were the same as people with low achievement needs

10. Which of the following theories of emotion contends that emotions are cognitive based and thought alone can elicit an emotion? (445)
    A.   Canon-Bard
    B.   Schacter-Singer
    C.   Valins-Reisenzein
    D.   James-Lange

After You Read, Practice Test #2

1. A state of physiological imbalance that is usually accompanied by arousal is a(n) _____.
   (417)
   A. Drive
   B. Need
   C. Impulse
   D. Trigger

2. Which theory of motivation assumes a need for balance or homeostasis? (417)
   A. Cognitive theory
   B. Arousal theory
   C. Drive theory
   D. Humanistic theory

3. A social need is an aroused condition that involves feeling good about each of the
   following, except _____. (421)
   A. Relationships
   B. Goals
   C. Self
   D. Others

4. Which of the following is a key element in expectancy theory? (421)
   A. Thoughts guide behavior
   B. Physiological drives are of little importance in human behavior
   C. Emotions can be motives
   D. Motives can be reinforced

5. According to Maslow's hierarchy of needs, the very first needs that must be met are
   _____ needs. (423)
   A. Love and recognition
   B. Recognition and approval
   C. Physiological and safety
   D. Cognitive and aesthetic

6. Which of the statements about hormones and sexual behavior is correct? (430)
   A. Hormones are solely responsible for sexual behavior
   B. Hormones interact with gender roles to impact sexuality
   C. Hormones are related to secondary sex characteristics but not adult sexual behavior
   D. Hormones are best thought of as only a part of sexual behavior in humans

7. Which is the correct order of the stages of the human sexual cycle? (430-431)
   A. Plateau; excitement; orgasm; resolution
   B. Excitement; plateau; resolution; orgasm
   C. Resolution; excitement; orgasm; plateau
   D. Excitement; plateau; orgasm; resolution

8.   Studies of sexual practices find that men and women _____. (431)
    A.   Are becoming more similar with regard to sexual behaviors
    B.   Tend to differ with regard to the acceptability of oral sex
    C.   Are becoming less similar with regard to sexual behaviors
    D.   Have similar sex drives throughout their development

9.   A social need that directs people to work for excellence and success is called (435)
    A.   Inspiration
    B.   Achievement
    C.   Affiliation
    D.   Self-actualization

10. Neither the James-Lange nor the Cannon-Bard approach considered the idea that a person's _____ might alter their reaction/response to a situation. (440-441)
    A.   Motivation
    B.   Arousal
    C.   Emotional state
    D.   Thoughts

After You Read, Practice Test #3

1. The state that results when people have to make a difficult choice is called (418)
   A. Frustration
   B. Conflict
   C. Arousal
   D. Anxiety

2. A state that involve activation of the central nervous system, the autonomic nervous system and the muscles and glands is called (419)
   A. Motivation
   B. Expectancy
   C. Arousal
   D. Homeostasis

3. The overjustification effect applies to only inherently _____ tasks. (422).
   A. Difficult
   B. Interesting
   C. Routine
   D. Large

4. When you engage in behavior for some external gain, the behavior is said to be _____ _____. When you engage in behavior for the internal pleasure, the behavior is said to be _____ _____. (422)
   A. Social need; motive driven
   B. Extrinsically motivated; intrinsically motivated
   C. Goal directed; pleasure directed
   D. Self actualization; overjustification effect

5. One of the most powerful stimuli in the environment that affects hunger is _____. (426)
   A. Time of day
   B. Previous meal
   C. Type of food being served
   D. Location

6. Obesity is _____. (428)
   A. Not at all genetically caused
   B. Is related to the number of fat cells the individual has
   C. Is primarily caused by environmental factors
   D. Is unrelated to metabolism

7. A person who is attracted to and has a preference for members of the opposite sex is called. (433)
   A. Metrosexual
   B. Heterosexual
   C. Homosexual
   D. Bisexual

8. One way to measure the need for achievement is through the Thematic Apperception Test (TAT), which involves asking people to _____. (436)
   A. Tell about their childhood experiences
   B. Describe their own attitudes and opinions
   C. Select the alternatives that are more true for them
   D. Answer questions about vague, ambiguous pictures

9. What do polygraphs measure? (441)
   A. Arousal
   B. Honesty
   C. Lies
   D. All of the above

10. A person's evaluation of the significance of a situation or an event in terms of the person's well being is called their _____. (446).
    A. Opinion
    B. Appraisal
    C. Schema
    D. Assessment

After You Read, Comprehensive Self Test

1. Motivation is an internal condition that does each of the following to an organism's goal directed behavior, except _____. (416)
    A. Initiates
    B. Activates
    C. Maintains
    D. Improves

2. When Meghan's parents caught her aggravating her sister, she was given the option of two consequences, loss of a privilege or quiet time in her room. Meghan was faced with a _____.(419)
    A. Approach-Avoidance conflict
    B. Approach-Approach conflict
    C. Avoidance-Approach conflict
    D. Avoidance-Avoidance conflict

3. Cognitive theory focuses on _____ as initiators and determiners of behavior. (421)
    A. Sensory stimulation
    B. External cues
    C. Thoughts
    D. Arousal

4. Which term refers to behavior that people engage in for no reward other than the pleasure of the activity itself? (422)
    A. Achievement motivated
    B. Power motivated
    C. Extrinsically motivated
    D. Intrinsically motivated

5. If a behavior that is intrinsically rewarding is first rewarded and then those rewards are stopped, its occurrence is decreased. That is called the _____. (422)
    A. Overt cost of rewards
    B. Covert cost of rewards
    C. Overregularization effect
    D. Overjustification effect

6. How would early motivation theorists have described the needs at the base of Maslow's pyramid? (423)
    A. Social motives
    B. Drives
    C. Expectations
    D. Incentives

7. Human male's sex hormones are _____ while female sex hormones are _____. (430)
    A. Androgens; estrogens
    B. Estrogens; androgens
    C. Pheromones; cholesterones
    D. Cholesterones; pheromones

8. Vasocongestion, or engorgement of blood vessels in the genital area, is usually a sign of _____.(430)
    A. The beginnings of a person's orgasm
    B. An abnormally high level of hormones
    C. The beginnings of sexual arousal
    D. A problem that interferes with sexual activity

9. One general finding of most scientific research on American sexual attitudes and behaviors is that _____. (432-433)
    A. People have more sexual activities when they are younger
    B. Very few women engage in premarital sexual activity
    C. Most people are unsatisfied with the quality of their sex lives
    D. There are more male homosexuals than people realize

10. John feels like he is a good psychology student and generally feels like he will do well on his exams. John displays _____. (437)
    A. An overinflated ego
    B. Self-efficacy
    C. Confidence
    D. Schema control

11. Which of the following tests is used to measure achievement motivation? (436)
    A. Thematic Apperception Test
    B. Achievement-Affiliation Survey
    C. Self-Effacement Exam
    D. Intelligence and Achievement Test-3rd Edition

12. Which of the following is not included in the definition of emotion? Emotions _____. (440)
    A. Have motivating properties that impel and direct behavior
    B. Have a private, personal, unique, and subjective component
    C. Are the result of irrational thoughts
    D. Are generally accompanied by physiological changes

13. Whose theory states that people do not experience emotion until after their bodies become aroused? (440)
    A. Cannon's
    B. James-Lange
    C. Schachter-Singer
    D. Shaver's

14. Women _____. (448-449)
    A.   Are more emotional than men
    B.   Experience less anger than men
    C.   Have different rules for displaying emotion than men
    D.   Have stronger physiological responses to emotion than men

15. If we wanted to control our emotions, we would likely be able to do this best if we focused on _____ (449-450).
    A.   The situation that was making us angry
    B.   People who feel the same way that we do
    C.   Past experience with similar situation
    D.   Our cognitive interpretations

True or False

1. According to Miller's research on approach-avoidance conflicts, a person's tendency to approach or avoid is not correlated with the strength of one's motivation. (419)

2. According to the Yerkes-Dodson principle, optimal human performance requires matching the level of arousal to the tasks requirements. (420)

3. Research conclusively suggests that you should not provide external motivation (e.g., rewards) for tasks that a person is intrinsically motivated to engage in. (422)

4. A low-carbohydrate diet may work against losing weight because it is high in fat. (429)

5. In industrialized countries such as the United States, differences between men and women with regard to sexual behavior have been decreasing. (431)

6. Research on the need for affiliation and social support suggests that people seek out others both when they feel good and when they feel bad. (438)

7. The belief that men experience more anger than women is largely inaccurate and due to commonly held gender stereotypes. (448)

8. Behavioral research indicates the controlling one's emotion is relatively easy if people are motivated to do so. (449-450)

Essay Questions

1. Summarize the role of the hypothalamus in regulating eating behavior. (426)

2. Describe Tice's (2001) research on the role of emotions in impulse control. (449-450)

When You Have Finished!

Surf's Up!!

After you've read and reviewed, try these web sites for additional information about some of the topics covered in this chapter.

1. **The Kinsey Institute** (http://www.indiana.edu/~kinsey/)
    This site is dedicated to information about research in sex, gender, and reproduction that was developed out of the work of Alfred C. Kinsey. Kinsey was one of the first and most influential researchers within the field of human sexuality.
2. **Positive Psychology Center** (http://www.positivepsychology.org/)
    This site is dedicated to promoting the emerging field of positive psychology, which focuses on growth and positive emotions.
3. **Self-Determination Theory: An Approach to Human Motivation and Personality** (http://www.psych.rochester.edu/SDT/index.html)
    Here you will find information on a theory of human motivation which examines the role of voluntary behavior within social contexts. Of the many links of interest is a questionnaire on intrinsic motivation that you could take.
4. **Brain and Emotions Research, University of Wisconsin-Madison** (http://www.new.wisc.edu/packages/emotion/)
    At this site, you will find a number of interesting links to information about the relationship between emotions and brain functioning. One of the most fascinating sections is devoted to images and movies where you can watch the brain responding to various emotional states.
5. **Emotions Annonymous** (http://www.EmotionsAnonymous.org/)
    A twelve-step program that is similar to alcoholics anonymous and focuses on the recovery from emotional difficulties.
6. **Encyclopedia of Psychology: Motivation** (http://www.psychology.org/links/Environment_Behavior_Relationships/Motivation/)
    You will find a number of links to text articles on the web that further discuss some of the basic and more complex aspects of motivation and emotion.
7. **Controlling Anger Before it Controls You** (http://www.apa.org/pubinfo/anger.html)
    Here you will find information about what anger is, how you can manage it, and strategies to keep the anger in control.

Cross Check: Motivation and Emotion

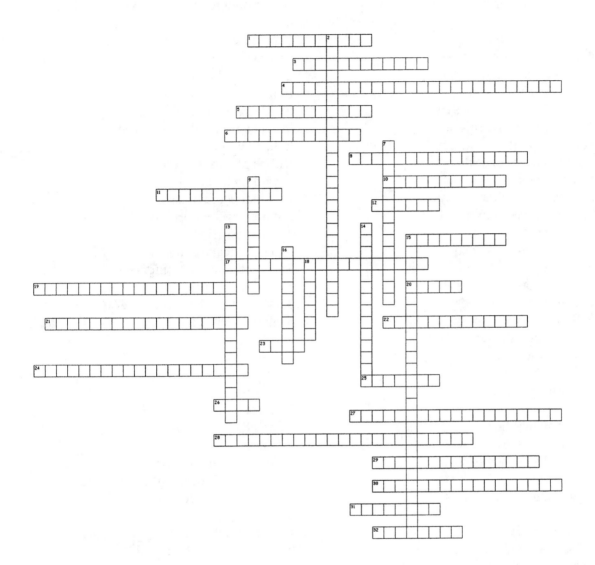

Across

1. Maintenance of steady state of inner balance
3. Rules for displaying emotion in different cultures
4. Choice between one good and one bad alternative
5. Person's belief that she can successfully engage in and execute a specific behavior
6. Second phase of sexual response cycle
8. Explains behavior in way that emphasizes growth and choice
10. Third phase of sexual response cycle
11. States that organisms are motivated to fulfill needs
12. Specific condition of arousal, which directs behavior toward a goal
15. Person's evaluation of the significance of a situation or event
17. Social need that motivates person to be with and establish relationships with others
19. Social need that directs person to strive for excellence and success
20. Internal condition that directs one to fulfill physiological need
21. Explains behavior by looking at what people expect from situations
22. Assistance from others, either emotionally or practically
23. Experience of becoming completely and pleasurably absorbed
24. Motive directed at reward from self

25. Subjective response with corresponding physiological change
26. State of physiological imbalance
27. Motive directed at reward from environment
28. Decrease in likelihood that an intrinsically motivated task, after being rewarded, will be performed when reward no longer given
29. Final phase of sexual response cycle
30. Highest level of psychological development
31. Emotional state generated by need to choose
32. Fixed behavior occurring in all members of species

Down

2. Choice between two good alternatives
7. Engorgement of blood vessels during sexual response cycle
9. Arousal that directs people to behave in way that makes them feel good about self and others
13. Stresses the role of thought in motivation
14. Initial phase of sexual response
15. Choice between two bad alternatives
16. Internal condition that initiates or motivates behavior
18. Physiological activation

Created by Puzzlemaker at DiscoverySchool.com

Chapter 13

Personality and Its Assessment

Before you read...

You may have spent time thinking about questions such as, "Who am I?" and "What things have influenced my sense of myself?" In addition, it is not uncommon to wonder about others and attempt to predict what others might do in certain situations. These questions are similar to those studied by psychologists in the area of personality psychology. In this chapter, you will be introduced to a wide variety of different theories regarding both how to describe personality and how personality might develop. In addition, you will find out how psychologists attempt to measure personality and some of the strengths and weaknesses of these approaches.

The chapter begins with an overview of personality and a discussion of the basic questions that are asked by personality psychologists. In addition, the important role of cultural influences on personality is also discussed. Following this brief introduction, you are introduced to one of the first, most comprehensive and influential theories of personality- the psychodynamic theory. In this section, Sigmund Freud's psychodynamic model of personality is reviewed in depth, and some of the psychodynamic theorists who broke from Freud, such as Adler and Jung, are also discussed. If you have ever acted in a certain way without really being sure what motivated you, these theories could help explain that experience!

Following the discussion of psychodynamic theories of personality, you will be introduced to the behavioral and trait theories of personality development. If you recall previous discussions of behavioral psychology from earlier readings, you might already suspect that behavioral approaches to personality are based on learning and that our personality is a result of learning from our environment. In contrast, trait theories of personality seek to describe rather than explain personality. You should be familiar with this approach from your own attempts to describe who you are or how you might respond to your environment. For example, if you say that you are conscientious (which you are if you are reading this!), then you have just described yourself using one of the "Big Five" supertraits that you will learn about in this section.

The final two theories of personality that are discussed include the humanistic and cognitive theories. Humanistic theories arose partly in response to Freud's theory and focus on a person's striving for growth and fulfillment versus seeking to satisfy basic sexual and aggressive needs. In addition, these theories introduce the importance of environmental and internal factors that influence one's struggle to fully realize one's human potential. In a similar way, cognitive theories focus on interactive role of thought process and behavior in the development of personality. In addition, cognitive psychologists (like their behavioral counterparts) focus on the importance of learning. However, the focus is more on how we learn to think about ourselves and our own abilities, versus learning to engage in certain behaviors.

The last section in this chapter looks at personality assessment. You have likely taken some sort of test in your lifetime that was aimed at telling you something about your personality. In this section, you will be introduced to some of the most common tests of this nature that are used by psychologists to understand people, explore the importance of personality, and help in applied tasks such as treatment planning and even career placement and advising.

Learning Objectives

After reading this chapter, you should be able to:

1. Define the term personality, and discuss the importance of viewing personality from within a cultural context.
2. Describe the three levels of thought described by Freud, list and define the three structures of the mind, and explain the relationship between the three primary structures of the mind and the different levels of thought as discussed in Freudian theory.
3. Summarize Freud's psychosexual stage theory of personality development and identify the conflicts experienced at each stage and the adult characteristics associated with each.
4. Identify the major defense mechanisms and explain how people use these to reduce anxiety.
5. Describe the 6 concepts of importance to Adler's personality theory and explain how his approach is different from Freud's psychodynamic theory.
6. Describe the similarities and differences between Jung and Freud and the four key archetypes discussed in Jung's theory.
7. Describe the behavioral approach to personality development, state how it differs from other personality theories, and discuss the role of reinforcement and punishment in personality development.
8. Name the three categories of traits defined by Allport, and compare this theory to Cattell's trait theory.
9. List and describe the three bipolar dimensions of Eysenck's type theory.
10. Describe the five "supertraits" in the Five-Factor Model.
11. Compare and contrast the humanistic approaches with other personality theories.
12. Explain Maslow's hierarchical model of personality development and discuss the characteristics of people who have achieved self-actualization.
13. Identify Rogers' basic assumptions about personality and the factors associated with its development, and explain the relationship between the self and personality.
14. Summarize the importance of positive psychology and explain how it is different from other humanistic theories of personality.
15. Characterize some of the assumptions made by cognitive personality theorists and explain how this theory differs from the traditional behavioral model.
16. Discuss the role of personal constructs in understanding personality according to Kelly.
17. Define and differentiate between an internal and external locus of control and state how this differentiation is important in understanding behavior.
18. Using Bandura's model, explain the importance of having a strong sense of self-efficacy, how this aspect of personality develops, and how gender norms can influence it.
19. Discuss how Mischel's self-regulatory process allows people to respond flexibly to various situations.
20. Define what is meant by a personality assessment, identify some of the most popular instruments used in personality assessment, and explain the difference(s) between objective and projective personality tests.

Key Terms

Personality
Psychodynamic Theory
Conscious
Preconscious
Unconscious
Id
Ego
Psychosexual Stages
Superego
Oral Stage
Anal Stage
Phallic Stage
Oedipus Complex
Latency Stage
Genital Stage
Libido
Defense Mechanism
Repression
Rationalization
Fixation
Regression
Projection
Reaction Formation
Displacement
Denial
Sublimation
Social Interest
Collective Unconscious
Archetypes
Trait
Type
Factor Analysis
Self-Actualization
Fulfillment
Unconditional Positive Regard
Self
Self-Concept
Ideal Self
Personal Constructs
Self-Efficacy
Assessment
Projective Tests

As you read...

What Is Personality?

1.   Personality is _____.

2.   List 5 questions personality research and theory should be able to answer.

13-1   **Personality in the Cultural Context**

1.   Define culture.

2.   Do cultural differences affect personality?

What is the Psychodynamic Approach to Personality?

1.   Freud's theory of personality is called the _____ theory, whereas the accompanying approach to therapy he developed is called _____.

2.   Describe the 5 key assumptions of psychoanalytic theory.

3.   Match the following levels of consciousness with the appropriate definition.
       Preconscious   *Unconscious*   *Conscious*

   a)   _____ The thoughts, feelings, and actions a person is *aware* of. This is the first level of consciousness and is very easy to study and understand.
   b)   _____ Mental activity (thoughts and feelings) that a person can become aware of if they closely pay attention to them. This is the second level of consciousness; it takes a little time and effort to study and understand it.
   c)   _____ Thoughts and feelings beyond normal awareness. This is the third level of consciousness; so deeply repressed, it can be studied and understood only by spending a lot of time and effort using a technique like psychoanalysis, according to Freud.

4.   List and describe the 3 basic structures of the mind.

5.   The id is guided by the _____ principle, whereas the ego is guided by the _____ principle.

6.   The ego ideal and conscience are related to which structure of the mind?

7.   Describe how the pleasure principle, reality principle, ego ideal, and conscience are related to one another in guiding and directing human behavior.

8.   List Freud's 5 stages of personality development and explain the conflicts associated with each stage.

9.   An adult who is overly flirtatious, vain, or promiscuous is likely to have had problems at which stage of development according to Freud's theory?

10.   The _____ complex involves the child's sexual feelings toward the opposite sex parent and jealousy of the same sex parent.

11.   Describe how the Oedipus complex is resolved.

12.   People tend to be motivated by two primary forces, a life drive referred to as the _____, and a _____ drive.

13.   What is a defense mechanism?

14.   List and describe the 8 types of defense mechanisms.

Psychology

15. Match the following defense mechanisms to the appropriate definition.

repression   *projection*   *denial*   *reaction formation*
rationalization   *sublimation*   *fixation*   *regression*   *displacement*

    a) _____ Making unreasonable feelings and behaviors seem reasonable by reinterpreting them.
    b) _____ Refusing to accept reality and the true source of anxiety.
    c) _____ Attributing one's own undesirable traits to others.
    d) _____ Behaving in a manner that is opposite to one's true, but anxiety-producing, feelings.
    e) _____ Anxiety-producing feelings are blocked from conscious awareness and pushed into the unconscious. For Freud this defense mechanism was the most important to understand.
    f) _____ Energy from an impulse that might be considered taboo is channeled or redirected into a socially acceptable form.

13-2   Adler and Individual Psychology

1. Define individual psychology and state how it is different than Freud's theory.

2. List and describe the 6 concepts of Adler's theory.

3. Adler terms the feeling of oneness with all of humanity _____ _____.

4. What is the role of early recollections in Adler's therapy?

13-3   Jung and Analytical Psychology

1. Compare and contrast Jung's theory with Freud's theory.

2. The _____ _____ refers to a shared storehouse of primitive ideas and images that reside in the _____.

3. Define archetypes and list and describe the 4 key archetypes in Jung's theory.

4.   The _____ _____ is the archetype of nourishment and destruction.

5.   What is a mandala and how is it related to the self-archetype?

Can Personality Be Learned?

1.   Describe the role of learning in personality development as described by behaviorists?

2.   According to _____ conditioning, behavior is more likely to reoccur if it is _____, and it is more likely to decrease in frequency if it is _____.

3.   How can you tell the difference between reinforcement and punishment?

13-4   Skinner and Behavioral Analysis: Acquiring a Personality

1.   Why are behavioral psychologists such as Skinner against the use of private events and concepts such as inner drives in describing personality?

2.   Describe the role of natural selection and cultural evolution in forming personality.

What Are Trait and Type Theories of Personality?

1.   A _____ is defined as any readily identifiable stable quality that characterizes how an individual differs from another individual.

2.   How is a type related to a trait?

13-5   Allport's Personal Disposition Theory

1.   Define personal dispositions.

2.   Describe the 3 categories of traits in Allport's Personal Disposition Theory.

3.   Describe Allport's cardinal, central, and secondary traits and give an example of each.
   a)   Cardinal traits
           Example

   b)   Central traits
           Example

   c)   Secondary traits
           Example

4.   We should look at a person's _____ of central traits in order to best understand that person.

13-6   Cattell's Trait Theory

1.   Factor analysis is _____.

2.   How might basing a theory on factor analysis be superior to models such as Allport's, which are based on theory and common sense?

3.   Describe the 2 types of traits in Cattell's theory.

13-7   Eysenck's Factor Theory

1.   List and describe Eysenck's 3 basic bipolar dimensions.

2.   People who are low in the neuroticism scale are said to _____
      _____.

3.   How can you explain a person who is a sensation seeker using Eysenck's theory?

13-8   The Five Factor Model

1.   List and describe the Big Five personality traits.

2.   Complete the table to describe the trait categories that have come to be known as the *Big Five* by modern day psychologists.

Trait Categories	Description
Extroversion-introversion	
	The extent to which people are good-natured or irritable, courteous or rude, flexible or stubborn, lenient or critical.
Conscientiousness-undirectedness	
Neuroticism-stability	
	The extent to which people are open to experience or closed, original or conventional, independent or conforming, creative or uncreative, daring or timid.

3.   Discuss some of the research findings that support the Five-Factor Model.

What Characterizes the Humanistic Approach to Personality?

1.   How are humanistic theories different from other personality theories?

2.   Humanistic theories suggest that people are motivated by _____.

3.   The approach to human personality that emphasizes the unique and individual meaning and experience is the _____ approach.

13-9   Maslow and Self-Actualization

1.   Describe the bottom, middle, and top ladder of Maslow's hierarchy of human needs.

2.   The realization of one's full human potential is called _____ _____.

3.   Describe the self-actualized person.

13-10 Rogers and Self Theory

1.   What are Roger's 3 basic assumptions about human behavior?

2.   Fulfillment is an inborn tendency that _____.

3.   What 3 things do humans need for growth?

4.   Describe the self.

5.   The person one would ideally like to be is called the _____ _____.

6. When does psychological stagnation occur?

7. According to Rogers' research, a fully-functioning person possesses what characteristics?

13-11 Positive Psychology

1. What is positive psychology and how is it different than traditional humanistic theory?

2. How have optimism, personality, and culture been studied within positive psychology?

What Is the Cognitive Approach to Personality?

1. Ways of understanding the world that are based on personal interpretation are _____ _____.

2. Kelly believed that personal constructs wee formed by combining what two factors?

13-12 Rotter and Locus of Control

1. Locus of control is defined as _____.

2. Describe people with an internal locus of control and those with an external locus of control, and provide some examples of how they might differentially interpret some events.

3. Summarize some of the research that links locus of control to certain behaviors.

13-13 Bandura and Self-Efficacy

1. Define self-efficacy and describe its impact and interaction with the environment and self-worth.

2. How do gender and culture impact self-efficacy?

13-14 Mischel's Cognitive-Affective Personality System

1. A psychologist who focuses on the relationship between stable personality traits and the situation are called _____.

2. Define self-regulation and provide one example.
3.

4. Mischel believes that a given individual's behaviors are relatively _____ from one situation to another, but basically _____ over time.

5. Describe Mischel's 5 cognitive-affective personality units.

6. Mischel's view of personality is different from the other views because it considers _____ and _____ more than other theories.

How Do Psychologists Assess Personality?

1. An assessment involves evaluating an individual using what means?

2. What is a projective test?

3. The _____ _____ Test is a series of inkblots that are presented to an individual who is then asked to describe what they see in the inkblot.

4.   What is the TAT?

13-15 Personality Inventories

1.   What is a personality inventory?

2.   Describe the Myers-Briggs Type Indicator.

3.   What personality inventories have been developed out of trait theory?

4.   What is the NEO-PI-R?

5.   The _____ _____ _____ is based on Maslow's humanistic theory of personality.

6.   Describe the Minnesota Multiphasic Personality Inventory-2.

After You Read, Practice Test #1

1. One of the key characteristics of personality is that it consists of traits or characteristics that are _____. (456)
   A. Environmentally determined
   B. Permanent
   C. Unstable across situations
   D. Independent of culture

2. According to personality research, which of the following statements about the relationship between culture and personality is true? (456-457)
   A. Cultural norms and values regarding such things as enforcing societal rules have been associated with certain behavioral tendencies such as conformity
   B. Culture tends to be more important in collectivist cultures as apposed to individualist cultures
   C. Very few personality characteristics have been shown to exist in cultures throughout the world
   D. Personality traits do not vary considerably across cultures

3. The _____ is the personality structure that serves as a person's conscience. (460)
   A. Ego
   B. Superego
   C. Id
   D. Defense mechanism

4. Georgia is very controlled in everything she does. Her desk must be neat at all times; she apologizes for the slightest hedging on someone's privacy; she cannot be spontaneous. In understanding Freud's psychosexual stages we could predict that Georgia is fixated in the _____ stage. (461)
   A. Oral
   B. Anal
   C. Phallic
   D. Genital

5. Clyde has a number of extremely hostile unconscious feelings. Unknowingly, he reduces the anxiety that these feelings produce by getting involved in highly aggressive sports, such as rugby. He is using the defense mechanism known as _____. (464)
   A. Sublimation.
   B. Denial
   C. Reaction formation
   D. Projection

6. Which of the following is an example of a "type?" (472)
    A. Energetic
    B. Apprehensive
    C. Prejudice
    D. Introverted, shy, withdrawn

7. According to Allport many people do not have _____. (473)
    A. Central traits
    B. Source traits
    C. Cardinal traits
    D. Secondary traits

8. Many modern day psychologists use the *Big Five* model to understand personality because: (474)
    A. They can identify over 100,000 different traits
    B. It provides them with a concise description of "super traits" which describes the dispositions that characterize most people
    C. It's based on Einstein's theory of relativity
    D. They can avoid placing personality labels on individuals

9. A person's view of themselves and how they see their own behavior is referred to as what in Rogers' theory of personality? (477)
    A. Self-thoughts
    B. Self-concept
    C. Self-esteem
    D. Self-efficacy

10. The _____ is one of the most widely used and researched personality tests. (488)
    A. 16 Personality Factors
    B. California Psychological Inventory
    C. Personal Orientation Inventory
    D. Minnesota Multiphasic Personality Inventory-2

After You Read, Practice Test #2

1. _____ refers to a pattern of relatively permanent traits, dispositions, or characteristics that lead to some consistency in an individual's behavior. (456)
   A. Patterns
   B. Persistence
   C. Persona
   D. Personality

2. The ego _____. (459)
   A. Is a preconscious behavior
   B. Manages the demands of the id and ego
   C. Acts like the moral branch for the id
   D. Works according to the pleasure principle

3. The Oedipus conflict arises and must be resolved during the _____ stage of psychosexual development. (461)
   A. Genital
   B. Phallic
   C. Anal
   D. Oral

4. Select the term used by Jung to refer to the store of images and ideas that we inherit from our ancestors and share with all human beings. (468)
   A. Primal representation
   B. Racial memory
   C. Psychic structure
   D. Collective unconscious

5. According to behaviorists theorists, personality _____. (470)
   A. Characteristics are stable and enduring
   B. Is the sum of a person's learning
   C. Characteristics are difficult to change
   D. Has a large genetic component

6. _____ differentiated between source traits and surface traits while _____ differentiated between cardinal, central, and secondary traits. (473)
   A. Carl Rogers; Gordon Allport
   B. Gordon Allport; Raymond Cattell
   C. Raymond Cattell; Carl Rogers
   D. Raymond Cattell; Gordon Allport

7. Select the most advanced level of Maslow's hierarchy of needs. (476)
   A. Self-actualization needs
   B. Physiological needs
   C. Acceptance needs
   D. Esteem needs

8. According to Rogers, unhappiness and maladjustment result from (478)
   A. Anxiety that is created by unconscious impulses
   B. Our inability to overcome our sense of inadequacy
   C. Discrepancies between the real self and the ideal self
   D. The conditioning of inappropriate behavior

9. For both men and women, research shows that their sense of self-efficacy is affected by their ability to _____. (484)
   A. Be independent and compete successfully
   B. Maintain good relationships with other people
   C. Fulfill social norms for the opposite gender
   D. Fulfill social norms for their own gender

10. According to Mischel, we base our responses on our past experiences and our assessment of the present situation, in a process he calls _____. (484)
    A. Internalization
    B. Behavior modification
    C. Self-regulation
    D. Reaction formation

After You Read, Practice Test #3

1. In Freud's view of the mind, things that we are not aware of at any moment but could be aware of easily are in the _____ mind (459)
   A. Preconscious
   B. Conscious
   C. Unconscious
   D. Nonconscious

2. What is the correct order for Freud's psychosexual stages of personality development? (460-462)
   A. Oral, anal, phallic, genital, latency
   B. Oral, anal, phallic, latency, genital
   C. Anal, oral, genital, latency, phallic
   D. Phallic, latency, genital, oral, anal

3. Freud theorized that people are energized and act the way they do because of two basic instinctual drives. They are _____. (463)
   A. Sex and aggression
   B. Instinctual gratification and minimizing punishment
   C. Release of anxiety and tension
   D. Life and death

4. A person who is a constant gossip yet considers everyone else a busybody, uses which defense mechanism? (464)
   A. Reaction formation
   B. Projection
   C. Sublimation
   D. Repression

5. According to Alfred Alder, people are motivated by feelings of _____, which leads them to strive for _____. (466)
   A. Sexual desire; gratification
   B. Social needs; recognition
   C. Feelings of inferiority; superiority
   D. Biological forces; conformity

6. Eysenck's Factor Theory argues that people have ____ basic personality traits. (473)
   A. Five
   B. Two
   C. Ten
   D. Three

7.   A person who is irritable, rude, critical would score low on which dimension of the Big
     Five model of personality (474)
     A.   Agreeableness
     B.   Introversion
     C.   Openness to experience
     D.   Neuroticism

8.   Rogers believed that _____ is an inborn tendency directing people toward self-
     actualization. (477)
     A.   Fulfillment
     B.   Idealization
     C.   Conditional regard
     D.   Phenomenology

9.   Mike always rationalizes his failures by blaming them on bad luck or the influence of other
     people. According to Rotter, he is demonstrating _____. (481)
     A.   Low self-efficacy
     B.   Faulty encoding strategies
     C.   Negative expectancies
     D.   An external locus of control

10. Select an example of a projective test of personality. (486-487)
     A.   Minnesota Multiphasic Personality Inventory-2
     B.   16 Personality Factor Questionnaire (16PF)
     C.   Rorschach Ink Blot Test
     D.   California Personality Inventory

After You Read, Comprehensive Test

1. Which of the following best defines personality? (456)
    A.   A collection of all behaviors an individual has ever emitted
    B.   The behaviors a person emits when he or she is with other people
    C.   Behaviors that a person emits over time and in most situations
    D.   Behaviors that make a person stand out in a crowd

2. Freud's model of personality and personality development is referred to as _____ theory. (458)
    A.   Psychoanalytic
    B.   Psychobehavioral
    C.   Psychosexual
    D.   Psychosomatic

3. During the oral stage of psychosexual development, the _____ is the focus of a child's primary pleasure. (460)
    A.   Anus
    B.   Same-sex parent
    C.   Opposite-sex parent
    D.   Mouth

4. Freud's theory of personality focused in two basic instincts. However, he focused mostly on sexual instincts, which he called _____ . (463)
    A.   Eroticism
    B.   Regression
    C.   Libido
    D.   The unconscious

5. The defense mechanism of rationalization involves (464)
    A.   Putting your own feelings unto someone else
    B.   Refusing to recognize that there is any problem or anxiety
    C.   Adopting behaviors that are opposite of your true feelings
    D.   Thinking of a logical, rational excuse for doing what you want

6. In Jung's view, _____ are inherited ideas and images that exist within the collective unconscious. (468)
    A.   Mandelas
    B.   Archetypes
    C.   Fixations
    D.   Actualizing tendencies

7. Jason beats his head against the walls of his room whenever his father yells at him because his father then stops yelling. From a behavioral point of view, Jason's self-destructive behavior is the result of _____. (470-471)
    A. Early childhood experiences
    B. A death wish
    C. A response that has been reinforced
    D. An overly strong libido

8. A stable defining feature of an individual's personality is a _____. (472)
    A. Factor
    B. Self-concept
    C. Type
    D. Trait

9. Hans Eysenck described personality in terms of three factors. These factors are _____. (473-474)
    A. Emotional stability, extroversion, psychoticism
    B. Introversion, openness, emotional stability
    C. Emotional stability, productivity, sensitivity
    D. Openness, extroversion, psychoticism

10. Phenomenological approaches focus on all of the following except _____. (476)
    A. Individuals unique experiences with interpreting the events in the world
    B. Examining immediate experiences rather than experiences from the past
    C. How people carve their own destinies through self-determination
    D. The controlling influence of environmental rewards and punishment

11. Self-determination is most closely associated with which of the following theories? (476)
    A. Psychoanalytic
    B. Trait
    C. Humanistic
    D. Behavioral

12. The major focus of humanistic psychology is on each individual's motivation to _____. (476)
    A. Defend against unconscious anxiety
    B. Overcome inferiority and achieve superiority
    C. Secure reinforcement and avoid punishment
    D. Achieve unique, personal goals

13. People with an external locus of control are more likely to _____. Than people with an internal locus of control. (481-482)
    A. Blame others for their mistakes
    B. Engage in preventative health measures
    C. Profit from psychotherapy
    D. Lose weight when they go on a diet

14. _____ tests are assessment instruments made up of a standard set of ambiguous stimuli. (486).
    A.   Objective
    B.   Projective
    C.   Personality
    D.   Invalid

15. Paula was asked to interpret a blob of color while a psychologist analyzed her answers Paula is likely taking what personality test? (487)
    A.   Rorschach Inkblot Test
    B.   Stochastic Modeling Test
    C.   Thematic Apperception Test
    D.   Minnesota Multiphasic Personality Inventory-2

True or False

1.   Personality traits tend to be pretty stable across cultures. (457)

2.   One of the main conflicts at the oral stage of development revolves around whether or not the child is able to receive oral gratification through activities such as cooing and thumb sucking. (461)

3.   Alfred Adler considered social interest as the primary means of judging the worth of a person's actions. (466)

4.   According to learning theories, if you want a behavior to occur less frequently, you should negatively reinforce it. (471)

5.   Research on the five-factor model suggests that there may be a genetic basis to the five supertraits described in this model. (474)

6.   According to Rogers, psychological stagnation is likely to occur when a person's behavior is inconsistent with their self-concept. (478)

7.   Mischel believes that a given individual's behaviors are relatively consistent from one situation to another, but basically inconsistent over time. (484)

8.   Systematic examinations of projective personality tests indicate that these tests are very accurate. (486)

Essay Questions

1.   Describe some of the ways that culture and personality are related. (456-457)

2.   In what ways do gender, culture, and self-efficacy interact with one another? (484)

When You Have Finished!

Surf's Up!!

After you've read and reviewed, try these web sites for additional information about some of the topics covered in this chapter.

1. **Five Factor Personality Test, the IPIP-NEO**
   (http://www.personal/psu.edu/faculty/j/5/j5j/IPIP/)
   At this site, you can take a test that assesses the big five personality traits, and you can receive feedback about how you scored.
2. **Sigmund Freud and the Freud Archives** (http://users.rcn.com/brill/freudarc.html)
   An interesting collection of internet links and resources devoted to Sigmund Freud and his work.
3. **The Personality Project** (http://www.personality-project.org)
   An excellent resource site devoted to the study of personality. You will find a lot of information on some of the current developments in personality research. In addition, you can find out where you might want to go if you are interested in a career studying personality.
4. **CG Jung Page** (http://www.cgjungpage.org/)
   Comprehensive site devoted to the work of Carl Jung.
5. **Society for Personality and Social Psychology** (http://www.spsp.org/)
   Dedicated to the study and dissemination of research in personality and social psychology.
6. **Mental Health Net-All About Personality Disorders**
   (http://mentalhelp.net/poc/center_index.php)
   Explains dysfunctional aspects of personality development and provides resources listing the symptoms associated with common personality disorders.
7. **Personal Construct Psychology** (http://repgrid.com/pcp/)
   This theory was first developed by George Kelly and is the cornerstone of the cognitive theories of personality. This site contains information about Kelly himself and a number of other links to information about, or related to, cognitive personality theories.

Cross Check: Personality

Across

2. Being stuck at a certain level of development
3. Theory of personality that focuses on unconscious processes
7. Category or broad collection of personality traits
9. In Adler's theory, a feeling of oneness with all humanity
10. Type of personality test made up of ambiguous stimuli
12. Unconscious that is shared with all others
14. Any readily identifiable stable quality of an individual
15. Defense mechanism where people redirect socially unacceptable impulses toward acceptable goals
17. Defense mechanism where person is driven by anxiety to return to earlier stage of development
21. Stage of development occurring between the ages of 7 and puberty according to Freud
22. Stage of development focused on adult sexuality
24. Type of analysis used for organizing a group of variables to detect which are related
26. Pattern of relatively permanent traits, dispositions, or characteristics
27. The self a person would ideally like to be
28. Region of mind that acts in accordance with reality
29. Stage of development related to toilet training
31. Level of mind we are currently unaware of, but may become aware of easily
33. Defense mechanism where people behave in a way opposite to what they feel
35. Defense mechanism where feelings are forced into unconsciousness

Down

1. Defense mechanism where people divert sexual or aggressive feelings onto another person or thing
4. Inherited ideas and images that exist in the collective unconscious
5. Stage of development focused on attraction to opposite sex parent
6. Thoughts occurring outside of awareness
8. Freud's developmental model consists of these
9. The conscience of the mind
11. Sexual life force
13. Region of mind that is instinctual and seeks pleasure
16. The realization of one's full human potential
18. Person's belief about whether they can successfully engage in and execute a specific behavior
19. How a person sees his behavior and internal characteristics
20. Mechanisms that guard against feelings of anxiety
23. Stage of development focused on the mouth
25. Inborn tendency toward actualization
30. Process of evaluating individual differences
32. Level of mind to which we are aware
34. Defense mechanism where people refuse to accept reality
36. Defense mechanism where people reinterpret undesirable feelings or behaviors
37. The perception that we have of ourselves

Created by Puzzlemaker at
DiscoverySchool.com

Chapter 14

Social Psychology

Before you read...

Social psychologists are interested in how individuals influence, and are influenced by, the thoughts, feelings, and behavior of others in social situations. In this chapter, you will be exposed to some of the major areas of study and interest in social psychology, including the social self, attitudes, interpersonal interactions, and the interactions between the group and the individual.

In the first part of the chapter, you are introduced to different aspects of the "self," and you will explore how these aspects relate to our ability to function within the social environment. One of the many key functions of the self that will be explored is attribution, the process of making judgments about the causes of behavior. In this section, you will find the explanation about why people tend to be harder on others than they are on themselves.

In the second part of the chapter, your attention will be turned to attitudes, the patterns of thoughts, feelings, and behaviors you have about things or people within your social environment. In this section, you will explore what an attitude is, how it might be expressed, and how you might go about producing attitude change. In addition, you will explore the relationship between attitudes and behavior, where you will find (maybe to your surprise!) that attitudes are good predictors of behavior only under certain conditions. You will also learn some of the "inside tricks" that people such as advertisers and politicians might use to sway your attitudes in their direction!

The next part of the chapter focuses in on some tried and true questions regarding social behavior such as: what is love, what attracts people to one another, why do some people engage in aggressive behavior, and is there really such a thing as a selfless act? To use the terms of social psychology, you will explore attraction and relationship formation, aggression and violence, and prosocial behavior. To all of you television watchers and video game players, you might be particularly interested in the section about the relationship between aggression and engaging in these two activities!

Finally, the chapter closes with a discussion of the mutual influence between the group and the individual. Specific issues that will be considered include how the group might facilitate or hinder individual performance, why individuals might do things within a group that they otherwise might not, and the impact of authority on group and individual decision-making. In addition, you will explore the socially relevant, and often problematic, existence of stereotypes, prejudice, and discrimination. Of particular interest is a study that reports on research indicating that our biases may be linked to specific parts of our brain!

Key Terms

Social Psychology
Self –Concept
Self-Esteem
Self-Presentation
Social Cognition
Attributions
Internal Attributions
External Attributions
Self-Serving Bias
Fundamental Attribution Error
Actor-Observer Effect
Attitudes
Implicit Attitudes
Explicit Attitudes
Social Norms
Self-Perception Theory
Elaboration Likelihood Model
Cognitive Dissonance
Self-Perception Theory
Interpersonal Attraction
Mere Exposure Effect
Friendship
Companionate Love
Consummate Love
Intimacy
Equity Theory
Aggression
Frustration-Aggression Hypothesis
Indirect Aggression
Prosocial Behavior
Altruism
Bystander Effect

Group
Social Facilitation
Social Loafing
Groupthink
Group Polarization
Deindividuation
Stereotypes
Ingroup
Outgroup
Prejudice
Discrimination
Social Learning Theory
Social Influence
Conformity
Reactance
Obedience

Learning Objectives

After reading this chapter, you should be able to:

1. Define social psychology and describe what topics might be of interest to social psychologists.
2. Identify the three aspects of the self that correspond to a person's thinking, feeling, and behavior.
3. Explain how people infer the motives and intentions of others through the process of attribution and discuss the three criteria people use to determine whether the causes of a behavior are internal or external.
4. Describe the common attribution biases and errors people make and discuss how they obscure other possible motives and intentions that drive people's behavior.
5. Define *attitude* and discuss the three dimensions of an attitude.
6. Discuss how attitudes might predict behavior and how behavior might influence attitudes.
7. List and describe the three factors that might influence the effect of attitudes on behavior.
8. Identify and explain the four components of effective persuasion, discuss how the elaboration-likelihood model might use these and other factors to account for attitudinal change, and compare and contrast central and peripheral routes to attitude change.
9. Explain how factors such as proximity, physical attractiveness, and similarity are related to interpersonal attraction.
10. Discuss the differences between friendship and different types of love, and discuss how Sternberg's theory of love and intimacy are related to these different types of relationships.
11. Discuss the role of equity and attachment in maintaining interpersonal relationships.
12. Identify and explain how biological, learning, and cognitive factors are related to aggressive behavior, and discuss whether or not aggression can be controlled.
13. Discuss the influence of television and gender on aggressive and prosocial behavior.
14. Define and differentiate between prosocial and altruistic behavior and discuss how the bystander effect may influence an individual's ability to engage in either of these behaviors in certain situations.
15. Define the concepts of social facilitation, social loafing, group polarization, groupthink, and deindividuation and discuss how these concepts are related to the performance of the individual within the group.
16. Describe the relationship between stereotypes, prejudice, and discrimination, summarize the four theoretical explanations of the causes of prejudice, and list several ways that people can work toward reducing and eliminating prejudice.
17. Explain how social influence is related to conformity, compliance, and obedience, and evaluate the methods, results and important conclusions of the classic studies by Asch and Milgram.

As you read...

Introduction to Social Psychology

1. Social psychology is interested in studying social behavior from the "inside out." Explain what this means.

2. Describe how social psychology is related to, and different from, other areas of study such as sociology and evolutionary, personality, and Gestalt psychology.

14-1   The Stanford Prison Experiment

Phillip Zimbardo conducted the Stanford Prison Experiment, and it has become a classic study within the field of social psychology. Visit the following website (http://www.prisonexp.org) and to read more about the experiment. After doing so, answer the following questions.

   a. What does this experiment tell us about attitudes and behavior?

   b. Do you think that the information gathered about social behavior was worth the ethical risks associated with conducting such a study? You might want to think about what it would have been like to be a prisoner in this study.

   c. How might we explain what happened in this experiment from the standpoint of a social psychologist versus a personality psychologist?

The Self in Social Psychology

1. According to evidence from social psychology, our sense of ourselves can be influenced by our own _____, _____, and _____ and _____.

2. Define and differentiate between self-concept, self-esteem, and self-presentation and describe how these terms are related to how we think, feel, and behave in relation to our selves.

14-2   Uncovering People's Sense of Self

You can try this activity with yourself, one of your friends or family, or even by watching your favorite television show. Start by making sure you understand the difference between the concepts of self-esteem, self-concept, and self-presentation. As you are interacting with the person that you have chosen to observe, notice the things that they do and say and keep track of whether these things represent their level of esteem, concept, or presentation. When you are done with your observation(s), write a brief description of what you know about that individual based on what they "revealed" during your interaction(s).

Thinking about Self and Others

1. Our attempts to explain the behavior of others is an example of _____ _____.

2. Define attributions and differentiate between internal and external attributions.

3. After dating someone for a month, that person suddenly and unexpectedly breaks off the relationship. How might you explain your partner's behavior using an internal attribution? An external attribution?

4. List and describe the three criteria people use to decide if a behavior is caused by internal or external factors according to Harold Kelly's theory of attribution.

5. You just got an "A" on a test in one class, and a "C" on a test in another class. How might you explain these two events using a self-serving bias? According to research, would you be more likely to use this bias if you were a male or a female?

6. Define and differentiate between the fundamental attribution error and actor-observer effect.

7. The fact that culture influences attributional style is evident from the finding that individuals from individualist cultures tend to make more _____ attributions, whereas individuals from more collectivist cultures tend to make more _____ attributions.

14-3   Biases and Attributional Errors

Read each of the following statements and decide whether it demonstrates a self-serving bias, actor-observer effect, or the fundamental attribution error.

a. A student just got the results of an examination back where they got a "C" and the class average was a "C-." When asked why they got a "C," the student responded, "the instructor didn't prepare me well enough." However, when asked why many of their classmates did poorly, the student replied, "they probably didn't study hard enough."

b. A member of a jury was asked what factors lead to him providing a guilty verdict even though the evidence suggested that there were strong situational factors related to the crime. The juror stated that he believed the person on trial was a "natural born criminal" who had very little chance of "changing his ways" in the future.

c. A famous pianist was playing his new piece with a full orchestra on two nights. The first night went very well, however, the second evening she had a number of errors during the performance. After the show, the pianist concluded that the orchestra must have had a bad night and influenced her performance.

Dimensions of Attitudes

1. Define and provide an example of an attitude.

2. List and describe the three dimensions of an attitude.

3. An _____ attitude is one that we are consciously aware of and able to describe, whereas a _____ attitude is one that we are not aware of that is automatically activated and uncontrollable.

14-4   De-constructing an Attitude

Listed below are two attitudes. Read each of them carefully and pick out the cognitive, emotional/evaluative, and behavioral/action components of each attitude.

a. John is an avid fan of the Cleveland Indians baseball team, but he dislikes their current coach. At a recent baseball game, John booed every time the coach came out of the dugout.

b. Olivia loves the Broadway musicals and attends at least 5 shows a year. When asked why she likes musicals so much, she stated, "they just seem to capture the essence of life."

The Relationship Between Attitudes and Behavior

1. Describe four variables that affect whether or not attitudes predict behavior.

2. You smoke cigarettes. However, you are with a group of friends who does not smoke and dislikes smoking. According to what you know about social norms, what would you predict about your smoking behavior that night? If you have a really strong belief that you should be able to smoke wherever you want, your response to the first question might differ. Explain why.

3. Behaviors are not predicted well by _____ attitudes.

4. Define self-perception theory and describe how it is different than the "common sense" view of the interaction between attitudes and behavior?

5. According to cognitive dissonance theory, what conditions must be present to produce the motivation to change one's behavior or attitudes?

14-5	**Problems with Parenting**

One of the problems that parents of adolescent children often experience is that their child seems to form even more positive feelings toward a certain activity or people <u>after</u> their parents prohibit them from that activity or person. The child's shift in attitude often happens after they have angrily protested and discussed the values of that activity or person. How would you explain the adolescent's shift in attitudes based on your knowledge of self-perception theory and what advice might you give to parents in dealing with this situation in the future?

Attitude Change through Persuasion

1. Describe Hoveland's four key components of effective persuasion.

2. A communicator needs to be _____, _____, and _____ to be effective at changing a person's attitudes.

3. Advertisers frequently run the same ads over and over again within a program and over time with the hope that your attitudes toward that project will _____. What persuasion effect are advertisers using?

4. Television, radio, and face-to-face communications are all examples of types of _____ that may be used to persuade people to change. Of these three examples, which is likely to be the most effective?

5. List some aspects of the audience that influence attitude change.

6. The _____ _____ model suggests that people who are highly motivated to think about issues logically and who have the time to do so, are more likely to be influenced via the _____ route to change.

7. Define and differentiate between the central and peripheral routes to change and list some factors that might influence when you would use one versus the other.

14-6   **Watch TV and Learn!**

Pick two different types or times to watch television. It will be helpful if you pick programs that might be aimed at different audiences (e.g., young children vs. old, educational programming vs. prime time programming, etc.). Record two commercials from each program and describe what the commercial was attempting to sell you. Once you have done this, see if you can figure out what methods of influence they were trying to use. Also identify whether they used a central or peripheral route to change.

14-7   **Change**

Attempt to design a program that is intended to change other students attitudes about a proposed increase in the number of credit hours needed to graduate. Use what you know about (a) Hoveland and colleagues model, (b) Elaboration-likelihood model, and (c) Cognitive dissonance theory.

Interpersonal Relationships

1. According to social psychology research, individuals are likely to form relationships with people who share what three factors?

2. Relationships with others have been linked to a variety of outcomes for the individual. What are those outcomes? (Hint: there are 4 of them!).

3. If you were interested in increasing the likelihood that someone might develop positive feelings toward you, you might want to use a certain strategy based on the principal of proximity. What is that strategy?

4. What factors influence people's judgments regarding physical attraction? Are there cultural differences in what people find attractive?

5. Many people who do not like drinking might find it difficult to find a mate by going out to bars and meeting people. Based on your knowledge of similarity, why might this be and what suggestions might you give that individual for finding a mate?

6. Discuss the differences between friendship, companionate love, and consummate love and discuss how Sternberg's theory of love and intimacy are related to these different types of relationships.

7. According to equity theory, relationships are likely to be maintained when _____.

8. Bowlby described three types of attachment styles, including _____, _____, and _____.

9. Individuals with _____ attachment styles tend to be more secure in relationships.

10. Psychologists have attempted to explain aggressive behavior through what three factors?

14-8   **Why War?**

How might you explain the occurrence of war from a biological/evolutionary, learning, and cognitive perspective?

11. The authors of your book state, "violent TV programming can affect children and adults." What evidence is provided to support this statement?

12. Your book mentions two prevention programs that have been successful in reducing aggression. Explain why those programs are effective from a cognitive and learning perspective.

13. _____ is NOT an effective at reducing aggression. Explain why or why not.

14. Name a prosocial behavior and state why it is a prosocial behavior.

15. Why might behavioral and evolutionary psychologists argue that altruism does not exist?

14-9   Will You Help Me?

Below is a list of individuals or situations. Indicate if that individual would be more (M) or less (L) likely to help someone in a social situation based on what you know about the bystander effect.

    a. A man faced with a situation that requires physical action.
    b. A person witnesses a crime against a person who is a stranger to them.
    c. An off-duty police officer who sees a crime.
    d. A person with a strong sense of self-esteem.
    e. A person who witnesses an emergency in a large urban area.
    f. A man witnesses another man being robbed in the street.
    g. A person in a large group of people who witnesses a crime.
    h. A person who perceives that there is a great deal of concern by others in the group.

Groups & Group Membership

16. Describe the characteristics of a group.

17. According to Zajonc's (1965) drive theory of social facilitation, the presence of others is likely to facilitate your behavior when _____, and impair your behavior when _____.

18. What things increase and decrease social loafing?

19. The tendency for groups to seek agreement with one another when reaching a decision, rather than effectively evaluating the options is referred to as _____.

20. Making school children all wear the same uniforms to school is an example of _____.

21. The process of stereotyping can be both adaptive and maladaptive. Explain how this is true.

22. Every time I go walking in the woods, I carry a bottle of water with me. I have never been attacked by a bear in the woods. As a result, I conclude that there is a relationship between my bottle of water and being protected from bears. This would be an example of an _____ _____.

23. Describe the relationship between stereotypes, prejudice, and discrimination and summarize the four theoretical explanations of the causes of prejudice.

24. Prejudice involves both a _____ and a _____ component, whereas discrimination involves a _____ component.

14-10   Implicit Biases

Many students become confused when discussing implicit versus explicit associations and biases. Got the Implicit Association Test at http://implicit.harvard.edu/implicit and take this test. After taking the test, describe the results and briefly discuss your thoughts about the existence of implicit biases. If you have such biases, what might you do to decrease their effect on your behavior?

25. List several ways that people can work toward reducing and eliminating prejudice.

The Influence of Others on the Individual

26. What three factors might influence whether someone conforms to a group?

27. After reading the following examples, write down the type of persuasion technique that is being used in each.

   a. You read an ad telling you that computers will be on sale for $200 this Saturday. When you get there, you find that it will cost you another $500 to get the needed software, however, you buy it anyway because you had already made the decision to purchase it before leaving the house.

   b. You ask your roommate to borrow their car for the weekend for a road trip with three other friends (knowing full well that they will say no). The next day, you ask to borrow $20 because you are low on cash and they agree.

   c. You want your friends to help you hang flyers for an upcoming event all around campus. However, you start by asking them to hang the signs in their dorm first and a week later you ask them to help you with the rest of campus.

   d. Public Broadcasting tends to run pledge drives during breaks in programming that have a particularly positive tone and content to them. During the breaks, individuals directly ask for money to support the "quality programming" available through public television.

28. List and describe four variables that affect conformity.

29. Compliance with the orders of others is called _____.

30. Describe Milgram's study and discuss what it tells us about obedience.

31. In Milgram's later studies, what factors did he find reduced the probability of obedience?

After You Read, Practice Test #1

1.   Social psychology is interested in the study of _____. (496)
     A.   How personality influences behavior
     B.   The influence of the group on the individual
     C.   Our evolutionary history and factors that have aided our survival
     D.   How social groups influence one another

2.   Your favorite movie star was just arrested for driving while intoxicated (DWI). When describing why this behavior occurred, the star stated, "the police are just out to arrest famous people." This person is making what type of attribution? (498)
     A.   Self-focused
     B.   External
     C.   Informational
     D.   Internal

3.   Which of the following is the behavioral component of the attitude that children should be respected as human beings? (502)
     A.   Believing that children are worthy of all the respect you would give to an adult.
     B.   Feeling very upset if you see the rights of a child infringed upon by an adult.
     C.   Acknowledging a child for holding his or her own opinion about a social issue even if it differs from your own.
     Having a sense of elation when you read about a child who is a computer wizard and has started his or her own business

4.   Which of the following does _not_ tend to contribute to a speaker's effectiveness in promoting attitude change? (505-506)
     A.   The speaker is attractive
     B.   The audience believes the speaker is powerful and prestigious
     C.   The speaker is able to surprise the audience with new and unexpected ideas
     D.   The audience trusts the speaker

5.   Physical attractiveness seems to play a role in attraction _____. (509)
     A.   Only in our youth-oriented culture
     B.   In the Western world, but not in primitive and agricultural societies
     C.   At least at first
     D.   To men in all cultures, but not to women in all cultures

6.   Consummate love involves the presence of intimacy, commitment, and _____. (511)
     A.   Concern
     B.   Passion
     C.   Jealousy
     D.   Care

7. _____ holds that people learn their prejudices through first observing those prejudices in others and then being rewarded for holding or acting on those prejudices (526)
   A. Personality theory
   B. Cognitive theory
   C. Motivation theory
   D. Social learning theory

8. What is meant by the term "social facilitation?" (520)
   A. Negative effects on one's performance due to the presence of others
   B. Both positive and negative effects on one's performance due to the presence of others
   C. Positive effects on one's performance due to the presence of others
   D. None of the above

9. The "ask-and-ye-shall-receive" approach to compliance is most effective when _____.
   (530)
   A. The person is in a good mood, regardless of the cause
   B. The person is asked to donate a specific amount of money
   C. The person is asked to donate small amounts of money first and large amounts of money later
   D. The person is asked first to donate a large amount of money and later asked to donate a smaller amount of money

10. An adolescent who wants their parents to buy them the same clothes that "everyone else is wearing" is demonstrating _____. (528)
    A. Obedience
    B. Compliance
    C. Objectivity
    D. Conformity

After You Read, Practice Test #2

1. _____ psychology is the scientific study of how individual thoughts, feelings, and behaviors are influenced by social situations. (496)
   A. Personality
   B. Evolutionary
   C. Social
   D. Gestalt

2. Cross-cultural research on attributional errors indicates that people from individualist cultures such as the United States tend to make more _____ _____ when explaining the actions of others. (501)
   A. Internal attributions
   B. Illusory correlations
   C. Negative judgments
   D. Self-serving

3. According to Petty and Cacioppo (1985),the peripheral route to attitude change _____. (506-507)
   A. Leads to deep processing of information and decisions that are long lasting
   B. Allows a person to attend to how logical a communication actually is
   C. Has an indirect, but powerful effect.
   D. All of the above

4. According to scientific evidence, you are most likely to be attracted to_____. (508)
   A. Your neighbors and work associates
   B. People you have met only once
   C. People you have met and have difficulty visiting often
   D. People who have ideas very different from your own

5. Friendship styles, especially early in development, tend to be characterized by ____. (510)
   A. Girls engaging in friendships at an earlier age than boys
   B. Boys relying less on friendships than girls
   C. Boys engaging in more activity-based friendships
   D. Girls engaging in more age-appropriate activities with friends

6. What concept has been used by behaviorists to explain altruism? (517)
   A. Intermittent reinforcement
   B. Stimulus generalization
   C. Intrinsic rewards
   D. Successive approximation

7.   Each of the following is likely to influence whether a bystander is likely to offer help in a particular situation, except _____. (518-519)
   A.   The number of other people that are present
   B.   The number of years of education they have achieved
   C.   Their gender
   D.   The type of community they are in

8.   You are sitting with a group of friends and someone comes up with a "get rich quick" idea that involves each of you investing a substantial amount of money in a new company that one of your friends claims, "is sure to make it big." The tendency for the group to seek an agreement versus thinking logically about all of the options is referred to as _____. (521)
   A.   Grouptalk
   B.   Groupthink
   C.   Group conformity theory
   D.   Group convergence

9.   You are on your way to an event at a local theater and when you arrive, you see a picket line and people protesting that the workers at that theater are not treated fairly. As a result of that picket line, you decide to go to another theater in town. This is an example of _____ _____. (528)
   A.   Social facilitation
   B.   Group coercion
   C.   Group loafing
   D.   Social influence

10.   Dissenting opinions within a group_____. (529)
   A.   Generally strengthen the group's influence upon individuals.
   B.   Can have a substantial influence on the decision making of an individual even if only a small number people are dissenting.
   C.   Become influential only when a majority of the members agree with the opposition.
   D.   Often lead to poor group decision-making

After You Read, Practice Test #3

1. You have just moved to a new apartment building. In order to show your neighbors that you are friendly, you invite them all over to your apartment for a party. You are attempting to manipulate your _____. (497)
    A. Self-concept
    B. Self-presentation
    C. Self-esteem
    D. Self-attribution

2. Unlike personality psychologists, social psychologists believe that self-esteem _____. (497)
    A. Is dependant on genetics
    B. Changes depending upon the time and situation
    C. Cannot be measured
    D. Is not important to understanding behavior

3. According to Harold Kelly's theory of attribution, people decide what causes behavior based on each of the following characteristics, except _____. (499)
    A. Confrontinveness
    B. Consensus
    C. Distinctiveness
    D. Consistency

4. That people will begin to think positively about a persuasive message if they hear is repeatedly is called _____. (506)
    A. Low balling
    B. Persuasive appeal
    C. The foot-in-the-door technique
    D. The mere exposure effect

5. According to equity theory, relationships are more likely to be maintained if _____. (512)
    A. Financial resources are available.
    B. A great deal of time has been invested in the relationship
    C. The couples attachment styles are similar to one another
    D. There is a relatively equal amount of give and take between partners

6. Which of the following conditions is most likely to reduce the tendency toward social loafing? (521)
    A. Holding each group member accountable for their performance
    B. Decreasing the size of the group to between 15-20 people
    C. Attempting to decrease group cohesion and highlight the need for competition
    D. All of the above

7. One of the first things that happens to military recruits is that they are given a standard uniform that they are required to wear at all times. One purpose of such tactics is to promote _____. (522)
   A. Independence
   B. Aggression
   C. Groupthink
   D. Deindividuation

8. Which of the following does not provide an explanation for why people conform? (529)
   A. Through attribution processes an individual is able to identify causes for the behavior of people in the group
   B. People want to do whatever is generally accepted as "right"
   C. The risks of being independent are high
   D. People want to avoid the stigma of being different or deviant

9. If Barb's mother tells Barb that she has to go to college, and Barb responds by moving out of the house, taking a full-time job in a restaurant, and spending her free time doing aerobic exercises, the concept of reactance would suggest that Barb _____. (530)
   A. Has a rebellious attitude
   B. Needed to maintain consistency with her beliefs and behaviors
   C. Behaved as she did in order to maintain a sense of freedom and choice
   D. Was not open to parental advice or suggestions

10. In Milgram's classic studies on obedience, "background authority" referred to _____. (533)
    A. The setting in which the research was conducted
    B. Whether or not the researcher was visible to the participant during the study
    C. The type of music that was playing in the background
    D. What day of the week the research was conducted

After You Read, Comprehensive Practice Test

1. Which of the following is *not* of major concern to social psychology? (496)
   - A. How and why people establish cultures.
   - B. Why people sometimes use the standards of others to measure their own feelings of self-worth.
   - C. How one adult can influence the behavior of another adult.
   - D. How to minimize or maximize the factors that affect behavior that are present when two or more people are together.

2. When Carolyn walked in the door, home late from work, Steve lost his temper. According to attribution studies _____. (500)
   - A. Steve will explain his behavior by reference to some situational factor such as his concern that the company would show up before his wife did.
   - B. Carolyn will explain his behavior by reference to some internal characteristic such as Steve is too dependent.
   - C. Steve and Carolyn will realize that the world is not always a just world.
   - D. A and B

3. Which of the following is a good example of a self-serving bias? (500)
   - A. Bryant wants to appear more competent to others, so he lies about his previous successes in the business world.
   - B. Ted has had four accidents in three months and he tells Sue that other people are just terrible drivers.
   - C. Rayna sees Alex slip something under the bed and decides that he is hiding something from her.
   - D. Sheila buys a new outfit so that she can look terrific for her new job interview.

4. Which of the following is not true? Psychologists feel fairly confident about predicting the behavior of an individual if they know his/her attitude about something and _____. (503)
   - A. A decision that closely matches the attitude needs to be made
   - B. There are few competing forces, and the attitude is strongly held by the individual
   - C. The individual has described the attitude-behavior sequence
   - D. The attitude was established through personal experience

5. Kim's arguments are logical and convincing. What persuasion route should she use in order to be better able to produce attitude change in her audience? (506)
   - A. Heuristic
   - B. Central
   - C. Peripheral
   - D. Elaborative

6. According to the self-perception view put forth by Bem (1972), the situations individuals find themselves in lead to _____. (504)
    A. The experience of dissonance and ultimately decisions that will influence their future behavior
    B. Inferences concerning their emotions, attitudes and the causes of their behaviors
    C. Paying attention to the reinforcements and punishments associated with change
    D. Establishing friendships that allow them to maintain a consistency in their belief systems

7. When it comes to liking someone, people tend to_____. (508-509)
    A. Keep a distance until they have evidence about the person they like
    B. Assume that the person they like is like them and likes them
    C. Almost always choose people who are slightly less attractive then themselves
    D. Seek friends who are less attractive and socially skilled than they perceive themselves to be

8. According to research on attachment theory and relationships, individuals with _____ attachment tend to be more satisfied in their relationships. (513)
    A. Avoidant
    B. Secure
    C. Ambivalent
    D. Serene

9. Which theory says that people attempt to maintain interpersonal relationships in which the ratio of costs and benefits are equal for both parties? (512)
    A. Social exchange
    B. Group balance
    C. Equity
    E. Justice motive

10. Research on the effectiveness of punishment in reducing aggressive behavior indicates that _____. (516-517)
    A. It is effective when the aggression being punished is physical aggression, but not indirect aggression
    B. It is not effective for women, but is effective for men
    C. It is as effective as prevention programs
    D. It is not effective

11. Randy helped a homeless family because he would be featured in the newspaper. His behavior was motivated largely by personal rewards. Larry helped a homeless family because he was concerned for their welfare. What motivated Larry's behavior? (517)
    A. Egoism
    B. Bystander apathy
    C. Sociobiology
    D. Altruism

12. _____ are fixed, overly simple, and often erroneous ideas about traits, attitudes, and behaviors of groups of people. (523)
    A. Prejudice
    B. Stereotypes
    C. Schemas
    D. Discrimination

13. A friend of yours comments that "all police officers are just out to feel a sense of power and control over people." Your friend's evaluation of all police officers is an example of _____. (524)
    A. Prejudice
    B. Discrimination
    C. Sentimentality
    D. Social loafing

14. People tend to comply when _____. (529-530)
    A. They like or are attracted to the individual making the request
    B. When the person making the request is an authority figure
    C. If the person making the request has previously done something for you
    D. All of the above

15. Many commercials for products use "experts" to promote their product and to influence your decision to buy and use that product. This tendency relies on people's tendency to comply with the requests of people they deem to be _____. (506)
    A. Attractive
    B. Authorities
    C. Likable
    D. Energetic

True or False

1. According to social psychologists, our sense of self is stable over time and situations. (496)

2. The tendency to assume that other people's behavior is caused by external situations and to underestimate the role of internal dispositions is referred to as the fundamental attribution error. (500)

3. According to the elaboration likelihood theory, attitude change is more likely to occur via the central route when people have the ability and energy to think through arguments carefully. (506)

4. Research indicates that one of the best ways to develop intimacy in relationships is through self-disclosure. (511)

5. Prevention programs aimed at reducing aggressive behavior have not been shown to be effective. (516)

6. According to Zajonc's drive theory of social facilitation, heightened arousal will impair performance for more complex and less well-practiced responses. (520)

7. A person who normally performs very well on tests performs poorly on a current test because they believe their performance might confirm a negative stereotype. This is an example of what psychologists refer to as a stereotype threat. (525)

8. The tendency to obey authority is not consistent across cultures. (533

Essay Questions

1. Describe cognitive dissonance theory and describe how it is related to attitude and behavior change. (504)

2. Explain how the bystander effect and diffusion of responsibility cause people not to help others. (518)

When You Have Finished!

Surf's Up!!

After you've read and reviewed, try these web sites for additional information about some of the topics covered in this chapter.

1. **The Social Psychology Network** (http://www.socialpsychology.org/).
   This is a general resource center for information about social psychology. It contains various links to psychology related resources, online social psychology research studies, and lots more! An impressive site for all that is social psychology!

2. **The Stanley Milgram Web Site** (http://www.stanleymilgram.com/)
   This site is devoted to the pioneering work of Stanley Milgram, whose studies have had tremendous impact on the way we think about conformity in social situations.

3. **Introduction to Social Influence** (http://www.workingpsychology.com/intro.html)
   This site provides a comprehensive overview of social influence and provides you with numerous examples, both past and present, about how our attitudes are influenced by those around us.

4. **Social Psychology Experiments Online** (http://www.socialpsychology.org/expts.htm)
   This site contains a number of studies on a variety of topics related to social psychology. In addition, there are a variety of links related to topics relevant to social psychology.

5. **The National Association for Self-Esteem** (http://www.self-esteem-nase.org)This site is completely devoted to spreading information about self-esteem and providing resources to enhance one's self-esteem. You might be interested in taking their brief self-esteem rating scale. Once you have completed it, take some time to write down your thoughts about the results of that test. Did they surprise you at all? If you were to develop strategies to enhance your self-esteem, what might you do?

6. **World War II Posters & The Power of Persuasion**
   (http://www.archives.gov/exhibit_hall/powers_of_persuasion/powers_of_persuasion_home.html)
   This site has a collection of propaganda that was used in World War II to motivate soldiers and civilians alike. How do these posters use the principles you learned about with regard to changing attitudes? Is similar propaganda used in today's society and governments to swing sentiment of soldiers (or potential soldiers) and the public?

7. **Multimedia Learning Center: Museum of Tolerance**
   (http://motlc.wiesenthal.com/index.html)This site contains information regarding the holocaust, one example of the severe negative effects stereotypes, prejudice, and discrimination in our world's history. Included on this site is both visual and written information about the holocaust and its consequences.

Cross Check: Social Psychology

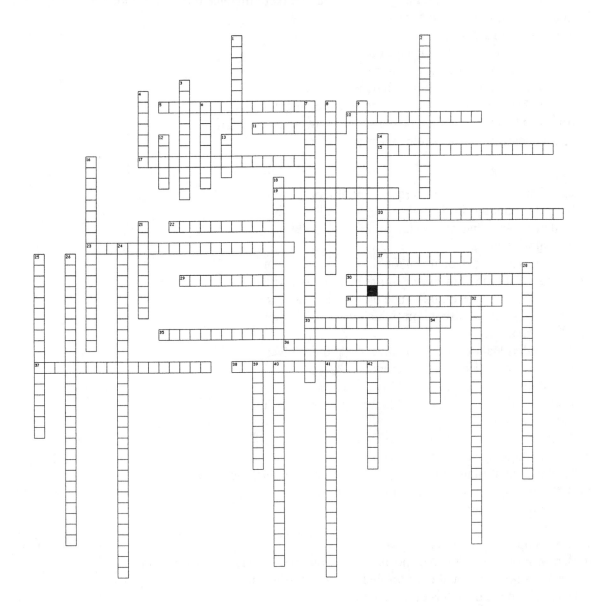

Across

5. The way others influence the individual
10. Being around others reduces your performance
11. What you may do when you realize someone wants you to do something and you don't like it
15. Attitudes that we are consciously aware of
17. Giving up your seat on a bus would be an example
19. Ratio of giving to receiving
20. Being around others improves your performance
22. Fixed, simplistic thoughts about others

23. Attitudes and emotions come from observing our own behavior
27. Evaluative thoughts about things in environment that influence future behavior
29. Behavior that intended to harm
30. Harm through a third party
31. Loss of personal identity in a group
33. Acting on stereotypes and prejudice
35. Descriptions of the causes of behavior
36. People thinking together just because they are together
37. Attitudes that we might not be consciously aware of
38. The tendency to not act if others are around

Down
1. Compliance with orders and requests of others
2. Thoughts about the world
3. Standards and values of a social group
4. The majority group
6. Behavior with no personal benefit
7. Predicts what type of influence might be effective when
8. Study of how people are influence by social situations
9. Discrepancy causes discomfort, which leads to change
12. Two or more people
13. What individuals know and believe about themselves
14. The image people portray to others
16. The more I see you, the more I love you
18. Taking credits for success but blaming others for failure
21. Judging before knowing
24. Aggression stems from frustration
25. Shift in thinking caused by a group
26. Tendency to attribute other peoples behavior to internal dispositions
28. Behavior originates and is controlled from within
32. Evaluating another positively
34. The minority group
39. How people feel about themselves
40. Behavior of others due to disposition, but your behavior is due to situation
41. Behavior originates and is controlled by the environment
42. Giving in to the demands of the group

Created by Puzzlemaker
at DiscoverySchool.com

Chapter 15

Stress and Health Psychology

Before you read...

Being a college student, there is no doubt that you are aware of what stress is and how it can impact your life and well being! This chapter is all about the understanding of these important constructs and how they impact individuals and even whole communities and cultures. In addition, you will be introduced to some constructive ways that psychologists have found that people cope with challenging situations and events in their lives. Finally, you are introduced to some new and exciting fields in psychology such as health psychology and psychoneuroimmunology.

The chapter begins with a basic, but important, distinction between stress and stressors. From there, you go on to explore different theories of stress and its impact and different approaches to measuring stressors in the environment. As you read, make sure to attend to the ideas regarding where stress comes from and the consequences or impact that stress has on the individual. As you will see, some theories tend to stress the physiological and physical aspects of stress, whereas other models tend to focus on the cognitive and psychological aspects of stress.

After discussing some of the theories about stress and stressors, you will lean more about specific sources of stress. As you will see, different types of stressors have different effects on human behavior and health. You will also lean about how personal, cultural, and environmental factors impact both the types of stressors we encounter and how we deal with those stressors. Toward the end of this section, you will learn that one of the reasons stress has become such a "hot topic" in psychology is because it has multiple effects on our psychological and physical functioning. For example, you might have noticed that often times when you are "stressed out," you become more likely to suffer from colds or other illnesses. In this part of the chapter, you will come to understand why.

So, now you know about stress and stressors. Now what? Some might tell you to just, "Deal with it!" However, the important question becomes how you "deal with it" and whether these coping strategies are effective at managing the stress and stressors you experience. In the next part of the chapter, you will come to understand what coping is, the various ways to cope with stress, and some of the factors that influence coping attempts

In the final part of the chapter, you will learn about health psychology, an emerging field that looks to incorporate the principles of health enhancement, prevention, diagnosis, and rehabilitation into a more holistic approach. You will learn how professionals in this field are coming to understand complex issues such as how to reduce the spread of HIV, getting people to adopt healthier lifestyles, and engaging people in the process of complying with treatments. Who knows, you might even find a new career path for yourself that you did not know existed! Or, at least, you will learn why it is sometimes hard to get yourself to actually make that doctors appointment!

Learning Objectives

After reading this chapter, you should be able to:

1. Define and differentiate between the terms *stress* and *stressor*, and discuss the importance of cognitive appraisal in the determination of what is stressful.
2. Compare and contrast Selye's general adaptation syndrome to Lazarus' view of stress and cognitive appraisal.
3. Describe the Holmes-Rahe Social Readjustment Rating Scale and compare it to the Hassles scale.
4. List the four broad sources of stress, and state how these stressors contribute to the experience of stress.
5. Identify the possible causes and symptoms of posttraumatic stress disorder.
6. Describe some of the physiological and behavioral responses to stress.
7. Summarize what is currently known about the relationship between stress and heart disease, infectious diseases, and health related behaviors.
8. Define coping and outline the relationship between coping and such personal factors as personal resources, a sense of control, and social support.
9. Differentiate between emotion-focused, problem-focused, and proactive coping strategies, and list some examples of each type of coping strategy.
10. Explain stress inoculation and summarize the processes involved in the three stages of this technique.
11. Describe the fields of health psychology and behavioral medicine and explain what individuals in such fields might study.
12. Discuss how health psychologists help explain why people do or do not engage in healthy behavioral acts.
13. Describe how health psychologists involved in AIDS prevention are educating the public about high-risk behaviors.
14. Explain what is meant by the psychology of being sick, focusing on when people seek medical care and adopt a sick role and under what circumstances they may comply with medical advice.
15. Explain how health psychologists help individuals adopt a healthier lifestyle and encourage people to engage in healthier behaviors related to pain management, substance use, and condom use.

Key Terms

Stress
Stressor
Post Traumatic Stress Disorder
Environmental Psychology
Burnout
Type A Behavior
Type B Behavior
Psychoneuroimmunology
Coping
Resilience
Coping Strategies
Social Support
Emotion-focused Coping
Problem-focused Coping
Stress Inoculation
Proactive Coping
Health Psychology

Psychology

As you read...

1. A _____ is an environmental event that affects an organism, whereas _____ is a response to that event that is interpreted as a challenge or threat.

2. The General Adaptation Syndrome was developed by _____, who described it as consisting of three stages. List and briefly outline each of those stages.

3. The Social Readjustment Rating Scale was developed by _____ and _____ to measure what?

4. Describe some of the common criticisms of the Social Readjustment Rating Scale.

5. Explain how Lazarus defined the interaction between the individual and the environment and define the role of cognitive appraisal in this interaction.

6. What are 3 things that influence a person's cognitive appraisal?

7. Describe the Hassles Scale and provide some examples of hassles.

15-1 Sources of Stress

1. An event of massive proportion and destruction is defined as a _____.

2. List the common symptoms of Posttraumatic Stress Disorder.

3.   The field of Environmental Psychology is interested in studying _____.

4.   Describe some common environmental factors that might be hazardous to people's health.

5.   How does discrimination lead to stress?

6.   Describe the conclusions of Fang and Myer's (2001) experiment on the effect of racist remarks on the cardiovascular system.

7.   Explain how work, personal relationships, and lack of time are related to stress and discuss some of the research findings related to these relationships.

15-2   Responses to Stress

1.   Describe the typical physiological response to stress.

2.   The adrenal glands release the hormones _____ and _____ in response to stress. List the function(s) of these hormones in the stress response.

3.   Describe the behavioral response to stress.

15-3	Stress and Health

1.   Differentiate between Type A and Type B behavior and state which of these behavior patterns is linked to heart disease and how.

2.   What behaviors and attitudes are linked with heart disease?

3.   How is stress related to infectious diseases?

4.   Psychoneuroimmunology is defined as _____.

5.   What 3 factors of stress are important in vulnerability to infection?

6.   How does stress impact health related behaviors?

How Do People Cope with Stress?

1.   Define coping.

2.   List the 5 assumptions of coping.

15-4	Factors that Influence Coping

1.   Define resilience.

2.   List and describe 3 factors that influence coping.

3.   People who have the _____ of control show health benefits.

4.   What is learned helplessness?

5.   What is the importance of social support?

15-5   Coping Strategies

1.   _____ refers to the process of taking action in a stressful situation, whereas _____ _____ refer to the type of action that is taken.

2.   Name three factors that influence coping ability and discuss how they might help one cope with stressors in the environment.

3.   Typically _____ coping strategies are more effective than _____ coping strategies.

4.   Describe the two types of active coping strategies.

5.   Some people believe that keeping a journal in which you write about and explore upsetting or confusing things in your environment is a good way of coping with stress. Support this argument using the results of research on emotion-focused coping.

6.   A strategy for dealing with stress that involves taking action in advance of a stressful situation is referred to as _____ _____.

7.   What are the 5 stages of proactive coping?

8.   List the three stages of stress inoculation and briefly describe the processes associated with each stage.

What is Health Psychology?

1. Health psychology is _____.

2. List 5 behaviors correlated with health and life expectancy.

3. Give 3 examples of health-impairing behaviors and describe their negative effects on health.

4. List the high-risk behaviors involved in getting AIDS.

5. Describe how health psychologists are attempting to prevent the spread of HIV.

15-6   The Psychology of Being Sick

1. List some reasons how one's beliefs might influence their decision to seek health care.

2. Why might women be more likely to seek medical care than men?

3. What cultural differences exist in seeking medical care?

4. A person who has accepted their illness and is taking steps to recover is said to have adopted a _____ role.

5. People are more likely to work toward getting well when their illness is _____ versus _____.

6. When are people more likely to comply with medical advice?

15-7	Adopting a Healthier Lifestyles

1. List and describe the 3 forms severe pain can take.

2. How does behavior modification work in pain management?

3. Describe some direct and indirect ways that drinking on college campuses can be modified.

4. Was the safer sex campaign effective in changing behavior?

After You Read, Practice Test #1

1. An environmental stimulus that affects an organism in physically or psychologically injurious ways is called _____. (540)
    A.   A stressor
    B.   Stress
    C.   Anxiety
    D.   Arousal

2. In Selye's General Adaptation Syndrome, the focus is on _____ responses and changes in response to stress. (540)
    A.   Physiological
    B.   Behavioral
    C.   Cognitive
    D.   Emotional

3. Cognitive appraisal is a process by which people _____. (543)
    A.   Develop emotional reactions to environmental events
    B.   Assess how successful they have been in the past
    C.   Evaluate a situation and their ability to deal with it
    D.   Try out various stress reduction strategies

4. Which of these factors seems to be most strongly associated with psychological and physical health? (544)
    A.   Major life events
    B.   Daily hassles
    C.   Feelings of control
    D.   Social support

5. Severe stress caused by some type of disaster is called _____. (545)
    A.   Psychogenic stress disorder
    B.   Delusional behavior
    C.   Catastrophic stress
    D.   Post traumatic stress

6. What do the physiological changes that accompany stress include? (551)
    A.   Elevation of blood pressure
    B.   Constriction of the pupils
    C.   Increased production of specific hormones
    D.   All of the above

7. The availability of comfort, recognition, approval, and encouragement from other people is called _____ and is extremely helpful when people are trying to cope. (558)
    A. Psychological manipulation
    B. Social support
    C. Friendship
    D. Mentoring

8. A subfield of psychology that emphasizes the application of behavioral science to enhance health and prevent illness is called _____. (563)
    A. Genetic psychology
    B. Behavioral medicine
    C. Health psychology
    D. Enhancement psychology

9. In general, people are more likely to seek medical care when _____. (567)
    A. They are men
    B. Their problem is psychological
    C. They believe their condition is curable
    D. They have visible symptoms

10. People who make changes in their normal routines and take specific actions designed to relieve illness and make them well are said to be _____. (564)
    A. Psychopathological
    B. Medically disturbed
    C. Adopting a sick role
    D. Securing a healthy schema

After You Read, Practice Test #2

1. You come home to find out that your apartment has been burglarized. This would be an example of a(n) _____. (540)
   A. Catastrophe
   B. Stressor
   C. Stress
   D. Hassle

2. According to the General Adaptation Syndrome, physiological and behavioral responses become more moderate and sustained in which stage? (540-541)
   A. Alarm
   B. Acceptance
   C. Resistance
   D. Exhaustion

3. Which term refers to the frequently occurring, repetitive sources of stress that happen to us on an almost daily basis? (544)
   A. Burnout
   B. Hassles
   C. Stressors
   D. Overload

4. A psychological disorder that is caused by exposure to extreme stress is called _____ disorder. (546).
   A. Posttraumatic
   B. Severe stress
   C. Adjustment
   D. Depressive

5. Stress management is the process individuals engage in to deal with varying stressful situations. Psychologists call this process _____. (556)
   A. Time management
   B. Resilience
   C. Defense mechanisms
   D. Coping

6. Taking steps to prevent a stressful event from occurring is an example of _____. (561)
   A. Defense-oriented coping
   B. Emotion-focused coping
   C. Proactive coping
   D. Anticipatory coping

7.   Which of the following behaviors has not been strongly linked to health and life
     expectancy? (564)
     A.   Smoking
     B.   Exercise
     C.   Sleeping
     D.   All of the above

8.   In most parts of the world, AIDS is spread from person to person through _____. (566)
     A.   Casual family contact
     B.   Contaminated food and water
     C.   Homosexual sex
     D.   Heterosexual sex

9.   Overall, the rate of non-compliance with medical advice is around _____. (569)
     A.   50%
     B.   25%
     C.   2%
     D.   75%

10. Pain which is long-lasting and ever-present is referred to as _____. (570)
     A.   Chronic pain
     B.   Never ending pain
     C.   Progressive pain
     D.   Acute pain

After You Read, Practice Test #3

1. A nonspecific response to real or imagined challenges or threats in the environment is called _____. (540)
    A. Stressor
    B. Alarm
    C. Stress
    D. Shock

2. According to Holmes and Rahe, stressful life events are _____. (541)
    A. Everyday hassles in a person's day-to-day experiences
    B. A combination of everyday hassles and irritations
    C. The build up of everyday hassles and irritations
    D. Prominent events in a person's life that necessitate change

3. The most important component in determining whether an event is stressful is _____. (543)
    A. Culture
    B. Appraisal
    C. Frequency
    D. Emotional stability

4. If we feel we have control over something that happens, in general that makes it _____. (544)
    A. Our responsibility, so it is more stressful
    B. Less interesting and challenging to us
    C. Harder to ignore and harder to deal with
    D. More predictable and less stressful

5. Which of the following environmental factors has not been related to stress? (546-547)
    A. Poverty
    B. A lack of time to complete activities
    C. Crowded living conditions
    D. The constant threat and fear of crime and violence

6. _____ is a state of emotional and physical exhaustion caused by work related pressures and stress. (549)
    A. Work overload
    B. Job press
    C. Burnout
    D. Interference

7. A physiological response to stress is characterized by arousal of the _____ nervous system. (551)
    A.   Central
    B.   Somatic
    C.   Autonomic
    D.   Bilateral

8. Type B behavior is characterized by _____. (553)
    A.   Anger
    B.   A sense of urgency
    C.   Patience
    D.   Competitiveness

9. Joan is upset due to the recent death of her family dog that has been with the family for 15 years. To cope with her feelings, Joan writes in her diary. This would be an example of which type of coping? (559)
    A.   Social support
    B.   Emotion focused
    C.   Supportive-expressive
    D.   Problem focused

10. Which of the following is not one of the stages of stress inoculation? (561-562)
    A.   Application
    B.   Skills acquisition
    C.   Conceptualization
    D.   Follow-through

After You Read, Comprehensive Test

1. Jim was just told that he will be training a new employee and he feels like he is not sure that he can do this. As a result, he is feeling increased anxiety. In this case, Jim's anxiety would be an example of _____. (540)
    A. A Stressor
    B. Stress
    C. Appraisal
    D. An Alarm

2. Cosmos has very high standards in accomplishing the tasks at his job. However, because of extreme work related pressures, he has been experiencing emotional and physical exhaustion lower productivity, and has felt isolated from the other employees. Cosmos is experiencing _____. (540-541)
    A. Reality
    B. Burnout
    C. Exhaustion
    D. Resistance

3. Which of the following theorists suggest that the most important component to dealing with stressful situations is our appraisal of those situations? (543)
    A. Holmes
    B. Lazarus
    C. Rahe
    D. Selye

4. Which of the following events contribute to post traumatic stress disorder? (546)
    A. Violence
    B. Natural disasters
    C. Man-made disasters
    D. All of the above

5. Which subfield of psychology studies how physical settings affect human behavior and stress levels? (546)
    A. Environmental
    B. Cultural
    C. Homeland
    D. Structural

6. Type A behavior _____. (553)
    A. Does not seem directly related to any physical illnesses
    B. Is marked by decreases physiological reactivity
    C. Is marked by competitiveness, happiness and patience
    D. Seems to be a risk factor for heart disease

7.	_____ is an interdisciplinary area of study that focuses on behavioral, neurological, and immune factors and their relationship to the development of disease. (554)
	A.	Psychonueroimmunology
	B.	Behavioral medicine
	C.	Clinical psychobiology
	D.	Immuniobiology

8.	According to Cohen's research, the _____ of stress are important in vulnerability to infection. (555)
	A.	Source and expression
	B.	Site and cause
	C.	Amount and duration
	D.	Visualization and experience

9.	Someone who is resilient is someone who responds to demanding situations by _____. (556)
	A.	Triggering a powerful defense mechanism
	B.	Reducing their level of immune system functioning
	C.	Exhibiting a high level of physiological reactance
	D.	Taking them in stride and dealing with them flexibly

10.	The strategies and systems we have developed to let us deal more effectively with stressful situations are called _____. (558)
	A.	Social support mechanisms
	B.	Coping strategies
	C.	Adaptation strategies
	D.	Health related behaviors

11.	Amy was the first one to comfort Tom when the news broke about the death of his father. Amy could be said to provide Tom with _____. (558)
	A.	Networking
	B.	Externalization
	C.	Interreactance
	D.	Social support

12.	According to Aspinwall and Taylor, the first step in proactive coping is to _____. (561)
	A.	Recognize that a stressful situation is up coming
	B.	Appraise the situation for potential difficulties
	C.	Accumulate resources
	D.	Devise a coping strategy

13. Stress inoculation refers to a set of strategies that are designed to help someone _____.
     (561-562)
     A.   Reduce their level of physiological reactance
     B.   Identify the original cause of their stress reaction
     C.   Measure the amount of stress they feel more accurately
     D.   Cope effectively with an upcoming stressful situation

14. With respect to AIDS, a high-risk behavior is one that _____. (565)
     A.   Exposes one to the blood or semen of someone who might have AIDS
     B.   Brings one into any contact, even casual, with an AIDS sufferer
     C.   Increases the likelihood of dying from the disease
     D.   Makes the symptoms of the disease more serious

15. People are less likely to comply with medical advice when _____. (569)
     A.   Advice is for wellness or prevention
     B.   When family and friends pressure the patient
     C.   An illness is tailored to them specifically
     D.   They have no fears of the possible diagnosis

True or False

1. One of the complaints about the Social Readjustment Rating Scale is that many people with high scores do not suffer negative effects of stress such as getting sick. (542)

2. Major life events tend to be more strongly correlated with psychological health than daily hassles. (544)

3. Heart disease is the number one killer of both men and women in the United States. (552)

4. People who are able to respond adaptively to both internal and external demands and stressors are said to be resilient. (556)

5. Proactive coping, emotion-focused coping, and problem-focused coping are all examples of active coping. (559-561)

6. Stress inoculation and proactive coping are both aimed at primarily reducing future stress. (561)

7. In the United States, almost 20% of known cases of AIDS are contracted through heterosexual sex. (566)

8. Males tend to seek help more frequently than females. (567)

Essay Questions

1. Describe the similarities and differences between Lazarus' and Selye's views of stress and coping. (540-543)

2. What are some ways that health psychologists help individuals and communities lead healthier lives? (563-567)

When You Have Finished!

Surf's Up!!

After you've read and reviewed, try these web sites for additional information about some of the topics covered in this chapter.

1. **National Mental Health Association.** (http://www.nmha.org/infoctr/factsheets/41.cfm)
   Information regarding resources and suggestions for dealing with everyday stressors and improving one's coping skills are provided at this site.

2. **American Psychological Association Division of Health Psychology.** (http://www.health-psych.org/)
   The Division of Health Psychology is devoted to the emerging field of health psychology and contains a great deal of information for professional and others interested in this area of study. Of particular interest to students is a whole section devoted to education and training in health psychology.

3. **Holistic Online.com** (http://www.holisticonline.com/stress/stress_home.htm)
   This site provides a great deal of information about managing one's stress. On the site, you will learn how to detect symptoms of stress, recognize diseases that are often mistaken for stress, and common sense ways to manage and prevent stress.

4. **United States Department of Health and Human Services.** (http://www.os.dhhs.gov/).
   This site contains information and guidelines for pursuing a healthier lifestyle. Some of the topics include diet and exercise, HIV/AIDS information, and addictions and substance abuse.

5. **The General Self-Efficacy Scale** (http://userpage.fu-berlin.de/~health/engscal.htm)
   This scale, developed by Jerusalem and Schwarzer, allows you to assess your own feelings about your self-efficacy.

6. **The International Society of Behavioral Medicine.** (http://www.isbm.info/)
   This organization is devoted to the interaction between psychosocial factors and medicine and the application of this information to health settings. There are numerous links to information of relevance to this field.

Cross Check: Stress and Coping

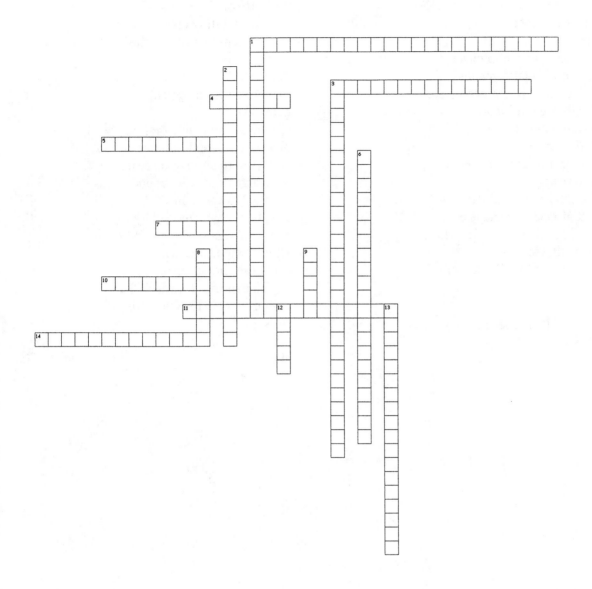

Across

1. Study of how physical settings affect behavior
3. Strategy for dealing with stress that focuses on preventing it
4. Taking action to manage environmental demands
5. Extent to which people are flexible and respond adaptively to demands
7. Nonspecific response to real or imagined challenges or threats
10. Environmental stimulus that affects an organism
11. Techniques people use to deal with stress
14. Comfort available from others

Created by <u>Puzzlemaker</u> at DiscoverySchool.com

Down

1. Concentrating on managing feelings associated with stress
2. Concentrating on solving the problem that causes the stress
3. Psychological disorder due to extreme environmental demands
6. Focuses on behavioral, neurological, and immune factors in relation to disease
8. A state of emotional and physical exhaustion
9. Pattern characterized by competitiveness and hostility
12. Pattern characterized by calmness and patience
13. Therapeutic approach that teaches people to cope with stress

Chapter 16

Psychological Disorders

Before You Begin...

The popular media is full of images and misinformation about mental illness. In addition, many students come into Introductory Psychology classes with many misperceptions about mental illness. In this chapter, you will be introduced to the field of abnormal psychology. Hopefully this information will give you a more accurate and realistic picture of what abnormal behavior and mental illness is all about.

The chapter begins by defining abnormal behavior. Specifically, the authors review the general criteria used in differentiating between normal and abnormal behavior. In addition to these general criteria, psychologists also examine the specific types of symptoms a client is experiencing. If both the general and specific criteria are met, an individual might receive a diagnosis. Following this broad discussion of defining abnormal behavior, you are introduced to the Diagnostic and Symptom Manual of Mental Disorders (DSM-IV), the current diagnostic system used by most mental health professionals.

In addition to making a good diagnosis, abnormal psychology is also interested in explaining why some people might experience mental illness and others might not. In this chapter, you are introduced to a variety of models in psychology, each of which have different ways of understanding mental illness. If you ever wondered why mental illness happens and how you might be able to explain it, this chapter should be very informative. It will also be interesting to see which of these models "fits" best with your own thoughts about this issue.

The bulk of the remaining chapter is devoted to more specifically exploring some of the most common and most interesting types of mental disorders. Included in this list are anxiety, mood, dissociative, psychotic, and personality disorders. For each of these groups of disorders, you will be introduced to the symptoms associated with them and the specific disorders that fall under these broad classes. You will also be introduced to some of the research that explores specifically what causes these disorders. Finally, you will come to understand how frequently some of these disorders occur and who might be at particular risk for experiencing these disorders. For example, do you think men or women experience more mental illness?

The chapter closes by examining the issue of the relationship between mental illness and violence. Many individuals think that all people with mental illness likely to commit violent acts. In this chapter, you will confront this popular opinion. You will also learn about how being a victim of violence might place someone at risk for experiencing a mental illness and what types of mental illness might be more common as a result of this violence.

Key Terms

Abnormal Behavior
Model
Abnormal Psychology
Diagnostic and Statistical Manual of Mental Disorders
Prevalence
Anxiety
Generalized Anxiety Disorder
Panic Attack
Phobic Disorders
Agoraphobia
Social Phobia
Specific Phobia
Obsessive-Compulsive Disorder
Mood Disorders
Depressive Disorders
Major Depressive Disorder
Delusions
Learned Helplessness
Vulnerability
Bipolar Disorder
Dissociative Disorders
Dissociative Amnesia
Dissociative Identity Disorder
Schizophrenic Disorders
Psychotic
Paranoid Type of Schizophrenia
Catatonic Type of Schizophrenia
Disorganized Type of Schizophrenia
Residual Type of Schizophrenia
Undifferentiated Type of Schizophrenia
Concordance Rate
Personality Disorders
Antisocial Personality Disorder
Insanity
Child Abuse
Rape

Learning Objectives

After reading this chapter, you should be able to:

1. List and describe five distinguishing characteristics of abnormal behavior.
2. Distinguish between the medical-biological, psychodynamic, humanistic, behavioral, cognitive, sociocultural, and evolutionary models of abnormal behavior.
3. State what the DSM-IV is, list the five axes of the multiaxial system, and identify what information is recorded on each axis. In addition, discuss some of the criticisms of the DSM system.
4. Discuss how diversity and diagnoses are related to one another.
5. Define the term *anxiety* and list and define the various anxiety disorders that are discussed.
6. Define phobic disorder and explain the differences between agoraphobia, social phobia, and specific phobia.
7. Differentiate between an obsession and a compulsion as each relates to the diagnosis of obsessive-compulsive disorder.
8. Describe the symptoms of major depressive disorder and describe its typical, onset, duration, and prevalence.
9. Summarize the causes of depression according to the biological, cognitive, and biopsychosocial theories.
10. Identify the two phases of bipolar disorder and discuss its prevalence and typical course.
11. Define dissociative disorder and identify and differentiate between dissociative amnesia and dissociative identity disorder.
12. Describe the common symptoms of schizophrenia and identify the characteristics associated with the different types of schizophrenia.
13. Describe the hereditary and environmental factors that contribute to schizophrenia and identify its most likely causes.
14. List and describe the three broad classes of personality disorders and then define the six personality disorders that are discussed in your text.
15. Explain the relationship having a psychological disorder and violent behavior. In addition, distinguish between suicide attempters and completers, citing some of the factors that may influence a suicide attempt.
16. Describe how being a victim of a violent act might increase one's risk for experiencing psychological problems, and identify what types of problems have been associated with certain types of violent acts.

Psychology

As you read...

| What is Abnormal Behavior? |

1. List the 5 characteristics of abnormal behavior.

2. _____ _____ is the subfield of psychology concerned with the assessment, treatment, and prevention of maladaptive behavior, whereas behavior characterized as atypical, socially unacceptable, distressing, maladaptive and/or the result of distorted cognitions is called _____ _____.

3. The cognitive _____ consists of a set of related concepts that helps scientists organize data and make predictions about behavior. There are _____ such _____ discussed in the text.

| 16.1   Models in Abnormal Behavior |

Match the names of the theories below with the description of the theory on the right.

A. Medical-Biological   _____ Focus is on learned maladaptive behavior and the role of reinforcement and punishment from the environment.

B. Psychodynamic   _____ Assumes that maladaptive behavior consists of adaptive behavior that has been taken to extremes.

C. Humanistic   _____ Belief that maladaptive behavior is guided by maladaptive thinking.

D. Behavioral   _____ Focuses on the physiological conditions and abnormalities that drive abnormal behavior.

E. Cognitive   _____ Places a primary emphasis on the context where the individual resides as a cause of abnormal behavior.

F. Sociocultural   _____ Maladaptive behavior occurs when someone's innate potential and needs are blocked.

G. Evolutionary   _____ Psychological disorders results from anxiety associated with unresolved conflicts and unconscious thought processes.

4. The current system used for making diagnoses is presented in the _____ manual.

5. Approximately 16% of the population will experience a depressive disorder at some time in their lives. This number is an example of the _____ of depression.

6. The DSM-IV is a _____ system that consists of how many axes?

7. Write in a description of what information goes on each axis of the DSM-IV and provide an example for each.

Axis	Description and Example
Axis I	
Axis II	
Axis III	
Axis IV	
Axis V	

8. What are some of the criticisms of the DSM?

9. How does culture impact diagnosis and treatment?

What Are Anxiety Disorders?

1. Anxiety is a generalized feeling of _____ that is often related to a _____ or object and is accompanied by increased physiological arousal.

2. Thinking back to the evolutionary model of abnormal behavior, how might you explain common anxiety reactions such as fear of heights and enclosed spaces?

3. In general terms, a phobia is characterized by both _____ and _____ of some specific object or situation.

4. A _____ phobia is a fear of a particular object or situation, whereas _____ phobia is a fear of being evaluated or embarrassed in front of others.

5. State the similarities and differences between agoraphobia, social phobia, and specific phobia.

6. What is the difference between an obsession and compulsion as it relates to obsessive-compulsive disorder?

7. A person with obsessive-compulsive disorder who washes her hands 200 times a day would be engaging in a _____.

8. Describe how the psychodynamic theorists, behaviorists and biopsychologists explain obsessive-compulsive disorder.

16.2	You Play The Doctor, Part I

Match the following case descriptions to the correct diagnostic label.

A. Social Phobia

_____ Tonia is constantly afraid for her children's safety and finds that if she constantly counts to 6 or in multiples of 6, her anxiety greatly diminishes.

B. Specific Phobia

_____ Luis is terrified of speaking in public to the point that he consciously avoids situations where there is even a possibility that he will be called on to speak.

C. Panic

_____ Maria is afraid of everything and states that she has felt this way for a very long time.

D. Generalized Anxiety

_____ Nathan is terrified of large crowds and is excessively fearful that he will get "caught" in the crowd and be unable to get out without extreme embarrassment or injury.

E. Agoraphobia

_____ Jenna is afraid of dogs and refuses to enter, or even walk by, a house where there is a dog present.

F. Obsessive-Compulsive

_____ Jim was at the movies with his friends when all of a sudden his heart started to beat faster and he was overcome with a sudden and intense fear.

What Are Mood Disorders?

1. List and define the three mood disorders discussed in your text.

2. List the symptoms of major depressive disorder and a bipolar disorder and identify the difference between them.

3. A friend of yours argues "depression is just being sad with a fancy name attached to it." What evidence would you use to refute your friend's statement?

4. How does the prevalence and onset of depression vary by age and gender?

5. According to research presented in your text, one reason women may experience depression more often than men is because they engage in more rumination. Define rumination and discuss why women may do this more than men do.

6. Both genes and neurotransmitters have been implicated as biological factors causing depression. Summarize the research that supports this statement.

7. Compare and contrast Beck's cognitive theory and Seligman's learned-helplessness theories of depression.

8. Describe the diathesis-stress model and state how it might explain the occurrence of depressive disorders.

9. Describe the 2 phases of the disorder and the symptoms associated with each phase.

10. Bipolar disorder is _____ common than major depression and occurs _____ in males and females.

What Are Dissociative Disorders?

1. Dissociative disorders are characterized by disturbances in what four areas?

2. Identify and describe the symptoms of the two dissociative disorders discussed in your text.

3. How is dissociative amnesia similar and different from amnesia that is caused by a physical injury to the head?

4. The disorder that is characterized by the presence of at least 2 personalities that are unaware of the existence of the other is called _____ _____ _____.

What is Schizophrenia?

1. What are schizophrenic disorders and how are they different than other disorders?

2. Describe the three essential characteristics of schizophrenic disorders and provide at least one example for each.

3. Perceptual experiences that occur without any physical stimulus are called _____.

4. Emotional responses that are not appropriate to the circumstances are referred to as displays of _____ _____.

16.3 You Play the Doctor, Part II

Match the following subtypes of schizophrenia with the appropriate description.

A. Disorganized Type   _____ Characterized by stupor in which individuals are mute, negative, and basically unresponsive. Characteristics can also include displays of excited or violent motor activity. Individuals can switch from the *withdrawn* to the *excited* state

B. Paranoid Type   _____ Characterized by prominent delusions, hallucinations, incoherence, or grossly disorganized behavior and does not meet the criteria for any other type or meets the criteria for more than one other type

C. Catatonic Type   _____ Characterized by a history of at least one previous episode of schizophrenia with prominent psychotic symptoms, a current state of being in touch with reality, and signs of inappropriate affect, illogical thinking, social withdrawal, or eccentric behavior

D. Residual Type   _____ Characterized by delusions and hallucinations of persecution and/or grandeur; irrational jealousy is sometimes evident

E. Undifferentiated Type   _____ Characterized by frequent incoherence, absence of systematized delusions, and blunted, inappropriate, or silly affect

5. Most researchers who study the causes of schizophrenia have concluded that it is caused by an interaction between _____ and _____ factors.

6. Both genetic factors and neurotransmitters have been implicated as potential causes of schizophrenia. Review the evidence that exists to support this conclusion.

7. _____ _____ estimates the degree to which a condition or trait is shared by two or more individuals or groups. How is the concept important to our understanding of schizophrenia?

8. What environmental factors influence schizophrenia?

What Are Personality Disorders?

1. Define personality disorders.

2. Describe the 3 broad classes of personality disorders.

3. List and describe the 6 personality disorders given in the chapter.

16.4   You Play the Doctor, Part III

Match the following personality disorder diagnoses with the correct descriptions.

A. Antisocial	_____ Brittany thinks very highly of herself and tends to bore others quite easily with incessant discussion of her life and interests. She also tends to be very demanding of others and gets easily upset if she thinks others are being critical of her.
B. Paranoid	_____ Mike is suave and confident. He tends to use these skills to steal from and cheat others. He does not feel regret for his actions and often states, "I can't help it if people are ignorant."
C. Borderline	_____ Monica tends to be the "life of the party" and is always in need of reassurance and praise from others.
D. Narcissistic	_____ Hector insists that others around him are generally no good and do not care for him or others. He is overly suspicious of people and always seems to feel the need to "watch his back" in relationships.
E. Histrionic	_____ Amanda tends to have a very difficult time making decisions for herself and she tends to look to others to protect her and make decisions for her. When she does not have such a person in her life, she is often overcome with anxiety and fear.
F. Dependant	_____ Heather is often described by others as "unstable." She is constantly in and out of activities and relationships and reports frequently feeling empty and alone even when she is with other people.

How Are Violence and Mental Disorders Related?

1. Identify the disorders and/or problems that have been associated with an increased risk for violent behavior.

2. _____ is the legal concept that refers to a condition that excuses people from responsibility and protects them from punishment. It is used as a defense in _____% of all felony defenses.

3. Distinguish between suicide attempters and completers.

4. Child abuse is defined as _____, _____, or _____ of a child.

5. Children who are the victims of abuse and neglect are at greater risk for experiencing what disorders and/or problems?

6. A forced sexual assault on an unconsenting partner is called _____.

7. What type of rape is most common, and what are some of the common effects of rape on the victim's mental health?

After You Read, Practice Test #1

1. John is an anti-war advocate. He routinely engages in anti-war protests and marches. Although you may disagree with John's stance on war, psychologists would not consider this "abnormal behavior" because it does not meet which of the five characteristics? (576)
    A. The behavior results in John feeling distress
    B. The behavior is socially unacceptable
    C. The behavior is odd
    D. The behavior is a result of distorted cognitions

2. Which perspective on abnormality focuses on the importance of one's family and community on the development and expression of maladaptive behaviors? (579)
    A. Psychoanalytic model
    B. Legal model
    C. The behavioral model
    D. The sociocultural model

3. Some abnormal behaviors, such as a fear of situations and objects, may occur because they increase the probability of survival and keep people away from danger. This type of belief is consistent with what model of abnormal behavior? (579)
    A. Cognitive
    B. Evolutionary
    C. Sociocultural
    D. Humanistic

4. Which of the following is a primary goal of the DSM-IV system? (580)
    A. Organize disorders into categories on the basis of etiological evidence
    B. Improve the reliability of diagnosis
    C. Improve the accuracy of treatments for mental illness
    D. Describe measures to prevent mental illness

5. Which of the following statements about diversity and diagnosis is correct? (584)
    A. All symptoms in the DSM-IV are expressed the same way in different cultures
    B. Caucasians are diagnosed at similar rates as individuals of other ethnic backgrounds
    C. The United States has culture-bound syndromes such as bulimia
    D. Culture is not addressed within the DSM-IV system

6. Which of the following best illustrates an obsessive-compulsive disorder? (587)
   A. Mary's desk is always neat because she spends fifteen minutes each day before leaving work putting things in order.
   B. Sam makes a point of checking to see that he has unplugged the coffee pot before going to work because he worries about small appliances causing fires.
   C. Mark loves sports and watches every television sports show he can
   D. Elida mops the kitchen floor three times before preparing a meal because she fears it is infested with mites, and she cannot feel comfortable exposing food until she has finished her mopping.

7. If a psychologist says that a depressed patient is experiencing delusions, we can assume that the psychologist means the patient _____. (590)
   A. Is displaying false beliefs
   B. Will talk excessively
   C. Is evaluating the consequences of suicide
   D. Has had a recurrence of a depressive episode

8. Those psychologists who explain the development of schizophrenic disorders as a combination of nature and nurture would suggest that_____. (593)
   A. If one twin has schizophrenia, the other twin also will develop the disorder.
   B. Contentious parents who minimize closeness and warmth will produce schizophrenic offspring.
   C. Brain impairment left undiagnosed will produce schizophrenia
   D. A genetic predisposition triggered by environmental stressors may lead to a behavioral pattern of schizophrenia

9. People diagnosed as having antisocial personalities _____. (606)
   A. Constantly blame themselves for their own problems.
   B. Violate the rights of others without feeling guilt or remorse
   C. Conform only so that they may avoid feelings of shame and guilt.
   D. Have insight into how their behavior affects others

10. A person who is judged legally insane _____. (609)
   A. Is typically suffering from a severe depressive disorder
   B. Can be held accountable for their actions only if they involve murder
   C. Is a diagnostic term used by psychologists
   D. Cannot be held responsible for a crime they committed while mentally ill

After You Read, Practice Test #2

1. Which of the following is not one of the defining characteristics of abnormal behavior? (576)
   A. It is not typical
   B. It is the result of distorted cognitions
   C. It is distressing to the person or others
   D. It is potentially dangerous

2. _____ psychology is the subfield of psychology concerned with the assessment, treatment, and prevention of maladaptive behavior. (577)
   A. Clinical
   B. Abnormal
   C. Psychopathological
   D. Insanity

3. A _____ model of abnormal behavior assumes that such behavior occurs because it is learned and reinforced in the environment. (578)
   A. Cognitive
   B. Behavioral
   C. Sociocultural
   D. Psychodynamic

4. The prevalence of a disorder refers to _____. (580)
   A. How frequently the disorder occurs
   B. The causes of the disorder
   C. The probability of a cure for that disorder
   D. The number of people who have recovered from the disorder

5. Lucy is sitting in class when suddenly she is overcome by extreme fear. She notices that her heart is beating rapidly, she is having trouble catching her breath, and she thinks, "I must be going crazy." Lucy is likely experiencing a _____. (585)
   A. Anxiety attack
   B. Obsessive fear
   C. Phobic fear
   D. Panic attack

6. People who exhibit symptoms of major depressive disorder _____. (544)
   A. Are usually unable to explain why their response is prolonged
   B. May need to be hospitalized
   C. Usually blame their loved ones for their problems
   D. Are too depressed to consider suicide

7. People who show symptoms of schizophrenia but who remain generally in touch with reality are diagnosed with which type of schizophrenia? (600)
    A. Disorganized
    B. Undifferentiated
    C. Residual
    D. Mild

8. Sam is convinced that he was sent to earth to convince people to follow him and reject all forms of organized government. He says that he used to be fearful that his views might cause him to be harmed by others, but recently he has started to see "guardian angels" that float in the corners of any room that he is in. These angels would be an example of _____. (599)
    A. Negative symptoms
    B. Delusions
    C. Catatonia
    D. Hallucinations

9. A disorder that involves unwarranted fear and feelings of persecution and mistrust is _____. (557)
    A. Histrionic personality disorder
    B. Paranoid personality disorder
    C. Inadequate personality disorder
    D. Dependent personality disorder

10. Approximately _____ of felony defendants attempt to use the insanity defense. (609)
    A. 1%
    B. 10%
    C. 5%
    D. 25%

After You Read, Practice Test #3

1. Models in abnormal psychology help scientists _____. (577)
    A. Make the correct diagnosis
    B. Understand how family factors influence illness
    C. Organize data and make predictions about behavior
    D. Evaluate research

2. Whereas the _____ model places an emphasis on how people think, the _____ model places an emphasis on the role of unresolved conflicts and anxiety in explaining abnormal behavior. (578)
    A. Sociocultural; Cognitive
    B. Cognitive; Psychodynamic
    C. Evolutionary; Behavioral
    D. Psychodynamic; Humanistic

3. Axis IV of the DSM-IV is used to describe _____. (581)
    A. Current medical conditions
    B. Global assessment of functioning
    C. Clinical disorders
    D. Psychosocial or environmental problems

4. Agoraphobia involves the strong fear and avoidance of _____. (586)
    A. Being alone in a public places that are hard to get out of
    B. Any specific object or situation that is not really dangerous
    C. Interacting with or being observed by other individuals
    D. Any small, confined space with no obvious way out

5. Which of the following is *not* an explanation offered by learning theorists about the cause of major depressions? Depressed people _____. (592)
    A. Lack prosocial behaviors and are avoided or punished because of the behaviors they do emit.
    B. Have negative views and expectations about the human condition.
    C. Experience an imbalance in certain body chemicals when they are involved in stress inducing situations
    D. Feel they have no control over the consequences of their behavior

6. Jane has experienced a two-week period of extreme sadness and loss of interest or pleasure in activities. She is having a very difficult time understanding this, because the week prior to this she felt "on top of the world" and had so much energy that she felt like she could do anything. Jane might be experiencing a _____. (594)
    A. Delusional disorder
    B. Bipolar disorder
    C. Major depressive disorder
    D. Dissociative disorder

7. A disorder that is characterized a by person who exhibits two or more distinct personalities at various times is referred to as _____. (596)
    A. Disorganized schizophrenia
    B. Borderline personality disorder
    C. Dissociative identity disorder
    D. Bipolar disorder

8. A prominent characteristic in catatonic type schizophrenia is_____. (600)
    A. The presence of delusions of persecution and grandeur
    B. Extreme overt behavior that involves either excessive motor and verbal activity or a severe decline in motor and verbal activity
    C. The lack of good personal hygiene
    D. The absence of systematized delusions

9. A delusion is _____. (590)
    A. A false belief that is inconsistent with reality.
    B. A perceptual malfunction that causes a person to hear voices of people who are not present.
    C. An incoherent and random pattern of thinking
    D. All of the above

10. Missy is constantly complaining about her boyfriend and telling wild stories about how he treats her. She also flirts with other boys and asks about how they would treat her if they were dating. She might be diagnosed with _____. (606)
    A. Borderline personality disorder
    B. Narcissistic personality disorder
    C. Conversion disorder
    D. Histrionic personality disorder

After You Read, Comprehensive Test

1. Which subfield of psychology focuses on the assessment, treatment, and prevention of maladaptive behaviors? (577)
    A. Health psychology
    B. Personality psychology
    C. Community psychology
    D. Abnormal psychology

2. Practitioners who treat maladjusted behavior by teaching people how to develop new thought processes that instill new values are an example of the_____ model of abnormal behavior. (578)
    A. Behavioral
    B. Biological
    C. Humanistic
    D. Cognitive

3. A person who believes that all mental illness is caused by some dysfunction in our brains would likely endorse which model of abnormal behavior? (577)
    A. Behavioral
    B. Medical-Biological
    C. Psychodynamic
    D. Evolutionary

4. When working with the DSM-IV, a psychologist will use the third axes to describe the individual's (581)
    A. Clinical disorder
    B. Global level of functioning
    C. Current medical conditions
    D. Social and environmental stressors

5. Megan has become increasingly afraid of being alone in crowded places such as shopping centers, concerts, and even lecture halls. She is afraid that if something were to happen, she would have a difficult time getting out of these situations. Megan is likely experiencing symptoms of _____. (586)
    A. Panic
    B. Phobia
    C. Generalized anxiety
    D. Agoraphobia

6.   A specific phobia is _____. (587)
      A. Any phobia of a specific object or situation, along with a compelling desire to avoid it
      B. The normal everyday hesitations that we all experience
      C. Easy to diagnose but very difficult to modify
      D. A fear of having to put forth effort or commitment

7.   Which of the following is not an example of a mood disorder? (589)
      A. Bipolar disorder
      B. Dysthymic disorder
      C. Major depressive disorder
      D. Obsessive-compulsive disorder

8.   Which of the following statements regarding the causes of depression is correct? (591-593-593)
      A. Genetic factors play a role, but not neurotransmitters
      B. It is linked to an overly negative way of thinking about the self, environment, and future
      C. Negative life events are almost certain to bring on an episode of depression
      D. Only individuals with a family history of depression will experience a depressive disorder

9.   Dissociative disorders are characterized by a sudden but temporary alteration in consciousness, identity, and _____. (596)
      A. Emotion
      B. Thoughts
      C. Intelligence
      D. Memory

10.   Which type of schizophrenia is characterized by disturbed thought processes, incoherent speech, and blunted, inappropriate or silly affect? (601)
      A. Undifferentiated
      B. Paranoid
      C. Disorganized
      D. Catatonic

11.   Andy claims that he knows about the governments plan to influence people's minds via the internet. He fears that if he tells anyone, the government will have him assassinated. Andy may be diagnosed as having _____. (600)
      A. Paranoid schizophrenia
      B. Delusional disorder
      C. Disorganized schizophrenia
      D. Dissociative identity disorder

12. The words "superficially charming" and "irresponsible" would be used to describe and individual with which type of personality disorder _____. (606)
    A. Borderline
    B. Antisocial
    C. Histrionic
    D. Narcissistic

13. Which of the following is not one of the three broad classes of personality disorders? (606)
    A. Odd or eccentric
    B. Pessimistic and negative
    C. Fearful or anxious
    D. Dramatic, emotional, and impulsive

14. Which of the following disorders is *not* associated with an increased risk of violent behavior? (608)
    A. Paranoid schizophrenia
    B. Borderline personality
    C. Substance abuse
    D. Antisocial personality disorder

15. Which disorder is associated with the highest risk of suicide? (609
    A. Personality disorders
    B. Somatoform disorders
    C. Dissociative disorders
    D. Depressive disorders

True or False

1. Evidence indicates that culture does *not* make a difference in how people express maladjustment. (583)

2. People between the ages of 25 and 45 are most likely to be diagnosed with depression. (591)

3. Bipolar disorders occur more frequently than major depressive disorders. (594)

4. Dissociative amnesia is typically caused by some sort of physical injury, like a blow to the head. (596)

5. The concordance rate for schizophrenia is higher for identical twins than for fraternal twins. (603)

6. Personality disorders tend to be more stable across time compared to other mental disorders. (605)

7. Most people who have mental disorders are not violent. (608)

8. The population most at risk for completing suicide is Caucasian females between the ages of 14-22. (609)

Essay Questions

1. Describe the purpose and goals of the DSM-IV system, list the axes used in making a diagnosis, and identify what information goes on each axis. (580-582)

2. Explain the relationship between violence and psychological disorder from the perspective of a) whether having a psychological disorder increases the risk of becoming violent, and b) how being a victim of violence might increase one's risk for experiencing a psychological disorder. (608-612)

When You Have Finished!

Surf's Up!!

After you've read and reviewed, try these web sites for additional information about some of the topics covered in this chapter.

1. **Dr. John Grohl's Psych Central** (http://psychcentral.com/)
   One of the best developed sites on the internet with regard to information and resources about psychological disorders. You will find information about symptoms of various disorders, treatments of disorders (including information about medications), and even self-help quizzes regarding certain disorders.

2. **National Alliance for the Mentally Ill** (http://www.nami.org/)
   This mission of this organization is to provide accurate information about mental illness, provide support for individuals and families of individuals with mental illness, and to improve the quality of life for individuals afflicted with mental illnesses.

3. **Depression and Bipolar Support Alliance** (http://www.dbsalliance.org/)
   This is a non-profit organization that provides information and resources for individuals suffering from mood disorders.

4. **National Institute of Mental Health** (http://www.nimh.nih.gov/nimhhome/index.cfm)
   NIMH is a governmental organization that aims to "reduce the burden of mental illness" through research initiatives. At this site, you can find information about various research studies looking at the causes and treatment of mental illness. In addition, you can review breaking news related to research and other topics related to mental illness.

5. **Anxiety Disorders Association of America** (http://www.adaa.org)
   The ADAA is devoted to information and resources related to anxiety disorders and their treatment. There is great information and descriptions of the different types of anxiety disorders here!

6. **Schizophrenia Information Center** (http://www.schizophrenia.com)
   This site contains information and resources about schizophrenia that are intended for people with the disorders and friends and family members of individuals with schizophrenia.

Cross Check: Psychological Disorders

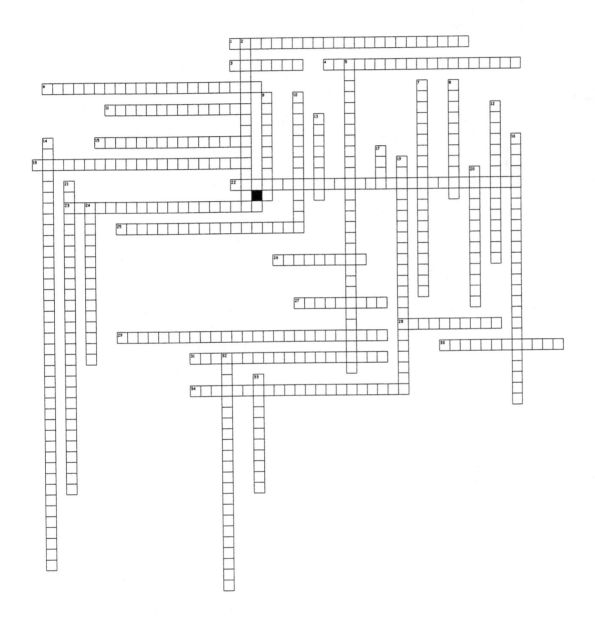

Across

1. Loss of interest and extreme sadness
3. Generalized feeling of fear
4. The behavior of giving up
6. Temporary disturbance in identity, memory, and consciousness
11. Fear of specific situation or object
15. Degree of agreement
18. Characterized by delusions of persecution
22. Used to be known as multiple personality disorder
23. Disorders characterized by extreme and persistent sadness
25. The study of abnormal behavior
26. Gross reality testing deficits that impair with ordinary life
27. False beliefs
28. How frequently a disorder occurs
29. Fear of multiple things and situations
30. Fear of scrutiny by others
31. Loss of memory
34. Symptoms of schizophrenia, but reality testing in check

Down

2. Opposite of normal behavior
5. Egocentric and irresponsible
7. Long standing disturbances
8. Fear of situations where escape may be difficult
9. The maltreatment of a child
10. Diminished ability to deal with demanding life events
12. Characterized by manic and depressive episodes
13. Legal definition of mental illness
14. Manual used to make diagnoses
16. Disturbed thought processes, emotion, and behavior
17. Forcible sexual act
19. Characterized by excited or violent motor activity or stupor
20. Either depression or bipolar disorders
21. Mixture of psychotic symptoms, with non dominant
24. Fear and avoidance
32. Class of disorders characterized by loss of reality testing
33. Intense and sudden fear

Created by Puzzlemaker at DiscoverySchool.com

Chapter 17

Therapy

Before You Begin...

You might think of psychotherapy as consisting of a client lying on a couch with an unresponsive therapist sitting next to them silently taking notes. In reality, this is only one rarely used type of psychotherapy called psychoanalysis. In this chapter, you will learn about a variety of different therapeutic approaches, how they differ from one another, and what techniques are used. You will also learn about other issues of importance in treating mental illness such as the role of medication, the influence of culture and gender on treatment efficacy, and the role of psychotherapists and treatment providers in the community.

The chapter opens by defining psychotherapy and providing you with a broad overview of the different approaches to psychotherapy. Like the last chapter, you will see that psychologists' understanding of the individuals they are working with is influenced by the model that they subscribe to. You will also learn that some psychologists believe there are common factors within all models that contribute to treatment being effective. Finally, you will explore the impact that gender, culture, and managed care have had on psychological treatments.

The heart of this chapter is devoted to then exploring the various models of treatment that are used by psychologists today. These models include psychodynamic, humanistic, behavioral, and cognitive treatment approaches. When exploring each model, you will learn about the underlying goals of each type of treatment, some of the common techniques used in each, and how practitioners in each model define psychotherapeutic effect. You will also practice those critical thinking skills by comparing and contrasting the different models and by reviewing some of the common criticisms of each model!

The final part of the chapter is devoted to exploring three other means of treating psychological problems: group and marital therapy, community interventions, and drug therapies. You will come to understand goals of each type of intervention and explore some of ways in which these treatments are conducted. When reviewing the biologically based treatments, you will be provided with a brief overview of the common types of medications and what types of disorders they are used to treat. In addition, you will learn about some of the less frequently used biological interventions and discuss when and why they might be used in modern treatment approaches.

Key Terms

Psychotherapy
Placebo Effect
Double-Blind Technique
Demand Characteristics
Eclectic Approach
Insight Therapy
Psychoanalysis
Psychodynamically Based Therapies
Free Association
Dream Analysis
Interpretation
Resistance
Transference
Working Through
Client-Centered Therapy
Behavior Therapy
Symptom Substitution
Token Economy
Time-out
Counterconditioning
Systematic Desensitization
Aversive Counterconditioning
Cognitive-Behavior Therapy
Rational-Emotive Therapy
Group Therapy
Family Therapy
Community Psychology
Empowerment
Biologically Based Therapy
Antianxiety Drugs
Antidepressant Drugs
Lithium Carbonate
Antipsychotic Drugs
Tardive Dyskinesia
Psychosurgery
Electroconvulsive Therapy
Deinstitutionalization

Learning Objectives

After reading this chapter, you should be able to:

1. Define psychotherapy and discuss whether it is effective, how we might study its effectiveness, and how managed care has changed therapy.
2. Identify the different orientations to psychotherapy and discuss what some psychologists consider to be the common factors among these therapies.
3. Discuss the role that culture and gender might play in therapy.
4. Distinguish between psychoanalysis and psychodynamically based therapy, describe the various techniques used in psychoanalysis, and identify some of the criticisms and problems surrounding psychoanalysis.
5. Outline the goals, techniques, and assumptions of client-centered therapy and discuss some common criticisms of this approach.
6. Define behavior therapy and differentiate among psychodynamic, humanistic, and behavior therapies by describing the reasons why behaviorists are dissatisfied with psychodynamic and humanistic therapies.
7. List the three general techniques used in behavior therapy. For each technique, define what it is, how it is implemented and what types of problems it might be used to treat.
8. State the three basic assumptions of cognitive therapy and identify how cognitive therapy is different than other therapy approaches.
9. Define and differentiate between rational-emotive, Beck, and Meichenbaum's approaches to cognitive therapy.
10. Compare and contrast individual and group approaches to treatment and discuss the structure of groups and the goals of group therapy.
11. Describe the assumptions and focus of family therapy and discuss some of the difficulties involved in the effort to change family systems.
12. Define community psychology and state how community psychologists are involved in empowerment and prevention efforts in the community.
13. Describe four classes of psychotropic drugs, give examples of each, and state types of disorders for which they might be prescribed.
14. Explain why psychologists might sometimes resort to biologically based therapies such as psychosurgery and electroconvulsive therapy.
15. Identify the benefits and costs associated with deinstitutionalization.

As you read...

What Is Psychotherapy, and What Types Are Available?

1.   Psychotherapy is _____.

2.   A _____ effect is an improvement that occurs as a result of a person's expectation of change rather than as a result of any specific treatment. Explain how a double-blind technique takes care of this and how it reduces demand characteristics.

3.   Is psychotherapy effective? Provide some evidence to support your answer.

4.   List and briefly describe the four major types of therapy.

5.   _____ approaches tend to use more than one type of therapy, whereas psychotherapy _____ has the goal of integrating theories to devise new ways to solve problems.

6.   According to Goldfriend's (2004) psychotherapy integration view, what makes psychotherapy effective?

7.   What are some of the common factors among therapy that have been identified by psychologists?

8.   Multiculturalism is defined as _____, whereas _____ recognizes the multiple cultural factors and experiences that may be involved in influencing the individual.

9.   How does culture affect therapy?

10.   Describe how gender might influence therapy.

11. What are the 3 key problems associated with managed care?

12. What benefit has managed care had on therapy?

13. How is planned short-term treatment different than traditional therapy?

How Do Psychodynamic Therapies Work?

1. _____ therapy is defined as any therapy that attempts to discover relationships between unconscious motivations and current abnormal behavior.

2. How is psychoanalysis different from and similar to psychodynamically based therapies?

3. What are the goals of psychoanalysis?

17.1   The Techniques of Psychoanalysis

Fill in the missing information from the chart below.

Dream Analysis	
	An unwillingness to cooperate with therapy, which the client signals by showing a reluctance to provide the therapist with necessary information
Free Association	
	The technique of providing a context, meaning, or cause for a specific idea, feeling or set of behaviors.
Transference	

4.   The repetitive cycle of interpretation, resistance to interpretation, and transference in psychoanalysis is referred to as _____ _____.

5.   What is ego analysis?

6.   How is ego analysis different than traditional psychoanalysis?

7.   What are the criticisms of psychoanalysis?

What Do Humanistic Therapies Emphasize?

1.   How are humanistic therapies different than psychodynamic therapies?

2.   _____ therapy seeks to help people evaluate the world and themselves from their own perspective by providing them with non-evaluative therapeutic relationship. It was developed by _____ _____.

3.   What are the three essential characteristics of successful client-centered therapy?

4.   When a therapist accepts the client and projects positive feelings toward a client it is called _____ _____ _____.

5.   What are the criticisms of client-centered therapy?

What Are The Methods of Behavior Therapy?

1.   Behavior therapy is_____.

2.   List the three reasons why behavior therapy has become so popular.

3.   What are the three general procedures involved in behavior therapy?

4.   How is behavior therapy different from the insight therapies?

5.   What are the 3 reasons behaviorists are dissatisfied with psychodynamic and humanistic therapies?

6.   _____ _____ refers to the appearance of one overt symptom to replace another that has been eliminated by treatment.

7.   What are the 3 general procedures of behavior therapy?

8.   How does operant conditioning work as therapy?

9.   Define and differentiate between token economies, extinction, and punishment.

10.   What is the problem with using punishment as a therapeutic technique?

11.   A time-out is an operant-conditioning procedure in which a person is removed from _____ of _____ in order to increase/decrease (pick one) the occurrence of desired/undesired (pick one) behavior?

12.   You feel anxious every time you think about speaking in public. In therapy, you are taught how to relax in response to this stimulus instead of feeling anxious. This would be an example of what therapeutic technique?

13.   _____ _____ is a multistage counterconditioning procedure in which a person is taught to relax when confronting a stimulus that formerly elicited anxiety.

14.   Describe aversive counterconditioning and provide an example.

15. Define modeling and discuss when it is likely to be most effective according to Bandura (1977).

Why is Cognitive Therapy So Popular?

1. Cognitive therapy is _____.

2. What are the 3 basic assumptions of cognitive therapy?

3. _____ _____ therapy is a type of cognitive therapy that emphasizes the importance of logical, rational thought processes. It was developed by _____ _____.

4. What is the major goal of rational emotive therapy?

5. The goal of Beck's approach to cognitive therapy is _____.

6. List the 4 stages that a successful client passes through according to Beck's cognitive therapy.

7. According to Meichenbaum, the goal of the therapist in cognitive therapy is to _____. The strength of this approach is that _____.

How Does Therapy In A Group Work?

1. _____ _____ is a treatment in which several people meet as a group with a therapist to receive help, whereas _____ _____ is a treatment where people who are committed to one another's well being are treated at once in an effort to change the ways they interact.

2. How are clients selected for group therapy, and what is the goal of this selection style?
3. Family therapy is _____.

4. Why is family therapy sometimes called relationship therapy?

5. Family therapists often attempt to change family systems. Describe what this means.

6. _____ is when the entire family becomes enmeshed in one family member's problem.

7. What characteristics might a person who is codependent have?

How Do Psychologists Reach Out to Communities?

1. Community psychology is _____.

2. _____ refers to facilitating the development and enhancement of skills, knowledge, and motivation in individuals so that they can gain control over their lives.

3. Name and describe the three types of prevention efforts that community psychologists are involved in.

How Do Biologically Based Therapies Create Change?

1. What are the three types of biologically based therapies?

2. Describe the key issues that clinicians should be aware of when prescribing drug therapies.

3. List the two types of antianxiety drugs describe and what these drugs treat.

4. Define the three classes of antidepressant drugs and name some of the drugs in each class.

5. Are antidepressant drugs effective?

6. The most common type of antimania drug is _____ _____.

7. Antipsychotic drugs are _____.

8. _____ _____ is a central nervous system disorder that is characterized by involuntary spasmodic movements of the upper body, especially the face and fingers.

9. Psychosurgery is _____. How frequently is it used and why?

10. _____ _____ is a treatment for severe mental illness in which a shock of electricity is applied to the head.

11. How frequently is ECT used, and when is it most likely to be used?

After You Read, Practice Test #1

1. Two clients are seeing a therapist for the first time. One client was referred to this therapist at the recommendation of a friend who said the therapist was "fantastic." The other person has heard that the therapist is "ok." Even though both clients receive the same treatment, the first client rates the treatment as being better because of the expectation they had coming in. This is an example of _____. (619)
   A. Demand characteristics
   B. Placebo effect
   C. Experimental control
   D. Double-blindness

2. The process of accepting and celebrating distinct cultural heritages and their influence on the therapeutic process is referred to as _____. (625)
   A. Ethnoculturalism
   B. Transculturalism
   C. Socioculturism
   D. Multiculturalism

3. The therapist is empathic, understanding, very attentive and yet the patient continues to respond to her as if he is not going to hear, care about, or accept what she has to say. Her behavior toward the therapist illustrates _____. (631)
   A. Interpretation
   B. Resistance
   C. Transference
   D. Reaction formation

4. An important difference between humanistic/client-centered and psychoanalytic therapies is that humanistic therapies emphasize (634)
   A. The environmental reinforcers that control behaviors
   B. The importance of achieving insight into one's problems
   C. The control of behavior by hidden, unconscious conflicts
   D. The uniqueness, creativity and free will of the clients

5. The basic concept of counterconditioning is to (641)
   A. Bring unconscious conflicts onto awareness to be dealt with
   B. Direct feelings at a therapist that are really for someone else
   C. Replace an undesired response with a new, more adaptive response
   D. Remove the reinforcers that are maintaining a behavior

6. When children are in time out, it is important that they receive (640)
   A. Negative reinforcement for their behavior
   B. No reinforcement at all for their behavior
   C. Token reinforcement for their behavior
   D. Positive reinforcement for their behavior

7. Which of the following involves changing the client's behavior by changing his thoughts or perceptions? (644)
   A. Behavioral therapy
   B. Biotherapy
   C. Cognitive therapy
   D. Client-centered therapy

8. Which of the following approaches to cognitive therapy focuses on teaching clients to uses self-instructions to help them cope better with stressful situations? (646)
   A. Beck's approach
   B. Rational-Emotive therapy approach
   C. Cognitive-Behavioral therapy
   D. Meichenbaum's approach

9. The specific composition of a group involved in group therapy usually _____. (648)
   A. Occurs by chance
   B. Is the result of one avid member who solicits others to join the group
   C. Depends on legal and medical referrals
   D. Is controlled by the therapist's selection of who can gain from and offer to the group's purpose

10. A patient who is experiencing mania is likely to be prescribed which drug? (656)
    A. Antianxiety
    B. Antipsychotic
    C. Lithium Carbonate
    D. Antidepressant

After You Read, Practice Test #2

1. _____ is the treatment of emotional or behavioral problems through psychological techniques. (619)
   A. Psychopathology
   B. Psychotherapy
   C. Electroconvulsive Shock Therapy
   D. Trephination

2. _____ are elements of an experimental situation that might cause a participant to perceive the situation in a certain way. (620)
   A. Control characteristics
   B. Placebo controls
   C. Demand characteristics
   D. Validity controls

3. One of the biggest benefits of managed care is that _____. (627)
   A. It has made therapy more accessible to more people
   B. Therapists now have to justify the need for additional treatment
   C. The outcome of therapies tends to be better
   D. It has led to the development of brief and effective treatments

4. A psychotherapist who urges a client to express freely thoughts and feelings and to verbalize whatever comes to mind without editing or censoring is using the technique of: (631)
   A. Transference
   B. Interpretation
   C. Free association
   D. Abreaction

5. The type of therapy developed by Carl Rogers is (634)
   A. Gestalt therapy
   B. Existential therapy
   C. Client-centered therapy
   D. Attributional therapy

6. An important criticism of client-centered therapies is that (636)
   A. There is not enough emphasis on biological factors
   B. Warm feelings may not be enough to help people change
   C. It focuses too much on behavior, not enough on feelings
   D. It makes clients feel too distant and uncomfortable

7.   In a token economy the number of tokens a person receives is usually dependent on: (639)
      A. A variable-interval schedule of reinforcement
      B. The time of day or the day of the week
      C. The number of privileges the person desires
      D. The level of difficulty of the behavior emitted

8.   Cognitive therapists believe that, for the most part, emotional disorders (644)
      A. Have physical causes
      B. Result from unconscious conflicts and motives
      C. Result from environmental stimuli
      D. Result from faulty thinking

9.   What is the primary aim of family therapy? (649)
      A. Identify maladaptive behavior in family members.
      B. Change the way the family interacts.
      C. Restructure the organization of the family.
      D. Balance the power in the family

10.   Electroconvulsive shock therapy is used to treat (603)
      A. Catatonic schizophrenia
      B. Paranoid schizophrenia
      C. Anxiety disorders
      D. Severe depression

After You Read, Practice Test #3

1. Psychotherapy is the _____. (619)
    A. First step in helping someone overcome their illness before medications are given
    B. Treatment of emotional problem through psychological techniques
    C. Process of helping people to understand their childhood better
    D. Attempt to help people understand what behavior is culturally appropriate

2. According to Kazdin, (2000), individuals in treatment are better off, on average, than _____ of untreated individuals. (620)
    A. 50%
    B. 25%
    C. 98%
    D. 80%

3. The type of psychotherapy that is rooted in Freudian theory is called _____. (621)
    A. Psychodynamic therapy
    B. Eclectic therapy
    C. Cognitive therapy
    D. Humanistic therapy

4. When aversive counterconditioning is used, the patient: (642)
    A. Is forced into a high anxiety state until he or she sees that the problem behavior is unreasonable.
    B. Gradually becomes less emotional.
    C. Learns a new behavior in response to a stimulus that needs to be avoided.
    D. Learns to challenge fear-producing stimuli

5. Through the process of systematic desensitization, a client is taught to _____ in response to a stimulus that normally creates anxiety. (641)
    A. Think differently
    B. Relax
    C. Act assertively
    D. Seek support from others

6. _____ prevention refers to reducing the number of new cases of a disorder and counteracting harmful circumstances before they lead to maladjustment. (651-652)
    A. Secondary
    B. Tertiary
    C. Intermediary
    D. Primary

7. When a symptom has been eliminated through therapy, but another symptom appears to take its place it is referred as _____. (638)
    A. Symptom realignment
    B. Symptom restructuring
    C. Symptom dissociation
    D. Symptom substitution

8. A person who has been taking antipsychotic medications over a long period of time may develop what disorder that is characterized by involuntary, spasmodic movements of the upper body? (656)
    A. Schizophrenia
    B. Parkinson's
    C. Tardive Dyskinesia
    D. Amnesia

9. In the 1940's, it was not uncommon for doctors to perform a surgery where parts of the brain's frontal lobes were severed in order to control symptoms of psychological disorder. This type of procedure would be an example of _____. (656)
    A. Psychosurgery
    B. Shock therapy
    C. Psychostimulant
    D. Aversive counterconditioning

10. Deinstitutionalization refers to _____. (658)
    A. The process of having treatments use less drug therapy and more talk therapy
    B. An attempt to have therapy conducted by professionals who are better trained
    C. A movement toward reducing the stigma associated with mental illness
    D. Transitioning of treatment from inpatient facilities to outpatient facilities

After You Read, Comprehensive Practice Test

1. Psychotherapy typically refers to treatment that involves a(n) _____. (619)
   a. The manipulation of diet and physical exercise
   b. The use of electroconvulsive shock and prescriptions for tranquilizers and antipsychotic drugs
   c. Techniques based upon psychological principles
   d. All of the above

2. A psychologist who works with groups and neighborhoods to develop an action-oriented approach to individual and social adjustment is a _____ psychologist. (621)
   a. Social
   b. Community
   c. Physiological
   d. Clinical

3. A client who was raised by a very critical father responds to his therapist's questioning by becoming angry with the therapist and accusing the therapist of being critical and not accepting him. The client's reaction is an example of _____. (632)
   a. Resistance
   b. Interpretation
   c. Working through
   d. Transference

4. Which of the following is not a criticism of psychoanalysis? (633)
   a. It fails to consider the important role of the family on the individual
   b. The approach tends to be unscientific and difficult to study
   c. Some of the basic tenets of psychoanalysis are sexist
   d. The effectiveness of its techniques has not been well established

5. The purpose of techniques such as dream analysis and free association is to _____. (631)
   a. Encourage the patient to talk about events in the "here and now"
   b. Observe the frequency of thoughts that arise from the reality principle
   c. Clarify the patient's point of view concerning his or her behavior
   d. Gain access to thoughts in the unconscious

6. A basic tenet of client-centered therapy is that the therapist must use _____. (635)
   a. Counterconditioning
   b. Interpretation
   c. Direct suggestion
   d. Unconditional positive regard

7.   The purpose of a time out is to _____. (640)
      a. Give the child time to think about what they did wrong
      b. Remove the child from sources of reinforcement
      c. Punish the child for bad behavior
      d. Teach the child better social skills

8.   Behavior therapists are dissatisfied with insight therapies for all of the following reasons except _____. (633)
      a. They find many of the terms used by insight therapists to be difficult to define and measure
      b. They disagree with insight therapist's belief that most maladjustment must be changed by the person with the behavior problem
      c. They feel that the labels used by insight therapists can themselves cause maladaptive behavior
      d. They question the effectiveness of insight therapies

9.   A behavior therapist knows that treatment has been effective when _____.(637)
      a. Symptom substitution can be noticeably measured
      b. The client says he has learned new coping skills
      c. Follow-up observations show that the new behavior is still occurring
      d. All of the above

10.   Behavior therapists would say a child's fear of dogs diminishes when she observes other children playing with dogs, because of which behavioral technique? (642)
      a. Operant conditioning
      b. Modeling
      c. Cognitive restructuring
      d. Time Out

11.   Rational-emotive therapy _____. (644-645)
      a. Tries to place a person's cognitive assumptions about their experiences in a reasonable framework
      b. Encourages people to put a high value on the things they want to get out of life
      c. Is based on the idea that abnormal behaviors cause irrational thoughts
      d. Is best described as a self-help technique

12.   From a family therapist's point of view, the patient in family therapy is _____. (649)
      a. The family member who is used as a scapegoat
      b. The family member or members who do the scapegoating
      c. The parents
      d. The family structure and organization

13. One of the advantages of group therapy is _____. (648)
    a. Members model behavior for one another
    b. A member can talk about a behavior problem without having to face social pressure to change
    c. The therapist is more directive, enabling therapy to proceed more quickly.
    d. All of the above

14. Psychosurgery is _____. (657)
    a. Used only with severe cases of depression
    b. Rarely used in the treatment of mental illness
    c. Not legal in some states
    d. A form of cognitive therapy

15. One of the unintended, negative effects of deinstitutionalization is that _____. (659)
    a. The number of people who experience mental illness has increased
    b. The number of people who have gone untreated has increased
    c. The cost of health care has decreased
    d. The development of new medications to treat mental illness has decreased

True or False

1. Research studies that compare traditional talking therapies with placebo treatments demonstrate that placebos are as effective as psychotherapies. (620)

2. Women tend to seek out therapy more often than men do; however, both genders tend to respond similarly to treatment. (626)

3. Unlike psychodynamic and humanistic therapies, behavior therapy does not encourage clients to interpret past events to find their meaning. (637)

4. Client-centered therapists believe that mental illness and problem behavior occurs when the environment prevents a person from developing their innate potential. (634)

5. One of the problems with punishment as a therapeutic technique is that only suppresses existing behaviors but does not establish new, desired behaviors. (640)

6. Research indicates that family therapy may be as effective as individual therapy. (650)

7. One of the main goals of community psychology is empowerment, which is defined as helping members of the community improve the quality of their environment. (651)

8. One of the benefits of deinstitutionalization has been that the cost of treating individuals with severe mental illnesses has been reduced. (659)

Essay Questions

1. Review the evidence about the effectiveness of psychotherapy and discuss the role of culture and gender in psychotherapy. (619-627)

2. Briefly describe the major types of drug therapy. (653-656)

When You Have Finished!

Surf's Up!!

After you've read and reviewed, try these web sites for additional information about some of the topics covered in this chapter.

1. **American Group Psychotherapy Association** (http://www.groupsinc.org/index.html)
   The AGPA is a group devoted to communication information and resources about group psychotherapy approaches. The site contains basic information about group therapy, resources for further reading, and referrals.

2. **Beck Institute for Cognitive Therapy and Research** (http://beckinstitute.org/)
   Aaron Beck is the founder of cognitive therapy. This site contains information about cognitive therapy, resources about cognitive therapy, and links to other sites related to cognitive therapy and emotional disorders.

3. **Albert Ellis Institute** (http://www.rebt.org/)
   Albert Ellis is the founder of rational-emotive therapy. This site is devoted to information, resources, and training in this form of cognitive-behavioral treatment.

4. **The American Psychoanalytic Association** (http://apsa.org/)
   This site is devoted to providing information to the public and professionals on psychoanalytic treatment and training.

5. **Association for Humanistic Psychology** (http://www.ahpweb.org/)
   The AHP is an organization devoted to all aspects of humanistic psychology, including treatment using humanistic methods. There is information here about humanistic theory and treatment, academic training in humanistic psychology, and links to other humanistic psychology sites.

6. **American Psychological Association Help Center** (http://www.apahelpcenter.org/)
   This site contains information about mental health issues and treatment for the general public. Included is information on current topics of interest and information regarding common interests and problems such as work and school, family and relationships, and managed care.

7. **Internet Mental Health** (http://mentalhealth.com/)
   A site filled with information about mental health and its treatment. A focus of this site is to increase the accessibility of such information to people all over the word, including professionals and laypersons. The site is also focused on presenting information that is empirically supported.

8. **Intranet Drug Index** (http://www.rxlist.com/)
   A site filled with information about commonly used drugs, including drugs used in the treatment of mental illness.

Psychology

Cross Check: Therapy

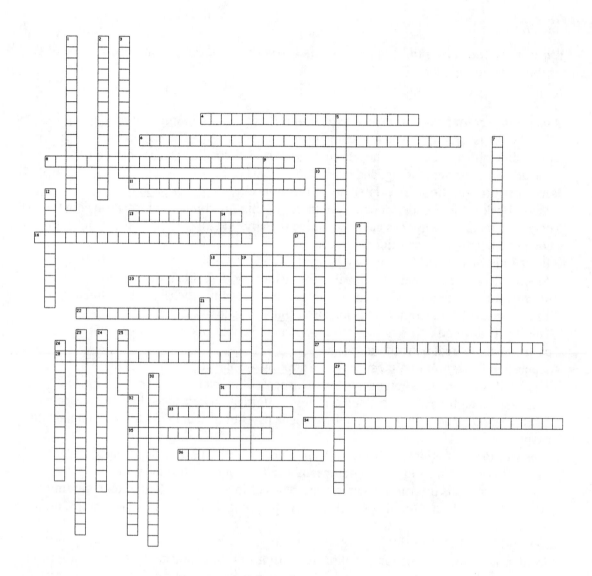

Across

4. When a client behaves a certain way because they believe they are supposed to
6. All therapies based on Freud's work
8. Also sometimes called "shock therapy"
11. Side effect of medication
13. Drug you would use to treat a phobia
16. Treatment developed by Carl Rogers
18. Treatment of emotional problems
20. Client refuses to give therapist what they want
22. Just say whatever comes to mind
27. Taking patients from inpatient to outpatient treatment
28. One of the major criticisms of behavioral therapy
31. Antimania drug
33. Reward(s) given for appropriate behavior
34. A form of counterconditioning
35. Process of making sense of client's material in therapy
36. Repetitive pattern in psychoanalysis

Down

1. Treatment focused on changing thoughts
2. Treatment focused on faulty learning
3. Improvement as result of expectations versus treatment
5. Treatments that focus on client becoming more aware
7. Developed by Albert Ellis
9. Pairing stimulus with negative contingency
10. Treatment through drugs, surgery, or ECT
12. Technique that reduces possibility of demand characteristics
14. A client responds emotionally to therapist the way they did to a parent
15. Type of therapy developed by Sigmund Freud
17. Making sense of what happens when you sleep
19. Replacing one response to stimulus with a more adaptive one
21. Removing person from chance to receive rewards
23. Branch of psychology focusing on empowerment
24. Drug you would use to treat a major depressive disorder
25. Therapy treatment of a group of family members at one time
26. Brain surgery that is used to treat mental illness
29. Treatment of more than two unrelated individuals at one time
30. The use of more than one therapeutic model at one time
32. Drug you would use to treat schizophrenia

Created by Puzzlemaker at DiscoverySchool.com

Chapter 18
Psychology in Action

Before you read...

      Throughout your journey through psychology this semester, you have been introduced to a number of areas of study and a number of actual and potential applications to every day life. This chapter more specifically examines four specific fields in which psychology is applied to modern life. These fields include industrial/organizational (I/O), human factors, forensic, and sport psychology.

      In the first part of the chapter, you will explore the question of how behavior is affected by the work environment. This question is explored by I/O psychologists who address a number of important areas related to the work environment. These areas include training, promoting, and evaluating employee performance, motivating people to perform better, and increasing job satisfaction. You will also be introduced to research exploring what makes for effective leadership and teamwork, two additional issues studied by I/O psychologists. Finally, if you will ever be out there interviewing for a job (and you will be!), this part of the chapter also provides some tips for effective interviewing.

      In the second part of the chapter, you will be introduced to human factors psychology, which combines information from perceptual and environmental areas of psychology. Human factors psychologists are concerned with the relationship between humans and machines, and their goals are to improve efficiency and safety on the job.

      In the third part of the chapter, you will explore the area of forensic psychology, which concerns the mix of law and psychology. You will see that psychologists play a number of roles in the legal arena, including researchers, policy or program evaluators, advocates, and expert witnesses. Although psychologists and lawyers do not always agree, the psychologist is being recognized as a key player in both the private and public sector.

      Finally, you will review the relatively new field of sport psychology. Sport psychologists apply psychological principles related to motivation, arousal and anxiety, and relaxation training to helping athletes maximize performance.

Key Terms

Industrial/Organizational Psychology
Job Analysis
Meta-analysis
Performance Appraisal
Goal-Setting Theory
Expectancy Theories
Equity Theory
Team
Transactional Leader
Transformational Leader
Human Factors
Forensic Psychology
Sport Psychology

Learning Objectives

After reading this chapter, you should be able to:

1. Define I/O psychology and describe its five broad areas: human resources psychology, motivation of job performance, job satisfaction, teamwork, and leadership.
2. Describe the personnel functions of human resource psychologists in the areas of job analysis, personnel selection, education and training, and performance appraisal.
3. Explain what factors might contribute to motivation on the job and describe characteristics of jobs that might cause stress or unhappiness.
4. Identify and distinguish between goal-setting, expectancy, and equity theories of motivation and job performance.
5. Describe the three approaches to management and discuss their influence on motivation.
6. Define a team and discuss the role of the team in companies.
7. Compare and contrast the three phases of research on leadership: traits, behaviors, and situations. For each phase, discuss some of the relevant research related to each phase.
8. Explain what constitutes effective leadership.
9. List five factors that should be considered when thinking about the future of I/O psychology.
10. Describe how human factors psychologists are involved in helping people and machines work together more efficiently.
11. Discuss the different types of designs that have been used to enhance workplace safety.
12. Name the multiple roles that psychologists play in the legal system, and provide a brief definition and example for each.
13. Describe how sport psychology attempts to bring order to the study of athletic performance.
14. State the relationship between arousal and athletic performance as it relates to athletic performance.
15. Distinguish between arousal and anxiety, and describe some of the stress management techniques used to relieve anxiety and arousal while increasing athletic performance.

As you read...

How Is Behavior Affected By The Work Environment?

1.   Industrial/organizational psychology is _____.

2.   I/O Psychology has its roots in what two areas of psychology? Explain.

3.   How might culture affect the work environment?

4.   List and describe the 5 broad areas of I/O psychology.

18.1   Human Resources

1.   A job analysis involves creating a detailed description of the ____.

2.   A job analysis specifies both _____ gets done and _____ it gets done.

3.   A _____ job analysis is appealing to I/O psychologists because, in a way, it is similar to a research study. Explain how.

4.   What is the basic goal of selection procedures?

5.   Name the types of selection procedures are typically used by I/O psychologists, and provide a brief description of each.

6.   _____ _____ are hands-on simulations of all or some of a job's tasks.

7. Describe the results of Huffcutt and Roth's (1998, 2003) research on job interviews and their relation to race.

8. A meta-analysis is _____.

9. _____ _____ is a process whereby companies and managers systematically teach employees knowledge and skills to improve their job performance.

10. Describe some different types of training and education corporations might use.

11. The process by which a supervisor periodically evaluates the job-relevant strengths and weaknesses of subordinates is called _____ _____.

12. A well done job appraisal should have what two qualities?

18.2	Motivation of Job Performance

1. What are the 4 dimensions that organizations and cultures vary on according to Hofstede (1983)?

2. Define intrinsically motivated behavior and provide one example of this construct as it related to work performance.

3. What factors might cause a worker to be unhappy or stressed?

4. The theory that asserts that setting specific, clear, attainable goals for a given activity leads to better performance is _____ _____ _____.

5. Define the following goals as they relate to smart theory:

    a. S:

    b. M:

    c. A:

    d. R:

    e. T:

6. According to the definition of expectancy theory, a person's desire to maintain goal-directed behavior is determined by _____.

7. According to Vroom (1964), motivation can be determined from a three part equation made up of _____, _____, and _____.

8. What are the key variables that determine performance?

9. According to equity theory, what a worker does should be reflected in what?

10. What are the 5 ways people alter inequalities?

11. Define self-efficacy and how it affects work performance.

12. Describe the 3 basic motivation management approaches.

18.3   Job Satisfaction

1. How is job satisfaction different than job motivation?

2. What are the 5 basic categories of job satisfaction?

3.   How do co-workers, personal dispositions, and mood affect job satisfaction?

18.4	Teams and Teamwork

1.   A team is a group of individuals who _____.

2.   The number of roles within a team is dependent on what 3 factors?

18.5	Leadership

1.   Leaders are _____.

2.   Name and differentiate between the goals of the three major phases of research on leadership.

3.   One defining trait of an effective leader is _____, the ability to quickly adapt to the ever changing environment.

4.   Describe employee-oriented, task-oriented, and transactional leaders.

5.   How does gender effect leadership?

6.   Describe Vroom's leadership model.

7.   A transformational leader is a person who _____.

8.   List the 8 guidelines to being an effective leader.

How Do Human Factors Affect Performance?

1.   The study of the relationship of _____ _____ to _____ and to workplaces and other environments is referred to as _____.

2.   Human factors researchers seek to design interfaces between people and machines that maximize _____, minimize _____ and _____, and are _____.

3.   What are the differences between an I/O psychologist and a human factors psychologist?

4.   To a large extent, _____ equipment has become the focus of human factors research rather than operating equipment.

18.6   Behavior-Based Safety

1.   Define behavior-based safety and its goals.

2.   Describe a good safety culture.

3.   A design in which it is impossible for a specific error to occur would be referred to as a _____ design.

4.   Name and describe the 3 types of designs that attempt to increase safe work environments.

5.   How has perception and environmental research helped improved work safety?

How Do Psychology and the Law Work Together?

1.   Forensic psychology is defined as _____.

2. List and describe the four roles psychologists might play in the legal system and provide an example of what they might do in each role.

3. Psychologist that help institutions determine if policies, agencies or programs work are called _____ _____.

4. How is the role of an advocate different than that of an expert witness?

18.7 Crime and Punishment

1. List the three common faulty assumptions that people hold in reference to capital punishment?

18.8 The Law and Psychology: An Uneasy Partnership

1. Why is the relationship between law and psychologists an uneasy one?

What Are the Goals of Sport Psychology?

1. Sport psychology is the systematic application of ____.

2. What are the 3 main goals of the sports psychologist?

3. How are sports psychologists trained?

18.9 Arousal and Anxiety in Athletic Performance

1. Define and differentiate between arousal and anxiety.

2.   How are arousal and anxiety related to performance?

18.10   Intervention Strategies for Athletes

1.   Describe progressive relaxation.

2.   How are hypnosis and meditation used with athletes?

3.   Having an athlete visualize a good performance would be an example of which type of intervention strategy?

4.   Both cognitive interventions and mental imagery involve teaching an athlete to think differently about their performance. Explain how they are different from one another, providing an example to illustrate your point.

18.11   Putting it Together: Go with the Flow

1.   What is the 4 step analysis to understanding what motivates a person?

2.   What is flow and when it is most likely to occur?

18.12   The Future of Sport Psychology:

1.   Describe the future of sports psychology.

After You Read, Practice Test #1

1. A detailed description of the tasks that will be required for employees to do a job, the resources and skills they will need, and how they will be evaluated is called a _____. (665)
    A.   Strategic plan
    B.   Screening test
    C.   Job analysis
    D.   Motivational system

2. Most psychologists see the paternalistic management style as being self-defeating because this style _____. (675-676)
    A.   Prevents slower workers from receiving rewards
    B.   Prevents employees from having any influence in establishing goals for the company
    C.   Does not encourage hard work because rewards are given without contingency
    D.   Requires hard work without adequate rewards

3. Which of the following tests might be used to test integrity? (668)
    A.   WAIS intelligence test
    B.   Scholastic Aptitude Test
    C.   A work sample test
    D.   MMPI-2 personality test

4. Meta-analysis is a statistical procedure that _____. (669)
    A.   Is used to evaluate the differences between effective versus non-effective work environments
    B.   Relies primarily on correlational data
    C.   Can be used only for examining questions related to I/O psychology
    D.   Is used to evaluate results from multiple studies that addressed the same topic or question.

5. The process called a 360-degree feedback refers to feedback that comes _____. (671)
    A.   By evaluating the employee in different situations
    B.   From multiple sources such as managers, co-workers, and customers
    C.   At specific times throughout the year
    D.   From managers and addresses personal and professional performance

6. Susan is paid by the number of boxes of apples she picks. This is an example of the _____ approach to motivating workers. (676)
   A. Behavioral
   B. Traditional
   C. Participatory
   D. Extrinsic

7. The process by which a supervisor or employer periodically evaluates how well an employee is doing on the job is called a (n) _____. (671)
   A. Job analysis
   B. Performance appraisal
   C. Employment review
   D. Worker evaluation

8. Currently, human factors researchers focus more on _____ equipment, rather that operating it. (685)
   A. Fixing
   B. Improving
   C. Controlling
   D. Describing

9. Psychologists working in the legal system may fill any of the following roles, except _____. (687-688)
   A. Researcher
   B. Program evaluator
   C. Advocate
   D. Consultant

10. According to sport psychologists, _____ occurs when a person becomes totally engrossed in overcoming a challenge or when a person is deeply engaged in an activity they enjoy. (693)
    A. Zoning
    B. Flow
    C. Exhilaration
    D. Leveling

After You Read, Practice Test #2

1. What is probably the most important goal of industrial/organizational psychology in the United States (665)
    A.   Stimulate the motivation of workers.
    B.   Increase productivity
    C.   Reduce the cost of labor
    D.   Provide a pleasant environment for workers

2. Research indicates that the best measures for helping employers make hiring decisions include each of the following, except _____. (666-667)
    A.   Test of general mental ability
    B.   Work samples
    C.   Tests of adjustment and mental stability
    D.   Integrity tests

3. The process by which a supervisor periodically evaluates the job-relevant strengths and weaknesses of a subordinate is called a _____. (671)
    A.   Job evaluations
    B.   Supervisory assessment
    C.   Performance appraisal
    D.   Personnel summary

4. Goal-setting theory says that better performance will result when we set goals that are _____. (673)
    A.   Specific, clear and attainable
    B.   General enough to apply to everyone
    C.   Too hard for anyone to reach
    D.   So easy there is no possible failure

5. Employees tend to experience a sense of self-determination and competence when they work under _____. (676)
    A.   Behavioral management styles
    B.   Participatory management styles
    C.   Boss-centered leadership
    D.   Task-oriented leadership styles

6. A leader who focuses on enhancing workers' self- worth is ____ oriented; one who focuses on getting the job done effectively is ____ oriented (680)
    A.   Satisfaction; motivation
    B.   Motivation; satisfaction
    C.   Task; employee
    D.   Employee; task

7. As a researcher, a psychologist may participate in the legal system by _____. (687)
    A.   Determining whether a specific person is mentally competent
    B.   Measuring the personality trait of an accused criminal
    C.   Studying the causes and treatment for aggressive behaviors
    D.   All of the above

8. A workplace environment in which a certain type of error is less likely to happen, but still might happen, exhibits a (n) design. (686)
    A.   Prevention
    B.   Exclusion
    C.   Fail-safe
    D.   Inclusion

9. An effort to design safe work environments that has the goal of making it impossible for a specific error to occur is called a(n) _____ design. (686)
    A.   Fail-safe
    B.   Exclusion
    C.   Prevention
    D.   Environmental

10. Athletes are taught to focus on changing the way they think about their performance, an upcoming event, or their own abilities in order to improve their performance. This technique is called _____. (693)
    A.   Progressive relaxation
    B.   Mental imagery
    C.   Cognitive interventions
    D.   Thought stopping procedure

After You Read, Practice Test #3

1. A functional job analysis (FJA) specifies three hierarchies for worker functions for each job. These hierarchies relate to _____. (666)
    A. Superiors, peers, and subordinates
    B. Preparation, performance, and evaluation
    C. Employment, promotion, and compensation
    D. Information, people, and things

2. A position analysis questionnaire is widely used to get information from workers about _____. (666)
    A. How they like their jobs and the companies they work for
    B. What changes would make their jobs easier or more pleasant
    C. What positions might be open in their organization soon
    D. The skills, activities and resources that their jobs require

3. According to Hofstede (1983) cultures and organizations vary on each of the following dimensions except _____. (672)
    A. Masculinity
    B. Uncertainty avoidance
    C. Femininity
    D. Power distance

4. A company that wants to increase workers' sense of self-efficacy should do all of the following EXCEPT _____. (675)
    A. Increase task complexity to increase intrinsic motivation
    B. Provide accurate descriptions of work to be accomplishes
    C. Suggest techniques to accomplish various tasks
    D. Increase the number of sub-goals for which a worker is paid

5. Which of the following situations is likely in an organization that has paternalistic management? (676)
    A. Workers compete for challenging jobs
    B. Bosses socialize with workers
    C. Companies provide amenities such as housing, schools, and recreation
    D. Pay is based on length of service

6. A key trait that seems to be common to most good leaders is _____. (680)
    A. Flexibility
    B. Self-confidence
    C. Sociability
    D. Assertiveness

7. _____ refers to effective safety management through a wide range of programs that focus on changing the behavior of workers and companies to prevent occupational injuries and illnesses. (685)
    A. Work-place management
    B. Behavior-based safety
    C. Environmental management and safety
    D. Employee prevention efforts

8. Research in the areas of _____ and _____ psychology have helped establish and maintain workplace safety. (686)
    A. Environmental and social
    B. Clinical and personality
    C. Perceptual and environmental
    D. Social and clinical

9. Working in forensic psychology typically requires a doctoral degree in _____ psychology. (687)
    A. Social
    B. Personality
    C. Counseling
    D. Clinical

10. The systematic application of psychological principles to several aspects of sports is called _____ psychology. (691)
    A. Athletic
    B. Sport
    C. Competitive
    D. Clinical

After You Read, Comprehensive Practice Test

1. The study of how worker's behaviors are affected by the work environment, by coworkers, and by organizational practices is called _____. (664)
    A.   Collective/productive psychology
    B.   Union/management psychology
    C.   Economic/managerial psychology
    D.   Industrial/organizational psychology

2. Selecting people for a job, determining benefits packages, and developing job training programs are all important functions for _____ psychologists (665)
    A.   Strategic
    B.   Human resources
    C.   Employment analysis
    D.   Forensic

3. Firefighter students have to pass a state proficiency test involving physical skills such as carrying a body, hooking up hoses, and setting up ladders. This is best described as _____. (667)
    A.   An intelligence test
    B.   A work sample test
    C.   A handwriting test
    D.   A test on integrity

4. The best way to reduce the effect of bias against minorities in interviews is _____. (668)
    A.   To have a highly structured interview
    B.   Probe for negative information in minority applicants' backgrounds
    C.   Reduce the size of the pool of applicants
    D.   Rely on ability tests scores to set a standard for comparing applicants

5. One of the most effective methods of training a new employee for a job is to have this person _____. (670)
    A.   Watch training videos produced by the management
    B.   Ask questions whenever something is not clear
    C.   Observe and interact with a more senior employee
    D.   Attend lectures on organization procedures and rules

6. A company that emphasizes the importance of getting the work done and puts less emphasis on relationships between co-workers demonstrates _____. (673)
    A.   Individualism
    B.   Masculinity
    C.   Collectivism
    D.   Femininity

7. According to expectancy theory, people are motivated by _____. (674)
    A.   Doing what they are expected to do
    B.   What they expect to get from performing an assigned task
    C.   Having the ability to make an assigned task a rewarding experience
    D.   B and C

8. Equity theory on the workplace emphasizes the importance of an employee's perception of _____. (675)
    A.   How much managers are paid compared to laborers
    B.   The balance between what they put in and their benefits
    C.   What others in the company think of their performance
    D.   How well the company does compared to other companies

9. Job satisfaction _____. (676)
    A.   Is a person's attitude about his or her job
    B.   Is directly related to job performance
    C.   Is solely determined by one's ability to do the job
    D.   A and B

10. Someone who influences the behavior of others toward attaining an agreed-upon goal is called a _____. (679)
    A.   Colleague
    B.   Supervisor
    C.   Manager
    D.   Leader

11. The study of how humans interact with machines and workplaces in an attempt to make these things more usable and safer is called _____. (684)
    A.   Industrial psychology
    B.   Robotics
    C.   Human factors
    D.   Engineering analysis

12. The application of psychological principles to phenomena or issues on the legal system is known as _____. (687)
    A.   Psychology jurisprudence
    B.   Forensic psychology
    C.   Legal psychology
    D.   Psycholegal research

13. As evaluators, psychologists may participate in the legal system by _____. (688)
    A.   Determining whether a particular program actually works
    B.   Studying factors that cause people to become criminals
    C.   Measuring the competence of prison guards and wardens
    D.   Assessing the mental competence of an accused criminal

14. Which of the following is not one of the goals of sport psychology? (691)
    A.   To improve the performance of athletes
    B.   Making communication between athletes and coaches better
    C.   Enhance the experience of sports for young participants
    D.   Assist with injury rehabilitation

15. Athletes are taught to focus their attention on one thought or idea in order to improve their performance. This technique is called _____. (693)
    A.   Mental imagery
    B.   Cognitive intervention
    C.   Hypnosis
    D.   Mediation

True or False

1. For complex jobs, differences between individuals of varying ethnicities tend to disappear, and both minorities and Whites are sought after equally vigorously. (668)

2. Constructing learning objectives for employee training tends to be effective because they allow employees to identify their own strengths and weaknesses. (670)

3. Research on motivation and job performance indicates that when intrinsically motivated behavior is reinforced with direct external rewards such as money, productivity often increases. (673)

4. Although teams tend to be complex, their behavior tends to remain relatively stable over time. (678)

5. Women leaders tend to be more employee-oriented and male leaders tend to be more task-oriented. (680)

6. Whereas I/O psychologists tend to focus on getting human beings to change their behavior to improve efficiency, human factors psychologists look at how equipment and machines can be improved to increase worker efficiency. (684)

7. Forensic psychology is a career choice that usually requires a Ph.D. or Psy.D. in social psychology. (687)

8. Competitive athletes often reach their peak of anxiety significantly before an athletic event begins. (692)

Essay Questions

1. What are the 5 broad areas of I/O psychology and how does each area help corporations succeed? (665)

2. Describe the 3 main areas where sport psychologists work to help athletes. (691)

When You Have Finished!

Surf's Up!!

After you've read and reviewed, try these web sites for additional information about some of the topics covered in this chapter.

1. **American Board of Sport Psychology**.
   (http://www.americanboardofsportpsychology.org/)
   This site is dedicated to communicating information regarding the practice and credentialing of sport psychologists. There is information about training, education, and readings related to a variety of areas in sport psychology.
2. **Internet Survival Guide of Industrial Organizational Psychology**
   (http://allserv.rug.ac.be/~flievens/guide.htm)
   This site contains links and information about internet sites valuable to both practitioners and researchers in the field of Industrial and Organizational Psychology.
3. **Careers in Applied Psychology**
   (http://www.wcupa.edu/_ACADEMICS/sch_cas.psy/career.htm)
   An interesting site filled with information about careers in applied psychology, such as sport psychology, I/O, and human factors.
4. **Society for Industrial and Organizational Psychology** (http://www.siop.org/)
   Organization of both the American Psychological Association and American Psychological Society dedicated to the study of I/O psychology.
5. **American Psychology-Law Association** (http://www.ap-ls.org/about/membershipIndex.html)
   This association is part of the American Psychological Association and is for individuals interested in the intersection between law and psychology. There is a very interesting and informative section devoted specifically to students.
6. **Center for Creative Leadership**. (http://www.ccl.org/CCLCommerce/)
   This organization has the goal of promoting the development of leadership through education, training, and research.

Cross Check: Psychology in Action

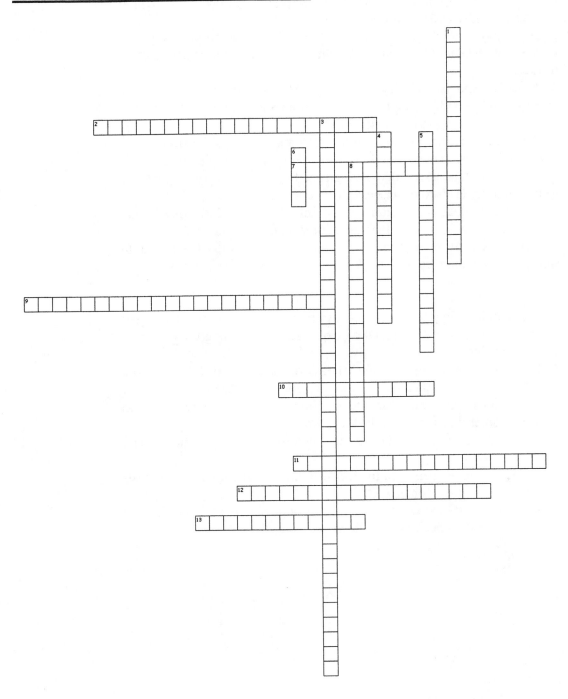

Across

2. The process by which a supervisor periodically evaluates the job relevant strengths and weaknesses of a subordinate

7. In I/O psychology, the theory that asserts that what people bring to a work situation should be balanced by what they receive compared to other workers

9. A leader who is typically charismatic and able to effect change by inspiring and providing intellectual stimulation and individual attention to followers, who respond with extra effort

10. Detailed description of the various tasks and activities that comprise a job, as well as the knowledge, skills, and abilities necessary to do it

11. The theory that asserts that setting specific, clear, attainable, goals for a given activity leads to better performance

12. The study of the integration of psychology and the law, focusing on such topics as the insanity defense and competence to stand trial

13. The study of relationship of human beings to machines and to workplaces and other environments

Down

1. Theories that suggest that a worker's effort and desire to maintain goal directed behavior are determined by expectations regarding the outcomes of that behavior

3. The study of how individual behavior is affected by the work environment, by co-workers, and by organizational practices

4. A statistical procedure used to combine and evaluate results from multiple studies that addressed the same topic

5. The systematic application of psychological principles to several aspects of sports

6. A group of individuals who interact with one another on a regular basis to accomplish a shared objective

8. A leader who seeks to motivate others by appealing to their self-interest and who focuses on performance outcomes

GRADE AID

ANSWER SECTION

PRACTICE TESTS

Practice Test #1		Practice Test #2		Practice Test #3		Comprehensive Test		Comprehensive Test True & False	
1	B	1	B	1	A	1	C	1	T
2	B	2	D	2	C	2	D	2	T
3	D	3	C	3	C	3	B	3	T
4	C	4	A	4	B	4	B	4	F
5	D	5	C	5	B	5	A	5	T
6	B	6	A	6	D	6	A	6	T
7	C	7	B	7	D	7	C	7	F
8	A	8	A	8	B	8	B	8	F
9	C	9	C	9	A	9	B		
10	A	10	B	10	D	10	A		
						11	A		
						12	C		
						13	B		
						14	C		
						15	D		

COMPREHENSIVE TEST, ESSAY QUESTIONS

1. The prevalence of women and minorities in psychology was relatively minimal until the later parts of the 21st century, although there have been significant and influential women and minorities throughout most of psychology's history. In regard to women, Mary Calkins and Margaret Washburn were two early leaders, with Washburn serving as president of the American Psychological Association. Today, women earn 73% of the bachelor's degrees, and 70% of the doctorates in psychology, compared to 1920-1975 where only 22.7% of ALL doctoral degrees in psychology were awarded to women.

2. The four recurring themes in psychology involve: a) the relation between the brain and behavior, b) the interaction of nature and nurture, c) the influence of human diversity, and d) the application of use of psychological research and knowledge. These four themes have been the basis for the development of a variety of questions within the field. Four such questions might be: 1) Is our need to sleep related and regulated to certain brain chemicals? 2) What is most important in determining our personality, our genetics or our early interactions with caregivers? 3) Do attitudes regarding appropriate interactions between men and women differ from culture to culture? 4) How might we apply our knowledge of group interactions to improve productivity of work groups?

PRACTICE TESTS

Practice Test #1		Practice Test #2		Practice Test #3		Comprehensive Test		Comprehensive Test True & False	
1	D	1	D	1	B	1	A	1	T
2	C	2	C	2	B	2	B	2	F
3	A	3	B	3	B	3	B	3	F
4	A	4	C	4	B	4	A	4	F
5	B	5	B	5	A	5	D	5	T
6	D	6	A	6	A	6	D	6	F
7	A	7	D	7	A	7	A	7	F
8	D	8	B	8	A	8	B	8	F
9	C	9	A	9	A	9	B		
10	C	10	A	10	D	10	C		
						11	B		
						12	B		
						13	D		
						14	B		
						15	C		

COMPREHENSIVE TEST, ESSAY QUESTIONS

1. There are many methods that psychologists use to study human behavior, and each has specific strengths and weaknesses. The strengths of the experimental method include being able to make strong causal interpretations and control over other factors that might influence the results that are observed. A primary weakness of this approach is that some variables cannot be manipulated. There are many descriptive methods used in psychology. Some of their weaknesses include not being able to manipulate variables and make cause and effect relationships, relying too heavily on self-reported data (surveys), and not being able to generalize the results to larger populations (case studies). Some of the strengths of descriptive methods include being able to make extensive observations on unique cases (case study), observing human behavior in its natural environment versus a laboratory (natural observation), and collecting large amounts of information in a very short time (surveys).

2. Psychologists study human behavior, and we know that human race consists of many people from diverse sociocultural backgrounds. In addition, we know that one of the main goals of research is to make conclusions about a population based on the sample we select. If the sample we use is not representative of the population, we must thus be careful about the conclusions we make. In addition, we must use diverse groups in our research so that we can make proper inferences. Characteristics that psychologists consider when conducting research include race, ethnicity, culture, social class, gender, sexual orientation, age, and disability status.

PRACTICE TESTS

Practice Test #1		Practice Test #2		Practice Test #3		Comprehensive Test		Comprehensive Test True & False	
1	C	1	D	1	C	1	A	1	T
2	D	2	B	2	C	2	C	2	F
3	D	3	C	3	A	3	B	3	F
4	C	4	D	4	D	4	C	4	F
5	B	5	A	5	C	5	C	5	T
6	D	6	C	6	B	6	C	6	T
7	C	7	C	7	D	7	D	7	T
8	D	8	B	8	A	8	B	8	F
9	B	9	B	9	D	9	B		
10	A	10	D	10	A	10	C		
						11	D		
						12	B		
						13	D		
						14	D		
						15	C		

COMPREHENSIVE TEST, ESSAY QUESTIONS

1. The action potential of a neuron is reached when the neuron is stimulated to its threshold. The "gates of the cell membrane open making it permeable and positive ions enter the neuron causing the neuron to be depolarized. The action potential itself is an electrical current that travels down the axon of the neuron. This firing occurs in an all-or-none fashion, it always occurs at full strength. After a neuron fires, there is a period of time, called a refractory period in which it cannot fire.

2. During the fight-or-flight state, the adrenal gland is stimulated by the sympathetic nervous system. The adrenal gland produces epinephrine producing a burst of energy. This in turn affects the somatic nervous system so that muscles can respond strongly and rapidly to the fight-or-flight situation.

PRACTICE TESTS

Practice Test #1		Practice Test #2		Practice Test #3		Comprehensive Test		Comprehensive Test True & False	
1	B	1	C	1	B	1	B	1	T
2	D	2	B	2	B	2	C	2	F
3	A	3	A	3	B	3	A	3	F
4	A	4	D	4	C	4	C	4	T
5	A	5	D	5	D	5	C	5	F
6	C	6	D	6	D	6	B	6	T
7	C	7	B	7	C	7	B	7	F
8	D	8	C	8	D	8	B	8	F
9	D	9	C	9	C	9	A		
10	A	10	A	10	B	10	A		
						11	D		
						12	C		
						13	C		
						14	C		
						15	B		

COMPREHENSIVE TEST, ESSAY QUESTIONS

1. Cross-sectional designs use different people at different ages and measure their differences on some dimension. Longitudinal studies use the same people at different time points to look for changes on some dimension. Cross-sectional studies take less time and are less expensive. The problem with cross-sectional designs includes that you cannot control people's backgrounds, so differences may be due to the different backgrounds of your sample, not just the dimension you are measuring. Longitudinal studies helps control for background differences, but subjects may not be available at all time points, people move away, stop participating or may even die. Also, practice effects may cause problems for some longitudinal research.

2. A father's involvement in childrearing is impacted by many factors including his work schedule and personal dispositions. More influential than either of these factors is the attitude of the child's mother. If the mother supports the father's involvement the other factors become important, but if she does not the father is unlikely to be involved regardless of his work schedule and disposition. Culture is also a factor in the father's involvement.

PRACTICE TESTS

Practice Test #1		Practice Test #2		Practice Test #3		Comprehensive Test		Comprehensive Test True & False	
1	B	1	D	1	D	1	D	1	F
2	C	2	B	2	B	2	D	2	F
3	C	3	C	3	A	3	A	3	T
4	B	4	D	4	B	4	B	4	F
5	D	5	B	5	C	5	C	5	T
6	B	6	B	6	D	6	B	6	T
7	C	7	B	7	A	7	D	7	T
8	A	8	A	8	C	8	C	8	F
9	B	9	A	9	D	9	B		
10	A	10	C	10	D	10	D		
						11	A		
						12	C		
						13	B		
						14	B		
						15	D		

COMPREHENSIVE TEST, ESSAY QUESTIONS

1.   The imaginary audience and personal fable are two cognitive distortions that occur as the result of adolescence becoming egocentric. The imaginary audience is characterized by adolescences feeling that they are always on stage and that everyone is watching them all the time. This often causes behaviors designed to not call attention to themselves. The personal fable is a belief in which the adolescent thinks they are so unique that no one understands them and that bad things will not happen to them. This cognitive distortion often leads to risky behaviors, like unsafe sex.

2.   The cognitive changes that occur after age 65 include decreases in vocabulary, reaction time, mathematic ability, and memory. These decreases are often minor and are less noticeable in people who are cognitively active. Also, these changes can be overcome through cognitive interventions. The cognitive changes that occur after age 65 do not have a large impact on elderly people because the changes are small and those that do occur can be overcome.

PRACTICE TESTS

Practice Test #1		Practice Test #2		Practice Test #3		Comprehensive Test		Comprehensive Test True & False	
1	D	1	D	1	B	1	B	1	T
2	D	2	A	2	A	2	B	2	T
3	D	3	A	3	A	3	A	3	F
4	A	4	B	4	B	4	D	4	F
5	C	5	A	5	A	5	D	5	F
6	A	6	D	6	B	6	B	6	F
7	A	7	D	7	C	7	A	7	T
8	C	8	D	8	D	8	A	8	T
9	D	9	B	9	A	9	D		
10	A	10	C	10	B	10	B		
						11	C		
						12	D		
						13	A		
						14	D		
						15	C		

COMPREHENSIVE TEST, ESSAY QUESTIONS

1. Bottom-up analysis starts at the most fundamental level of sensation. This approach starts at the receptor and moves up toward the more complex processes of interpretation. Top-down analysis starts at the more complex processes and focuses on the perceptual process such as selective attention.

2. Prosopagnosia is the inability to recognize faces. Research on patients with this form of agnosia has demonstrated that certain brain cells are only activated by facial stimuli. Other cells have been found that respond best to faces. This does not mean there is a neuron for every face. Taking all prosopagnosia research as a whole paints a picture of interacting and interdependent parts that create the whole visual experience.

PRACTICE TESTS

Practice Test #1		Practice Test #2		Practice Test #3		Comprehensive Test		Comprehensive Test True & False	
1	B	1	C	1	B	1	D	1	T
2	A	2	C	2	D	2	A	2	F
3	B	3	D	3	C	3	B	3	T
4	C	4	A	4	D	4	D	4	T
5	A	5	B	5	B	5	B	5	T
6	B	6	B	6	C	6	C	6	F
7	D	7	B	7	D	7	B	7	T
8	A	8	A	8	D	8	A	8	T
9	B	9	D	9	D	9	D		
10	D	10	C	10	A	10	C		
						11	C		
						12	A		
						13	C		
						14	A		
						15	B		

COMPREHENSIVE TEST, ESSAY QUESTIONS

1. There are a number of theories about why we sleep. However, none of these studies has been solely accepted as the only explanation for why we sleep. One theory is that sleep provides some sort of restorative function. A second theory, the evolutionary theory, suggests that we sleep to conserve energy and to keep us out of danger. A third theory emphasizes the role of circadian rhythms and the ability of the brain to regulate our sleep patterns and habits.

2. Substance abuse is evidenced by use for over one month; legal, personal, social or vocation problems that are the result of use, and use even when doing so is hazardous. Withdrawal symptoms are the physical reactions that occur when person that has become dependant on some substance stops taking that substance. Withdrawal symptoms are different for every drug and are usually the opposite of the drug's effect.

PRACTICE TESTS

Practice Test #1		Practice Test #2		Practice Test #3		Comprehensive Test		Comprehensive Test True & False	
1	D	1	A	1	A	1	D	1	T
2	B	2	A	2	C	2	A	2	T
3	B	3	D	3	B	3	D	3	T
4	D	4	B	4	C	4	C	4	T
5	B	5	B	5	D	5	A	5	T
6	C	6	C	6	A	6	C	6	F
7	C	7	B	7	B	7	B	7	F
8	C	8	C	8	C	8	A	8	F
9	D	9	D	9	D	9	B		
10	D	10	B	10	A	10	D		
						11	A		
						12	C		
						13	B		
						14	D		
						15	D		

COMPREHENSIVE TEST, ESSAY QUESTIONS

1. Allergies can be classically conditioned. Pet dander is the unconditioned stimulus for many people, this elicits an allergic reaction. If every time you go to a friend's house you have an allergic reaction due to the dog at their house, you can be conditioned to have the allergic reaction. Even if your friend gets rid of the animal you will still have allergic reactions because of the classical conditioning. The immune system of animals has been classically conditioned in the same way. These animals' bodies released antibodies in reaction to the conditioned stimulus of sweetened water after it had been paired with a toxin.

2. Hebb proposed that groups of neurons work together to form a recurring pattern. He termed this network of neurons a reverberating circuit. When learning takes place stimulation of a set of neurons occurs. With repeated stimulation, these neurons form a permanent circuit, referred to as consolidation. Differences in the ability of the neurons to consolidate may be the reason for different learning abilities.

PRACTICE TESTS

Practice Test #1		Practice Test #2		Practice Test #3		Comprehensive Test		Comprehensive Test True & False	
1	D	1	B	1	D	1	B	1	F
2	A	2	C	2	C	2	A	2	F
3	B	3	B	3	D	3	D	3	F
4	A	4	D	4	C	4	C	4	T
5	B	5	C	5	C	5	B	5	T
6	C	6	B	6	B	6	C	6	F
7	B	7	B	7	D	7	C	7	T
8	B	8	D	8	D	8	B	8	F
9	B	9	A	9	C	9	C		
10	A	10	B	10	D	10	A		
						11	D		
						12	C		
						13	D		
						14	A		
						15	B		

COMPREHENSIVE TEST, ESSAY QUESTIONS

1. Declarative memory is for specific information. Procedural is memory for skills. Declarative memory can be broken down into episodic and semantic memories. Episodic memory is memory of specific personal events and is tagged with information about time. Autobiographical memory is episodic memory of your own story. Semantic memory is memory for ideas, rules, words and general concepts.

2. Baddley and Longman looked at the effects of massed and distributed practice. Massed practice is where the subject practices intensively at one time, distributed practice breaks the practice session into several intervals. Baddley and Longman's study looked at the effects of the different types of practice on typing. Their results indicate that subjects who had practice sessions over several days, that is distributed practice had better performance than those with massed practice. Since all subjects had the same total hours of practice, this indicates that distributed practice is more effective.

PRACTICE TESTS

Practice Test #1		Practice Test #2		Practice Test #3		Comprehensive Test		Comprehensive Test True & False	
1	D	1	A	1	D	1	B	1	T
2	C	2	B	2	C	2	B	2	T
3	C	3	D	3	A	3	C	3	T
4	D	4	C	4	D	4	B	4	F
5	C	5	A	5	B	5	C	5	F
6	D	6	A	6	A	6	D	6	T
7	A	7	D	7	C	7	A	7	F
8	A	8	A	8	B	8	A	8	F
9	B	9	A	9	C	9	A		
10	A	10	B	10	A	10	A		
						11	B		
						12	C		
						13	B		
						14	A		
						15	C		

COMPREHENSIVE TEST, ESSAY QUESTIONS

1. Creative ideas are original, novel, and appropriate. Original ideas are those that are not imitations of some other idea, and come directly from the problem solver. Novel ideas are those ideas that do not have a precedent and that are new. Appropriate responses are those that are reasonable solutions to the problem and the given situation. Creative ideas break out of the mental set of the person and can be very effective in problem solving.

2. Language and culture interact. A belief that is held in a specific culture is often reflected in the language of that culture. Research with people who are bilingual has shown that how a person responds to personality tests depends on the language in which the test is written. Subjects will give answers that are more consistent with the values of the culture of the language of the test. If given the same test in a different language their responses will reflect the values of the culture of the second language.

PRACTICE TESTS

Practice Test #1		Practice Test #2		Practice Test #3		Comprehensive Test		Comprehensive Test True & False	
1	C	1	C	1	D	1	D	1	T
2	B	2	B	2	D	2	B	2	T
3	B	3	D	3	B	3	C	3	T
4	D	4	C	4	B	4	A	4	F
5	B	5		5	A	5	C	5	T
6	B	6	A	6	A	6	D	6	F
7	B	7	C	7	C	7	C	7	F
8	B	8	B	8	A	8	C	8	T
9	D	9	C	9	D	9	B		
10	B	10	B	10	A	10	B		
						11	A		
						12	D		
						13	B		
						14	D		
						15	B		

COMPREHENSIVE TEST, ESSAY QUESTIONS

1. Reliability is a tests ability to return the same score when the test is administered to the same person twice. If a test is not reliable, then it is context dependant and is not an accurate measure. Validity is the tests ability to measure exactly what it was designed to measure. If the test is not valid then the results cannot be used as a measure of the quality, trait or ability it was designed to measure. Without both reliability and validity a test is not useful for its designated purpose.

2. A deprived environment, such as one lacking in nutrition and cognitive stimulation may lead to retardation. This normally leads to mild retardation. Infectious diseases and physical trauma such as alcohol or drug use can also lead to mental retardation. Finally, genetic causes such as Down syndrome and fragile X can also lead to mental retardation.

PRACTICE TESTS

Practice Test #1		Practice Test #2		Practice Test #3		Comprehensive Test		Comprehensive Test True & False	
1	A	1	A	1	B	1	D	1	F
2	B	2	C	2	C	2	D	2	T
3	C	3	B	3	B	3	C	3	F
4	B	4	C	4	B	4	D	4	T
5	D	5	C	5	A	5	D	5	T
6	A	6	D	6	B	6	B	6	T
7	B	7	D	7	B	7	A	7	T
8	D	8	A	8	D	8	C	8	F
9	C	9	B	9	A	9	A		
10	B	10	D	10	B	10	B		
						11	A		
						12	C		
						13	B		
						14	C		
						15	D		

COMPREHENSIVE TEST, ESSAY QUESTIONS

1. Insulin and leptin are two important hormones in weight maintenance. Insulin allows glucose to be taken into body cells and is produced by the pancreas. Leptin in produced by the fat cells themselves. Both hormones send signals to the hypothalamus as part of the weight control process.

2. Tice and colleagues looked at impulse control from the perspective that break downs in impulse control are the result of a person's strategy to make themselves feel better. Her research showed that people who are not in a good mood are more likely to choose immediate rather than delayed gratification, eat unhealthy food and delay tedious tasks. This research supports the idea that we can control undesirable behaviors, but that when we are feeling bad, we often chose the quick fix over desirable behaviors.

PRACTICE TESTS

Practice Test #1		Practice Test #2		Practice Test #3		Comprehensive Test		Comprehensive Test True & False	
1	B	1	D	1	A	1	C	1	F
2	A	2	A	2	B	2	A	2	T
3	B	3	D	3	A	3	D	3	T
4	B	4	D	4	B	4	C	4	F
5	A	5	B	5	C	5	D	5	T
6	D	6	D	6	D	6	B	6	T
7	C	7	A	7	A	7	C	7	F
8	B	8	C	8	A	8	D	8	F
9	B	9	D	9	D	9	A		
10	D	10	C	10	C	10	D		
						11	C		
						12	D		
						13	A		
						14	B		
						15	A		

COMPREHENSIVE TEST, ESSAY QUESTIONS

1. Although the personality traits of people from different cultures can be measured with the same Five Factor Model, this does not mean that they have the same personalities. While researchers have found the Five Factors to exist across different cultures, the variance is substantial. Personality scores vary significantly across different cultures and the largest amount of variance is found in the individual. Further, personality must be viewed in the cultural context and the culture must also consider its own definition of personality. What one culture defines as *extraversion* may be different in another culture even though both are considered descriptive relative to their own culture.

2. According to Bandura's theory, gender and culture have a significant impact on self-efficacy. Two pieces of evidence support this theory. First, research indicates that women have lower expectancies for success in stereotypically masculine activities such as taking math tests. Second, women in some countries such as Hong Kong and Japan show substantially lower levels of self-efficacy when compared to other cultures.

PRACTICE TESTS

Practice Test #1		Practice Test #2		Practice Test #3		Comprehensive Test		Comprehensive Test True & False	
1	B	1	C	1	B	1	A	1	F
2	B	2	A	2	B	2	D	2	F
3	C	3	C	3	A	3	B	3	T
4	C	4	A	4	D	4	C	4	T
5	C	5	C	5	D	5	B	5	F
6	B	6	C	6	A	6	B	6	T
7	D	7	B	7	D	7	B	7	T
8	B	8	B	8	A	8	B	8	F
9	B	9	D	9	C	9	C		
10	D	10	B	10	A	10	D		
						11	D		
						12	B		
						13	A		
						14	D		
						15	B		

COMPREHENSIVE TEST, ESSAY QUESTIONS

1. Cognitive dissonance theory suggests that conflicts between a person's attitudes and behavior motivate an individual to act. More specifically, this theory suggests that when a person is engaging in a behavior that is contradictory to their reported beliefs, they will be motivated to either a) change their behavior or b) change their attitudes. The act of changing their behavior or attitudes then leads to dissonance reduction for the individual.

2. The bystander effect is that the willingness of people to help someone else decreases with the number of other bystanders that are present. This is in part due to the fact that people are less likely to determine that the event is in fact an emergency when others are apparently showing lack of concern over the event. Diffusion of responsibility also contributes to the bystander effect. Because other people are around who are also doing nothing the person feels they cannot be held responsible for not responding. Also, the presence of others makes it more likely that you think someone else has already responded (e.g., called 911).

PRACTICE TESTS

Practice Test #1		Practice Test #2		Practice Test #3		Comprehensive Test		Comprehensive Test True & False	
1	A	1	B	1	C	1	B	1	T
2	A	2	D	2	D	2	D	2	F
3	C	3	B	3	B	3	B	3	T
4	C	4	A	4	D	4	D	4	T
5	D	5	B	5	B	5	A	5	F
6	D	6	C	6	C	6	D	6	T
7	B	7	D	7	C	7	A	7	T
8	C	8	D	8	C	8	C	8	F
9	D	9	A	9	B	9	D		
10	D	10	A	10	A	10	B		
						11	D		
						12	A		
						13	D		
						14	A		
						15	A		

COMPREHENSIVE TEST, ESSAY QUESTIONS

1. Lazarus suggests that stress is the result of the interaction between the event itself and the person's evaluation of the event. He refers this interaction as an active negotiation between the demands of the events and a person's beliefs. Other cognitive researchers refer to the active negotiation as cognitive appraisal. Therefore, how a person view the stressor, whether in a positive or negative light, determines on how stressful the situation is. How familiar a person is with the event and if they believe the have the resources to deal with the event will impact that person's cognitive appraisal of the situation.

2. Health psychologists focus on health promotion. They do this through studying health related behaviors, such as eating habits and exercise. Also they educate people about prevention and wellness. Health psychologists are also involved in reducing risky behaviors and increasing compliance with orders from the doctor.

PRACTICE TESTS

Practice Test #1		Practice Test #2		Practice Test #3		Comprehensive Test		Comprehensive Test True & False	
1	A	1	D	1	C	1	D	1	F
2	D	2	B	2	B	2	D	2	T
3	B	3	B	3	D	3	B	3	F
4	B	4	A	4	A	4	C	4	F
5	C	5	D	5	C	5	D	5	T
6	D	6	B	6	B	6	A	6	T
7	A	7	C	7	C	7	D	7	T
8	D	8	D	8	B	8	C	8	F
9	B	9	B	9	A	9	D		
10	D	10	A	10	D	10	C		
						11	A		
						12	B		
						13	B		
						14	B		
						15	D		

COMPREHENSIVE TEST, ESSAY QUESTIONS

1. The goals of the DSM-IV-TR system include increasing the reliability of clinical diagnoses, focusing on observable behaviors in making diagnoses, and making diagnoses consistent with research and practical experiences of mental health professionals. There are five axes involved in a DSM-IV-TR diagnosis. The first is used to describe clinical disorders, whereas the second is for diagnosing more stable clinical conditions such as mental retardation and personality disorders. Axis three is used to diagnoses related medical conditions, whereas the fourth axis is used to record psychosocial or environmental problems that the individual is experiencing. Finally, axis five is used to indicate the global functioning of the individual.

2. Many people think that individuals with mental illnesses are violent. However, research evidence suggests that this belief is not true for the majority of individual diagnosed with a mental illness. However, there are some specific types of disorders that are more associated with violent behavior. These disorders include bipolar disorder (manic phase), paranoid schizophrenia, and antisocial personality disorder. In contrast, individuals who are exposed to violence tend to be more likely to experience some type of mental illness themselves. Typical problems that might follow victimization include depression, suicide, sexual difficulties, post-traumatic stress, and eating disorders.

PRACTICE TESTS

Practice Test #1		Practice Test #2		Practice Test #3		Comprehensive Test		Comprehensive Test True & False	
1	B	1	B	1	B	1	C	1	F
2	D	2	C	2	D	2	B	2	T
3	B	3	D	3	A	3	D	3	T
4	D	4	C	4	C	4	A	4	T
5	C	5	C	5	B	5	D	5	T
6	B	6	B	6	D	6	D	6	T
7	C	7	D	7	D	7	B	7	T
8	D	8	D	8	C	8	B	8	F
9	D	9	B	9	A	9	B		
10	C	10	D	10	D	10	B		
						11	A		
						12	D		
						13	A		
						14	B		
						15	B		

COMPREHENSIVE TEST, ESSAY QUESTIONS

1.   Broadly speaking, the evidence indicates that psychotherapy is effective. For example, one study indicated that those in therapy are better off than 80% of those who are not in therapy. Studies also indicate that the speed at which someone gets better may be related to the type of problem that the individual is experiencing. Research also indicates that both gender and culture should and do play a role in the effectiveness of therapy. For example, children being treated for anxiety were found to improve at a greater rate when culturally sensitive treatment was provided. In regard to gender, research indicates that females respond differently to therapy than men and that they seek out therapy more than men.

2.   There are 4 main types of psychotropic drugs, antianxiety drugs, antidepressant drugs, antimania drugs and antipsychotic drugs. Antianxiety drugs reduce feelings of stress and lowers excitability. Antidepressant drugs alter the levels of neurotransmitters and generally elevate the person's mood. Antimania drugs relieve the manic symptoms associated with bipolar disorder. Antipsychotic drugs reduce hostility and aggression as well as delusions.

PRACTICE TESTS

Practice Test #1		Practice Test #2		Practice Test #3		Comprehensive Test		Comprehensive Test True & False	
1	C	1	A	1	D	1	D	1	T
2	C	2	C	2	D	2	B	2	T
3	D	3	C	3	C	3	B	3	F
4	D	4	A	4	A	4	A	4	F
5	B	5	B	5	C	5	C	5	T
6	A	6	D	6	A	6	B	6	T
7	B	7	D	7	B	7	B	7	F
8	C	8	A	8	C	8	B	8	T
9	D	9	B	9	D	9	A		
10	B	10	C	10	B	10	D		
						11	C		
						12	B		
						13	A		
						14	B		
						15	D		

COMPREHENSIVE TEST, ESSAY QUESTIONS

1. The 5 broad areas of I/O psychology are human resources, motivation of job performance, job satisfaction, teamwork, and leadership. Human resource focuses on helping employers to hire, train and evaluate their employees. Motivation of job performance focuses on how rewards relate to successful performance and the relationship between management and employees. Job satisfaction of employees and managers are assessed and leadership looks at the define attributes of leaders. Teamwork focuses the interaction among teammates work with one another. Finally, leadership studies examine what constitutes effective leadership and the basic characteristics of good leaders.

2. Sports psychologists help athletes by improving sports performance. They do this by teaching athletes mental strategies that helps them be more effective and overcome obstacles. Second, sport psychologists try to enhance the sports experience for young participants. Finally, they help with injury rehabilitation.

NOTES

NOTES

NOTES

NOTES

NOTES

NOTES

NOTES

NOTES

NOTES

NOTES

NOTES

NOTES